THE CRACKLE OF THE FROST

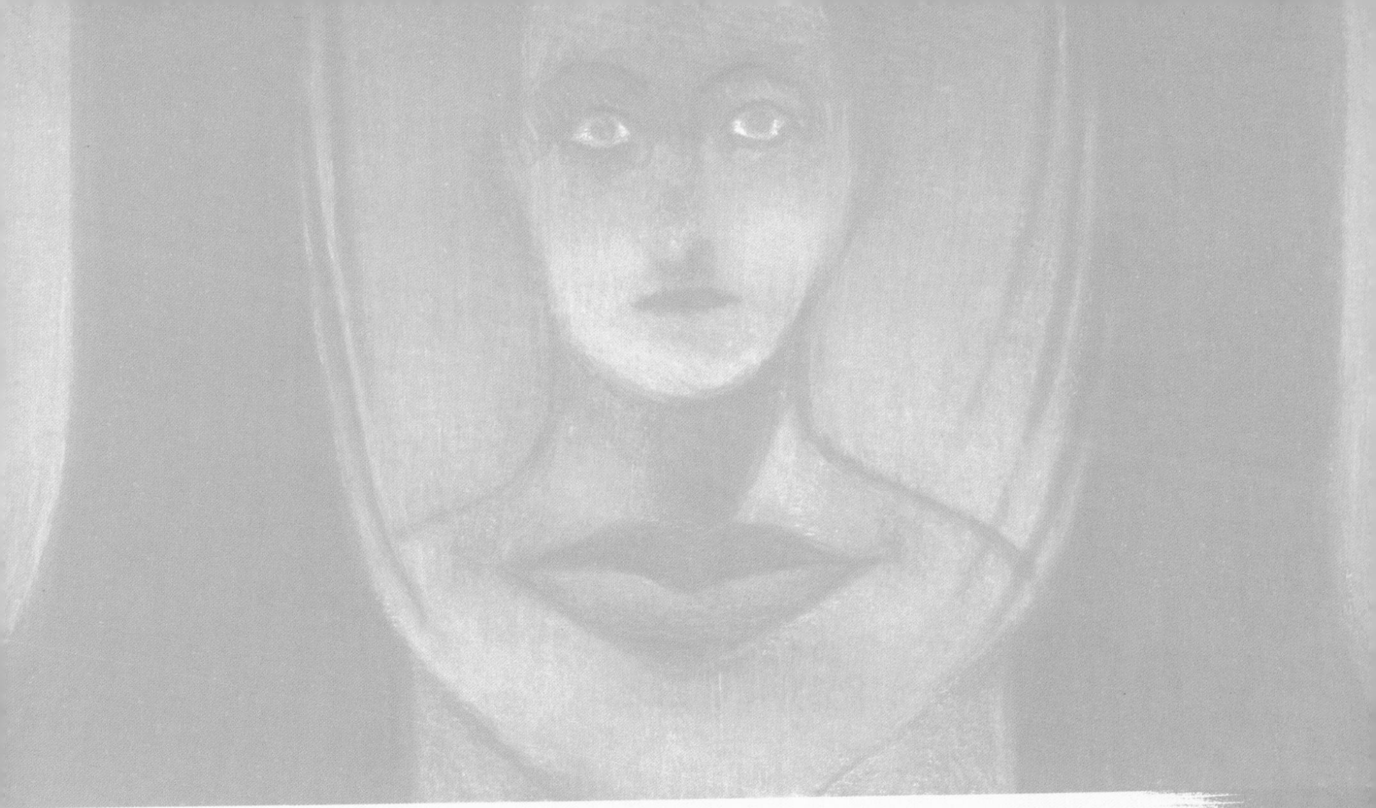

THE CRACKLE OF THE FROST

Lorenzo MATTOTTI and Jorge ZENTNER

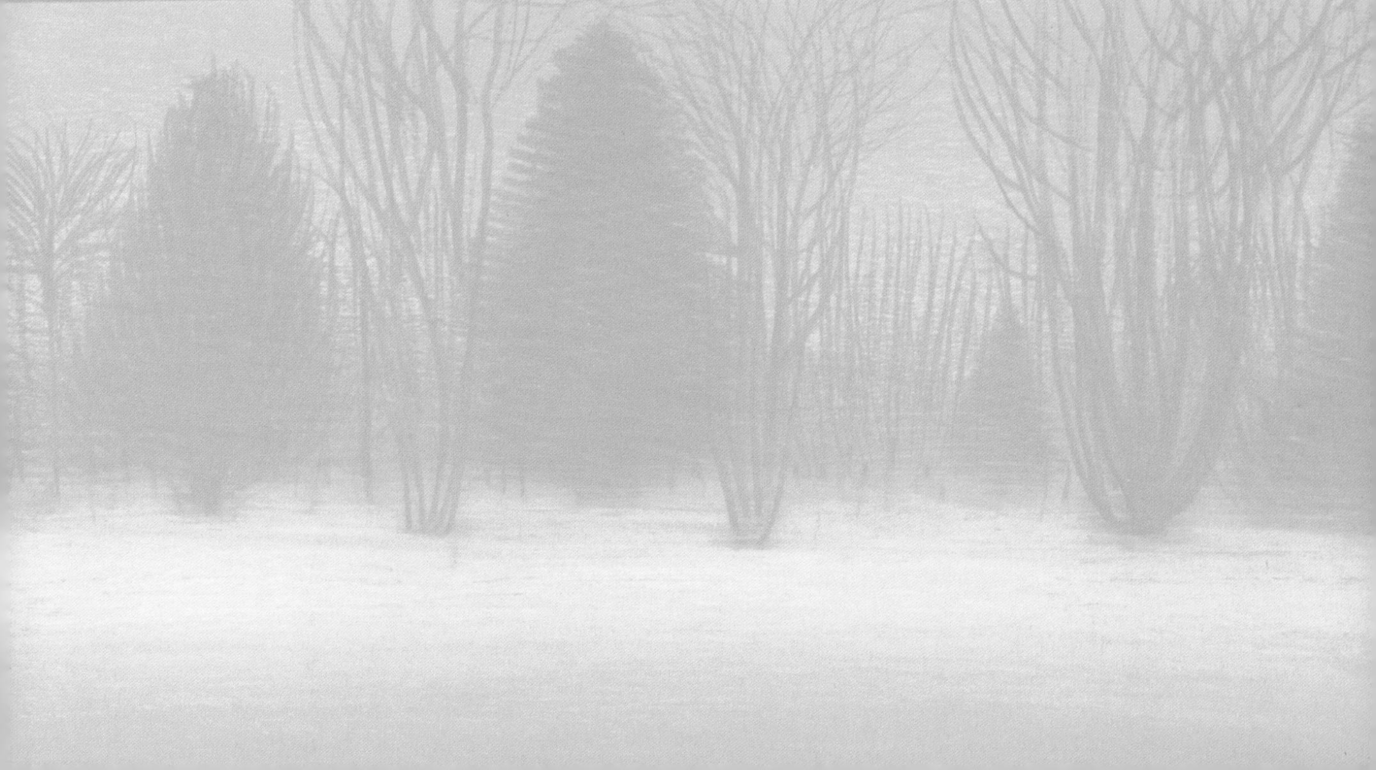

Jorge Zentner and Lorenzo Mattotti originally wrote and drew *The Crackle of the Frost* in 2001 to be serialized in the Sunday edition of the *Frankfurter Allgemeine Zeitung*, at the rate of a weekly eight-panel tabloid page, under the title *Der Klang des Rauhreifs*. The story was created with the eventual two-panels-per-page iteration used for the subsequent book editions in mind. For more information about the genesis of this project and a gallery of sketches and related art, and to view information about other Mattotti projects, visit fantagraphics.com.

FANTAGRAPHICS BOOKS
7563 Lake City Way NE
Seattle, WA 98115

Edited and translated by Kim Thompson
Designed by Emory Liu
Production by Paul Baresh
Proofeading by Jason T. Miles and Kristy Valenti
Associate Publisher: Eric Reynolds
Published by Gary Groth and Kim Thompson

To receive a free catalog of comics, call 1-800-657-1100, write us at
Fantagraphics Books, 7563 Lake City Way NE, Seattle, WA 98115,
or email us at fbicomix@fantagraphics.com .

Distributed in the U.S. by W.W. Norton and Company, Inc. (800-233-4830)
Distributed in Canada by Canadian Manda Group (800-452-6642 x862)
Distributed in the United Kingdom by Turnaround Distribution (020-8829-3002)
Distributed in the U.S. to comic book specialty stores by Diamond Comics Distributors (800-452-6642 x215)

Visit the Fantagraphics website at www.fantagraphics.com
Visit Lorenzo Mattotti's website at www.mattotti.com

First printing: July, 2012.
ISBN: 978-1-60699-543-3
Printed in Hong Kong

1

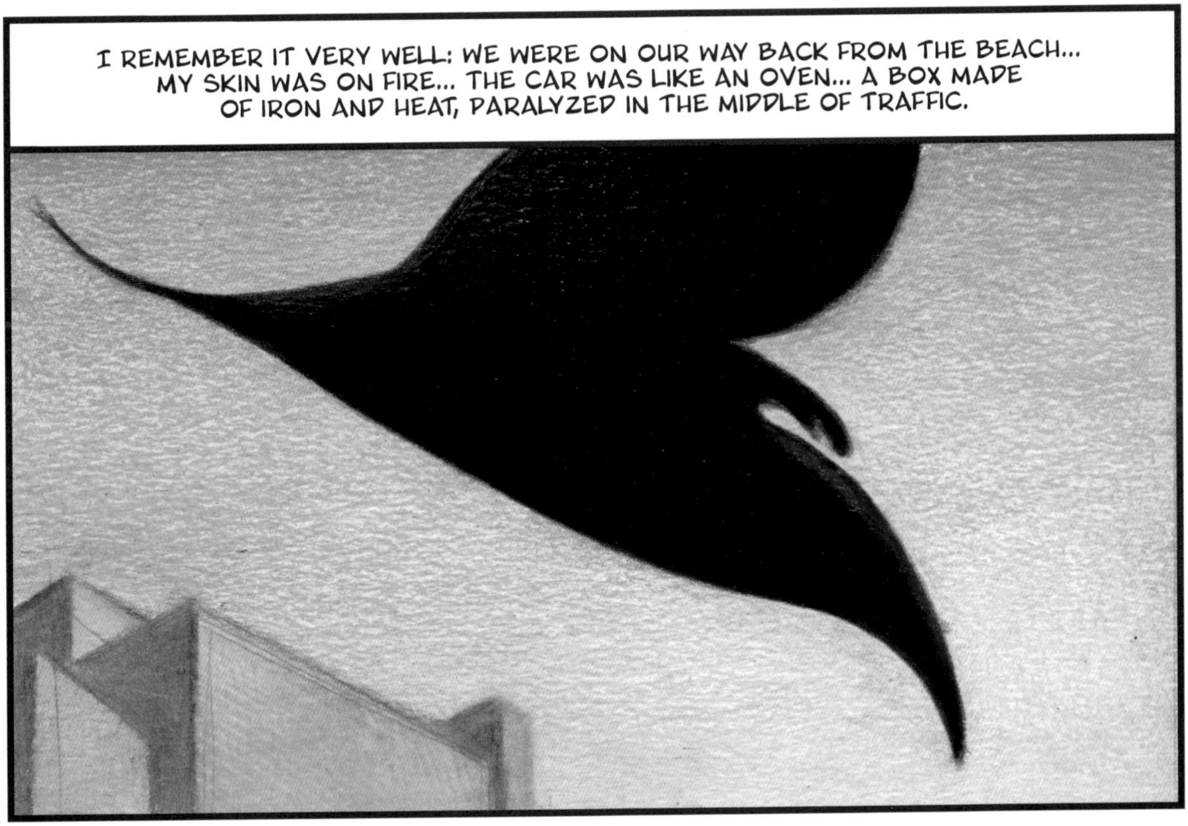
I REMEMBER IT VERY WELL: WE WERE ON OUR WAY BACK FROM THE BEACH... MY SKIN WAS ON FIRE... THE CAR WAS LIKE AN OVEN... A BOX MADE OF IRON AND HEAT, PARALYZED IN THE MIDDLE OF TRAFFIC.

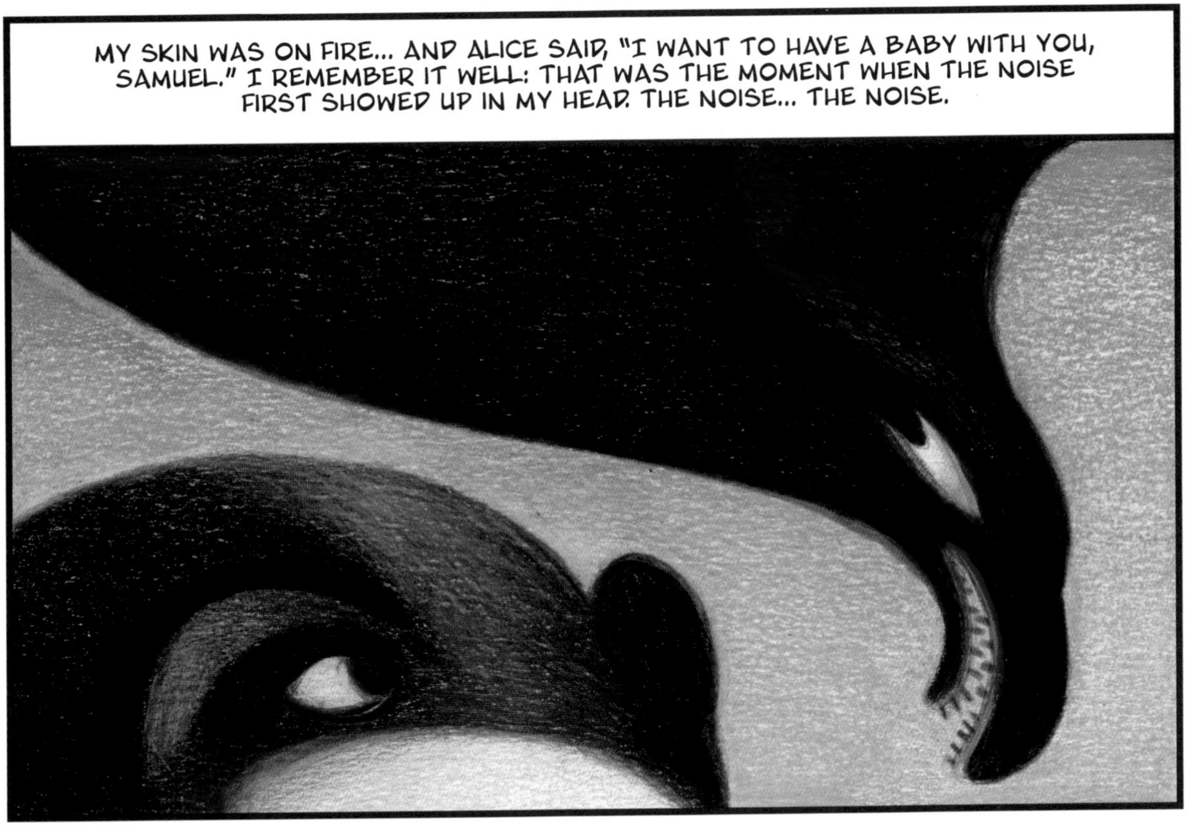
MY SKIN WAS ON FIRE... AND ALICE SAID, "I WANT TO HAVE A BABY WITH YOU, SAMUEL." I REMEMBER IT WELL: THAT WAS THE MOMENT WHEN THE NOISE FIRST SHOWED UP IN MY HEAD. THE NOISE... THE NOISE.

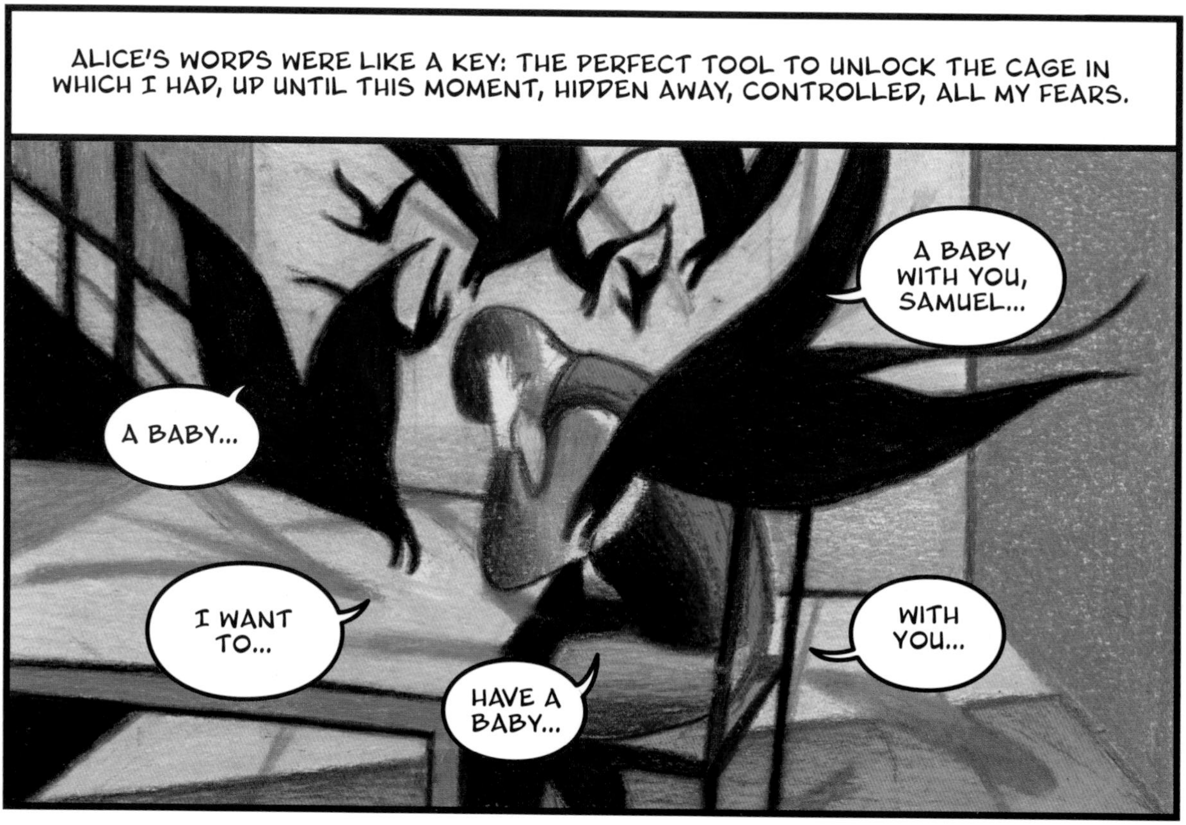
ALICE'S WORDS WERE LIKE A KEY: THE PERFECT TOOL TO UNLOCK THE CAGE IN WHICH I HAD, UP UNTIL THIS MOMENT, HIDDEN AWAY, CONTROLLED, ALL MY FEARS.
A BABY WITH YOU, SAMUEL...
A BABY...
I WANT TO...
HAVE A BABY...
WITH YOU...

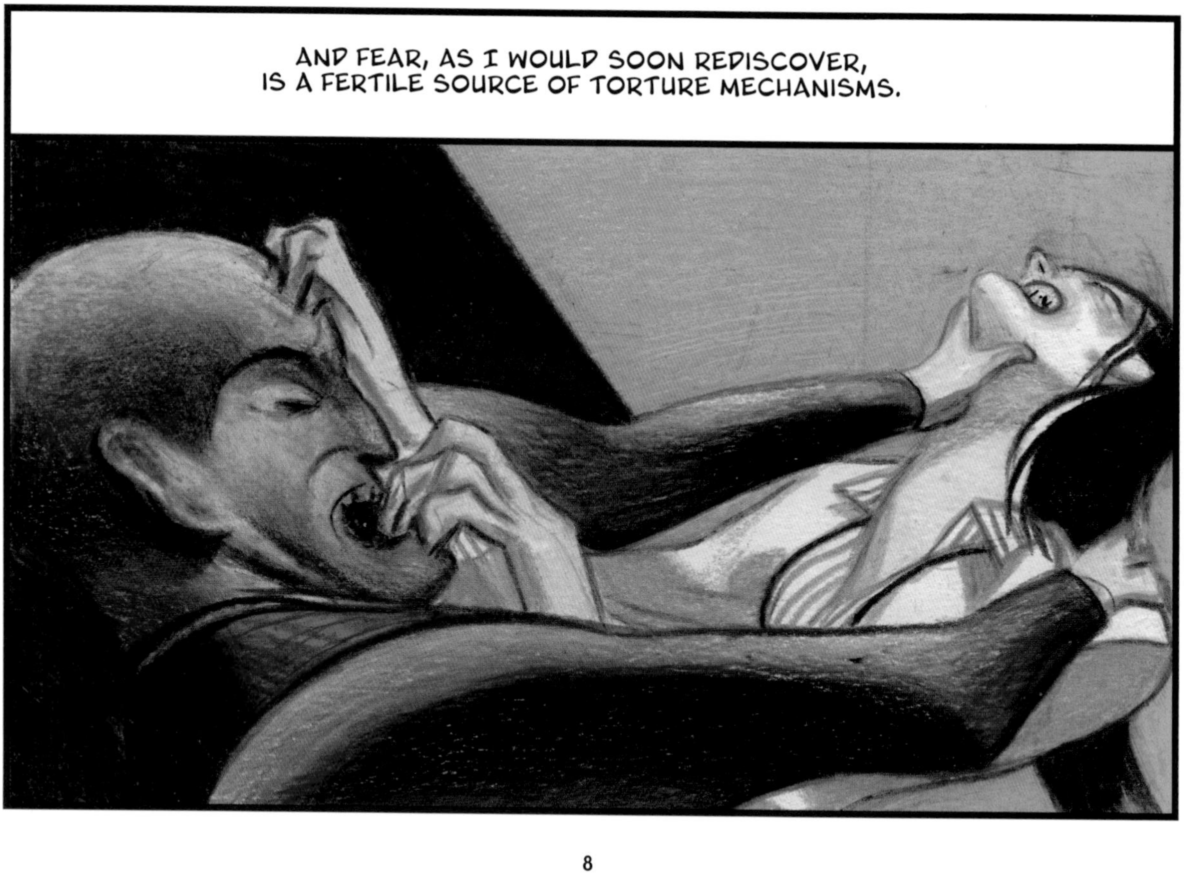
AND FEAR, AS I WOULD SOON REDISCOVER, IS A FERTILE SOURCE OF TORTURE MECHANISMS.

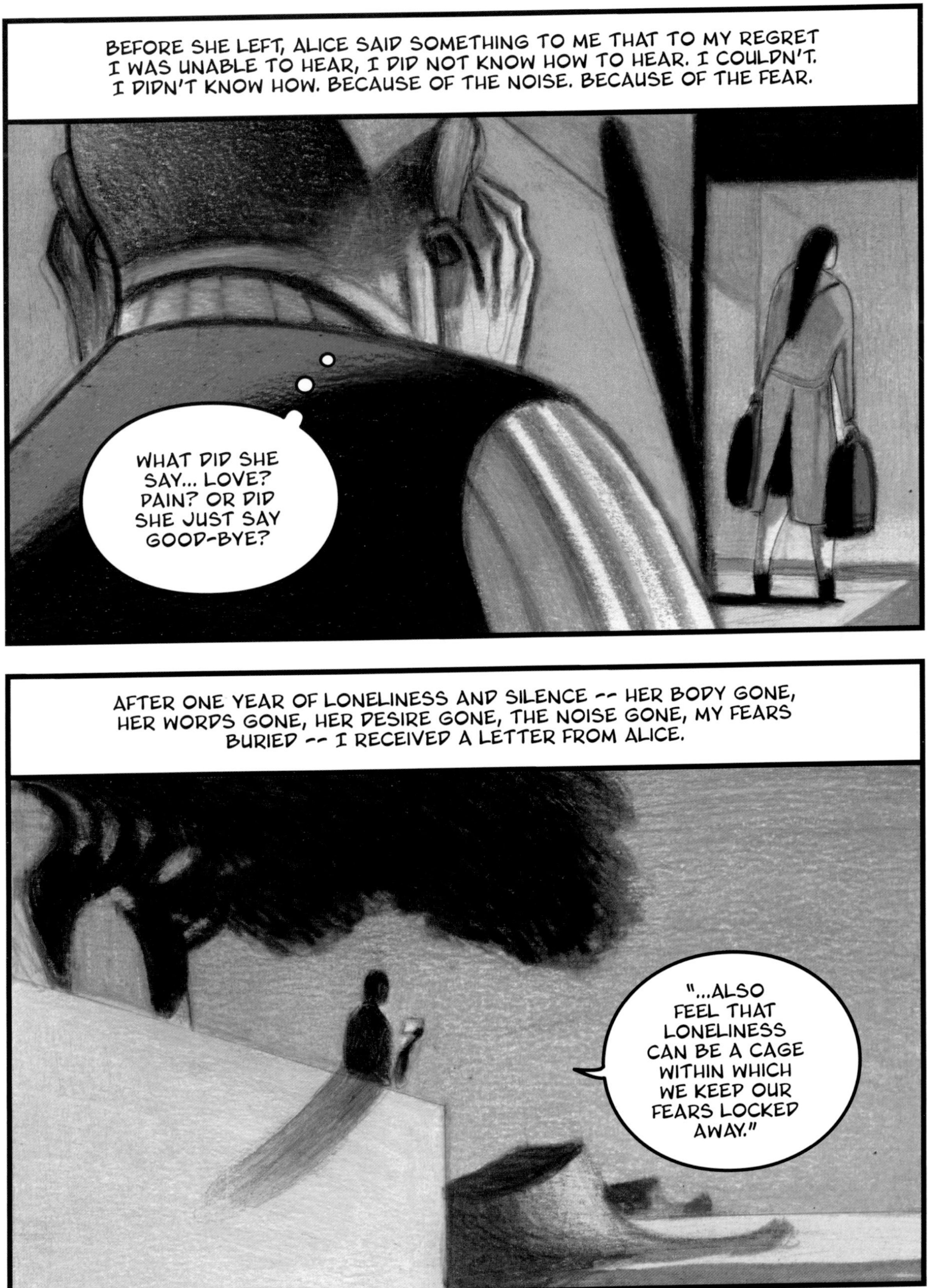
BEFORE SHE LEFT, ALICE SAID SOMETHING TO ME THAT TO MY REGRET I WAS UNABLE TO HEAR, I DID NOT KNOW HOW TO HEAR. I COULDN'T. I DIDN'T KNOW HOW. BECAUSE OF THE NOISE. BECAUSE OF THE FEAR.
WHAT DID SHE SAY... LOVE? PAIN? OR DID SHE JUST SAY GOOD-BYE?
AFTER ONE YEAR OF LONELINESS AND SILENCE -- HER BODY GONE, HER WORDS GONE, HER DESIRE GONE, THE NOISE GONE, MY FEARS BURIED -- I RECEIVED A LETTER FROM ALICE.
"...ALSO FEEL THAT LONELINESS CAN BE A CAGE WITHIN WHICH WE KEEP OUR FEARS LOCKED AWAY."

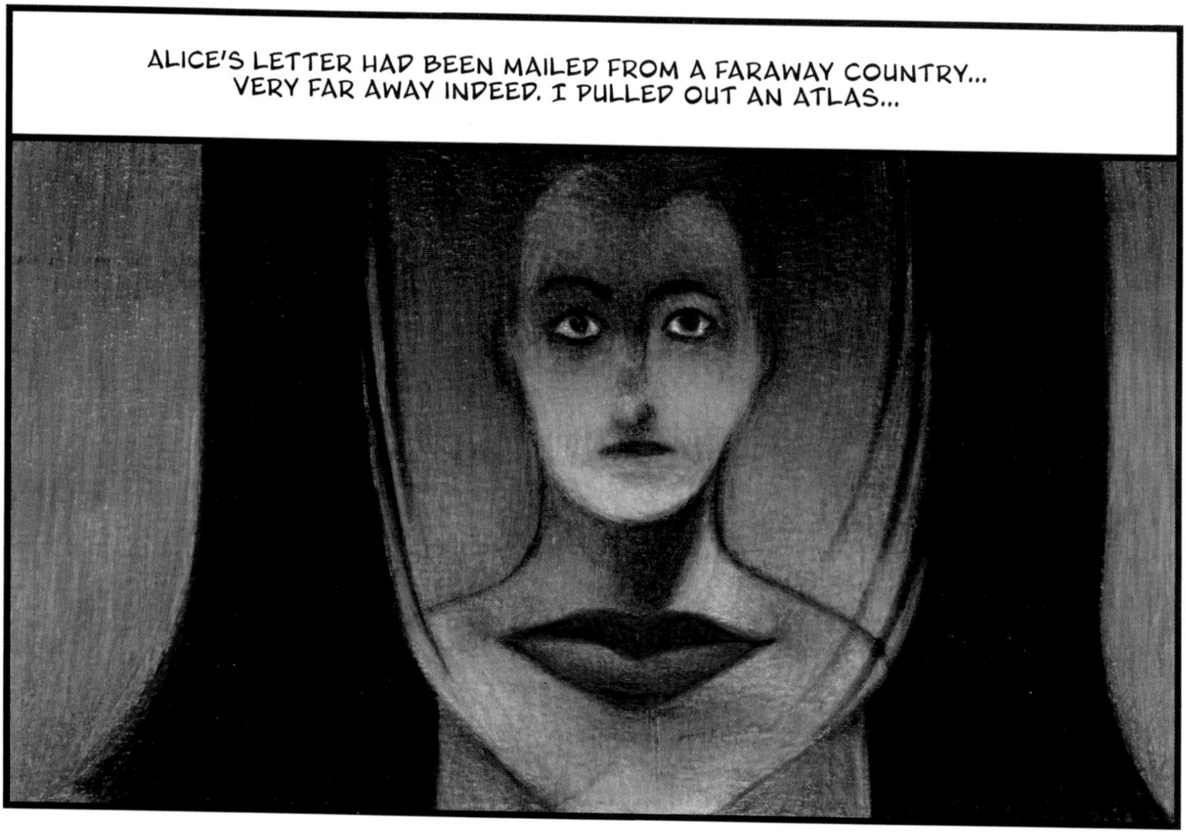
ALICE'S LETTER HAD BEEN MAILED FROM A FARAWAY COUNTRY... VERY FAR AWAY INDEED. I PULLED OUT AN ATLAS...

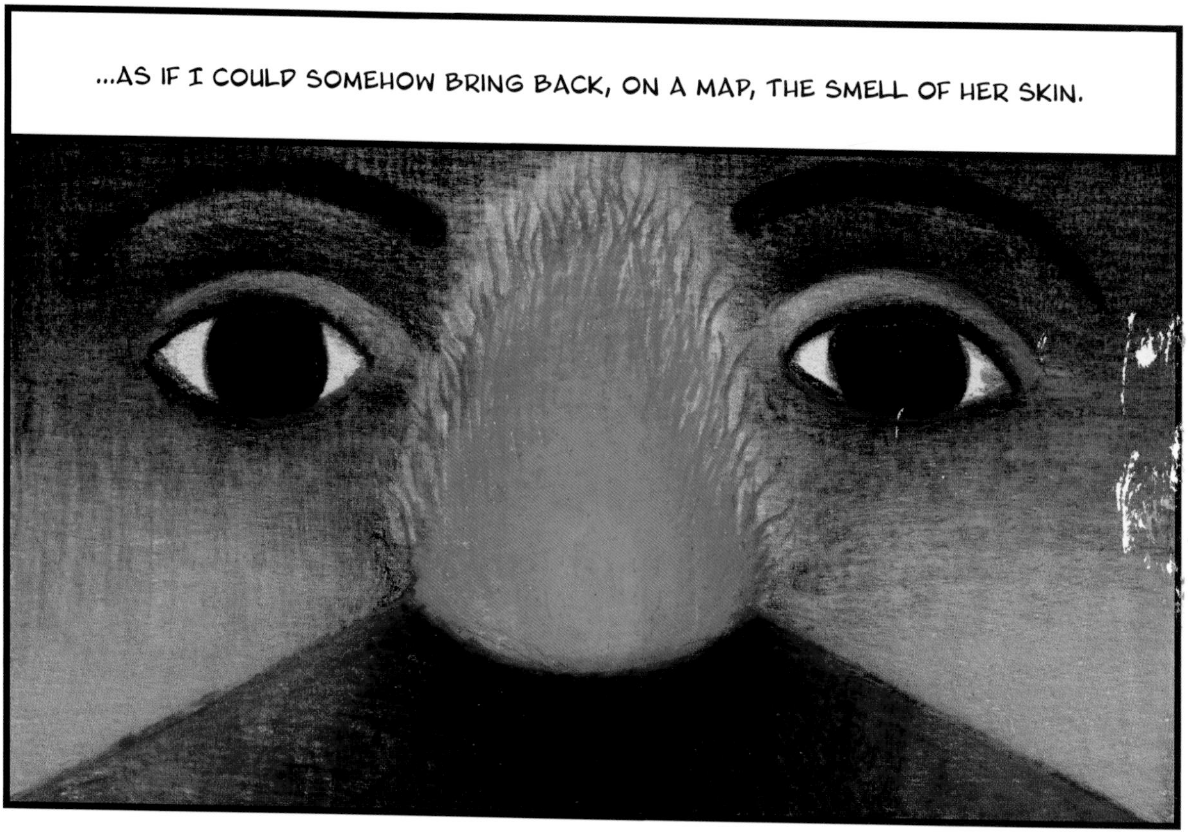
...AS IF I COULD SOMEHOW BRING BACK, ON A MAP, THE SMELL OF HER SKIN.

IN HER LETTER, ALICE DID NOT SAY "COME"; SHE DID NOT SAY
"I'M WAITING FOR YOU"; SHE DID NOT SAY "I WANT TO SEE YOU."

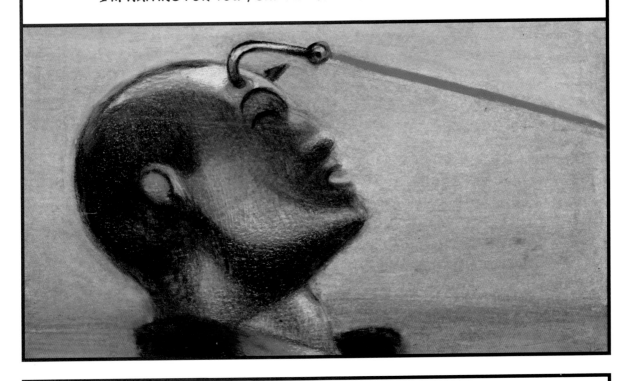

THAT IS SURELY THE REASON -- THE FACT THAT ALL THOSE
PHRASES WERE, SO FAR AS I WAS CONCERNED, MISSING FROM
HER LETTER -- FOR MY DECISION TO LEAVE, TO GO FIND HER.

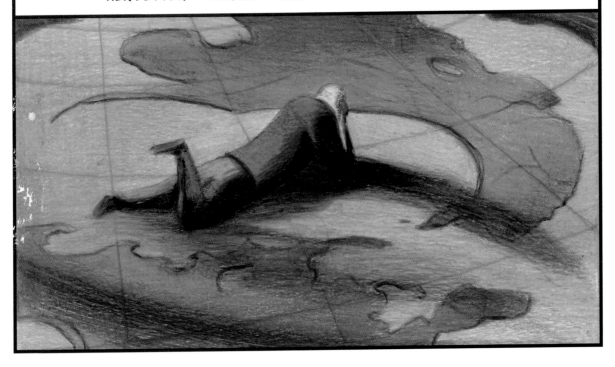

BEFORE UNDERTAKING THIS LONG JOURNEY, I PHONED MY FRIEND MARC. "I NEED YOU TO TAKE CARE OF CLEOPATRA. SHE'S VERY WELL-BEHAVED, AS YOU KNOW... SHE WON'T BE A NUISANCE."

I'M LEAVING YOU IN GOOD HANDS. TRY TO AVOID SAYING ANYTHING TOO FOOLISH, CLEOPATRA... MARC IS AN INTELLECTUAL, WITH A CRITICAL DISPOSITION.

I'D KNOWN DANA FOR SEVERAL YEARS. EVERY WEEK -- EVER SINCE ALICE HAD LEFT -- I WOULD SPEND A FEW HOURS AT HER APARTMENT. WE NEVER TALKED AND WE RARELY TOUCHED. ON THE OTHER HAND... WE LOVED LOOKING AT ONE ANOTHER.

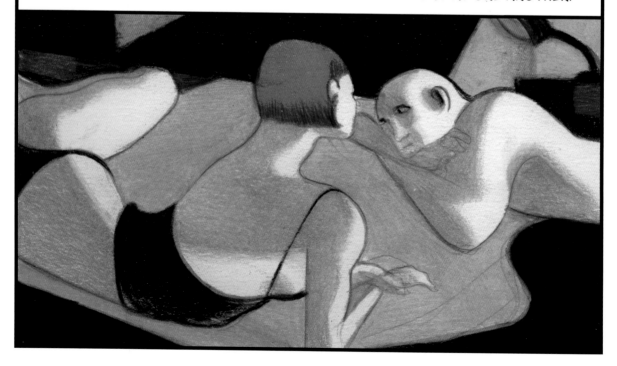

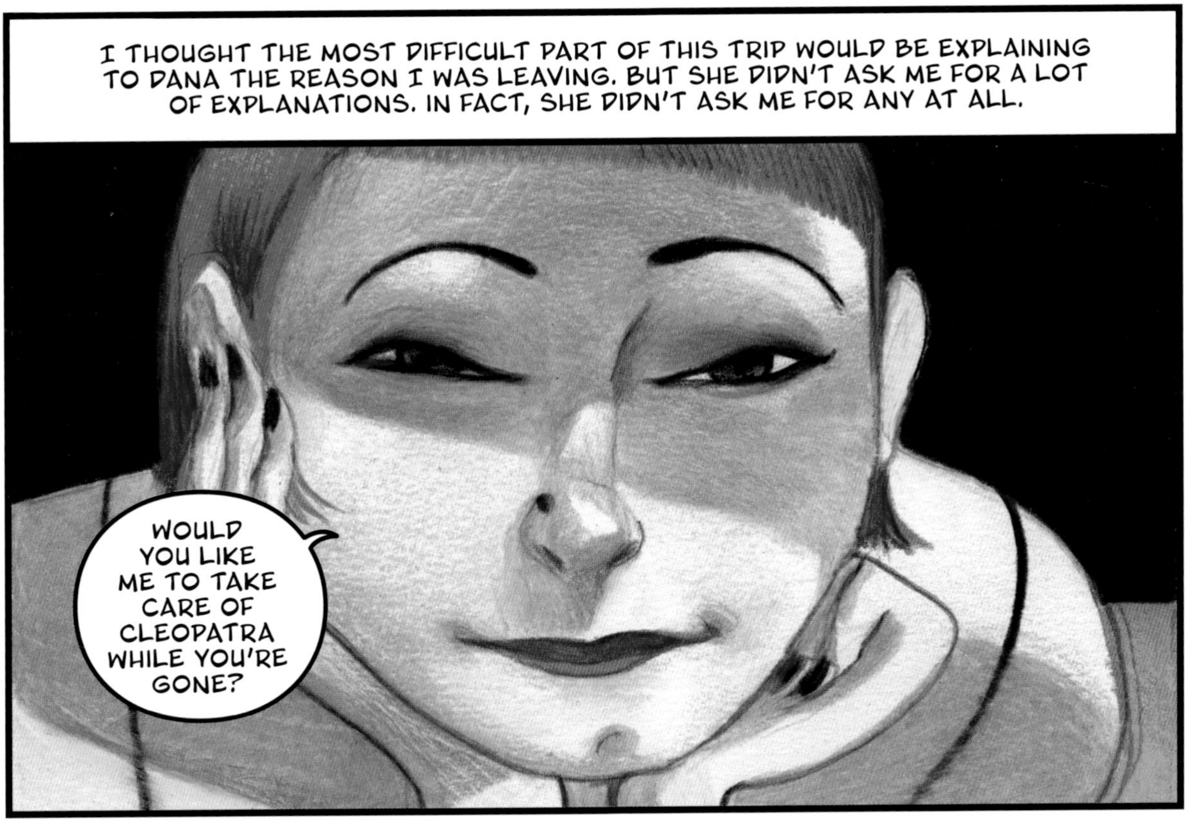
I THOUGHT THE MOST DIFFICULT PART OF THIS TRIP WOULD BE EXPLAINING TO DANA THE REASON I WAS LEAVING. BUT SHE DIDN'T ASK ME FOR A LOT OF EXPLANATIONS. IN FACT, SHE DIDN'T ASK ME FOR ANY AT ALL.
WOULD YOU LIKE ME TO TAKE CARE OF CLEOPATRA WHILE YOU'RE GONE?

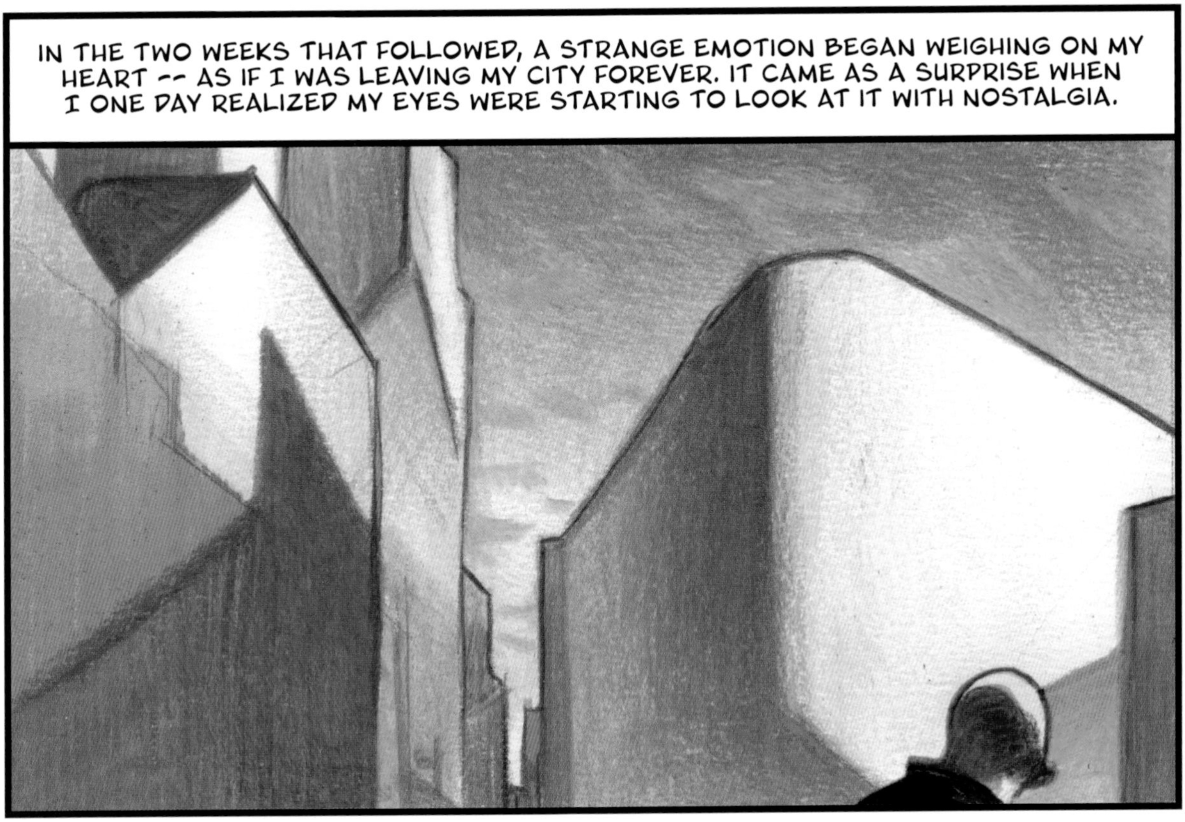
IN THE TWO WEEKS THAT FOLLOWED, A STRANGE EMOTION BEGAN WEIGHING ON MY HEART -- AS IF I WAS LEAVING MY CITY FOREVER. IT CAME AS A SURPRISE WHEN I ONE DAY REALIZED MY EYES WERE STARTING TO LOOK AT IT WITH NOSTALGIA.

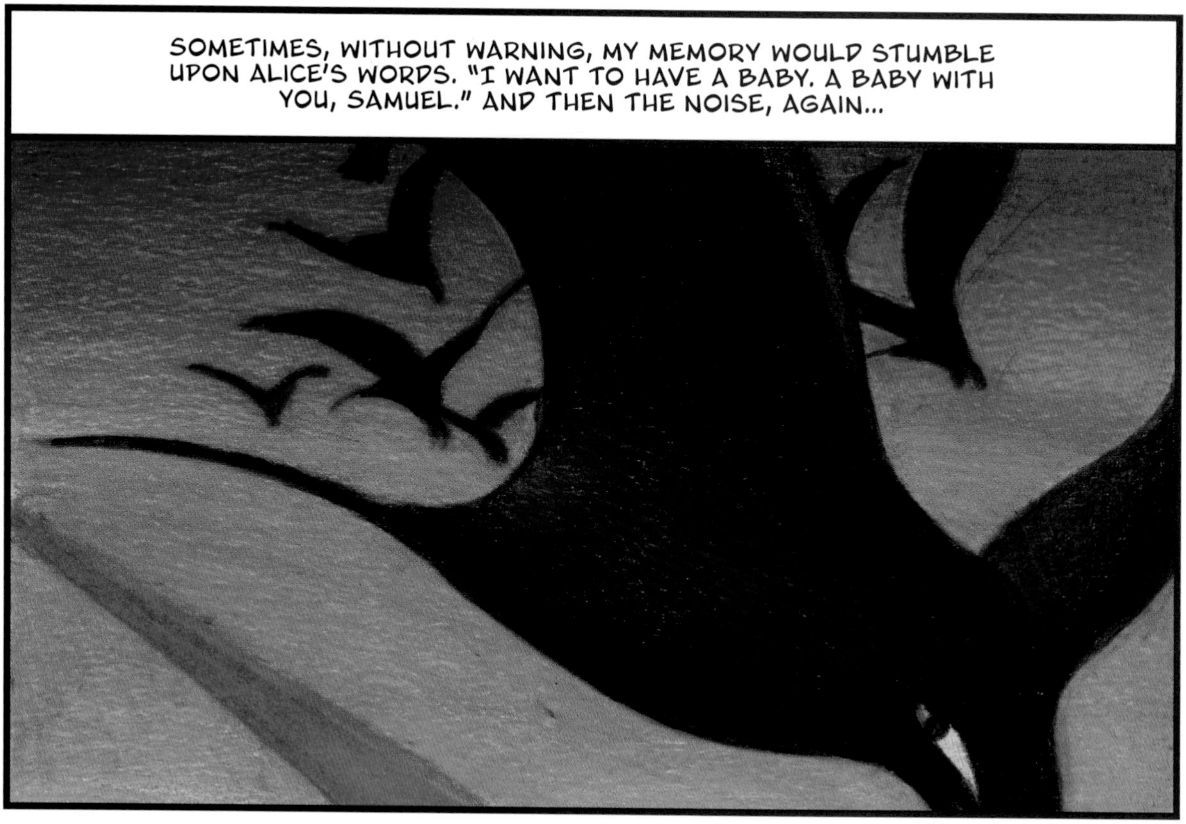
SOMETIMES, WITHOUT WARNING, MY MEMORY WOULD STUMBLE UPON ALICE'S WORDS. "I WANT TO HAVE A BABY. A BABY WITH YOU, SAMUEL." AND THEN THE NOISE, AGAIN...

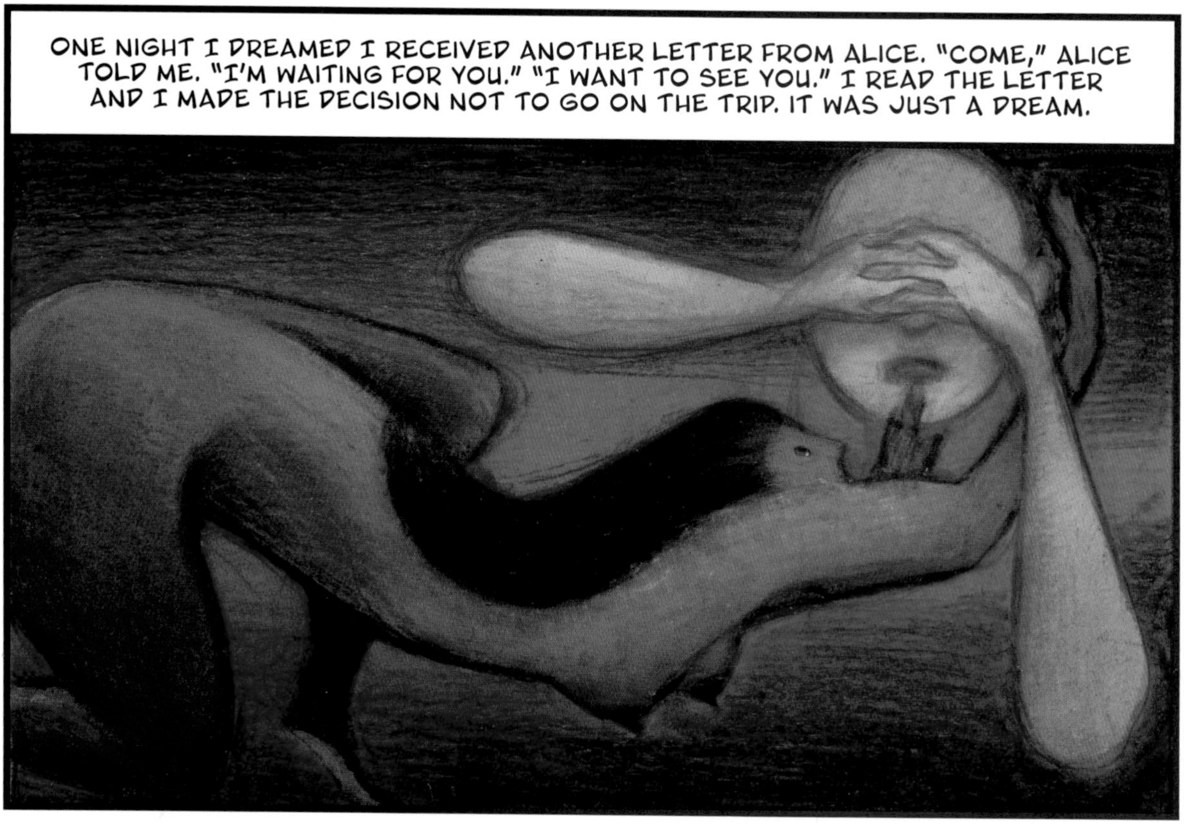
ONE NIGHT I DREAMED I RECEIVED ANOTHER LETTER FROM ALICE. "COME," ALICE TOLD ME. "I'M WAITING FOR YOU." "I WANT TO SEE YOU." I READ THE LETTER AND I MADE THE DECISION NOT TO GO ON THE TRIP. IT WAS JUST A DREAM.

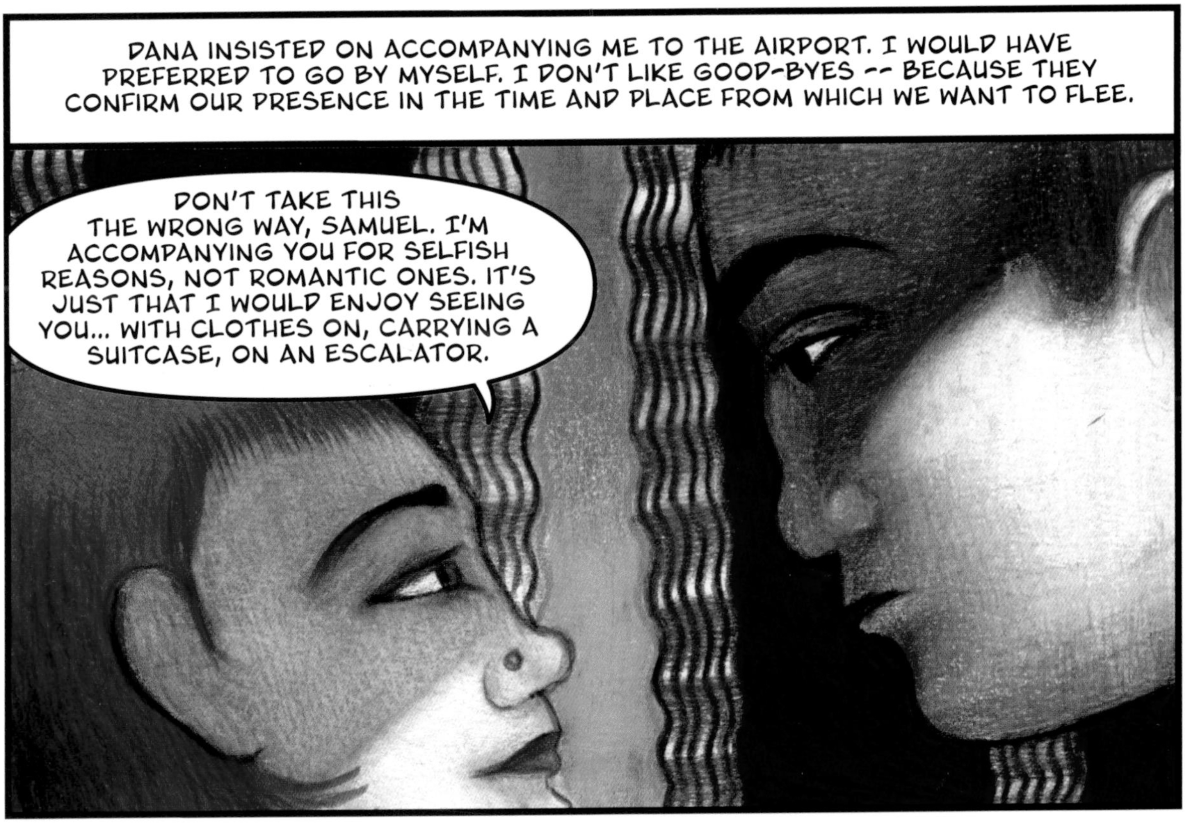
DANA INSISTED ON ACCOMPANYING ME TO THE AIRPORT. I WOULD HAVE PREFERRED TO GO BY MYSELF. I DON'T LIKE GOOD-BYES -- BECAUSE THEY CONFIRM OUR PRESENCE IN THE TIME AND PLACE FROM WHICH WE WANT TO FLEE.
DON'T TAKE THIS THE WRONG WAY, SAMUEL. I'M ACCOMPANYING YOU FOR SELFISH REASONS, NOT ROMANTIC ONES. IT'S JUST THAT I WOULD ENJOY SEEING YOU... WITH CLOTHES ON, CARRYING A SUITCASE, ON AN ESCALATOR.

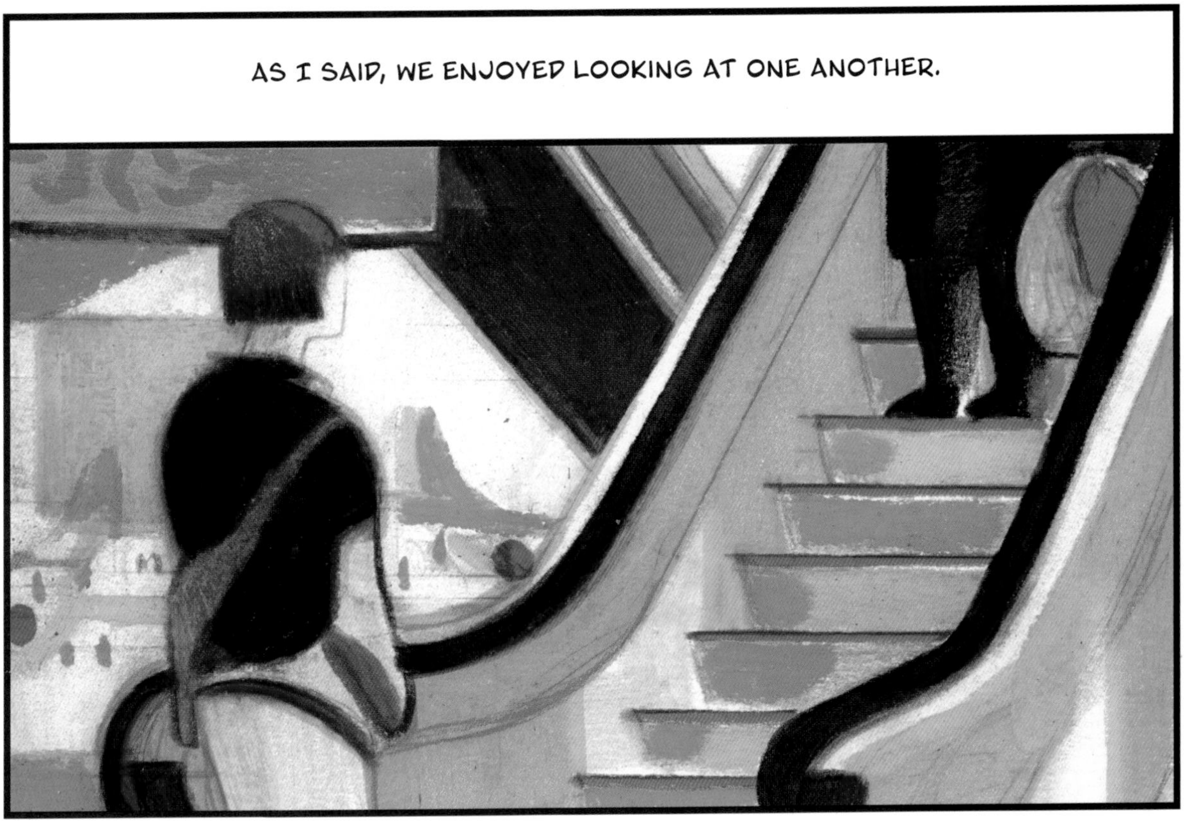
AS I SAID, WE ENJOYED LOOKING AT ONE ANOTHER.

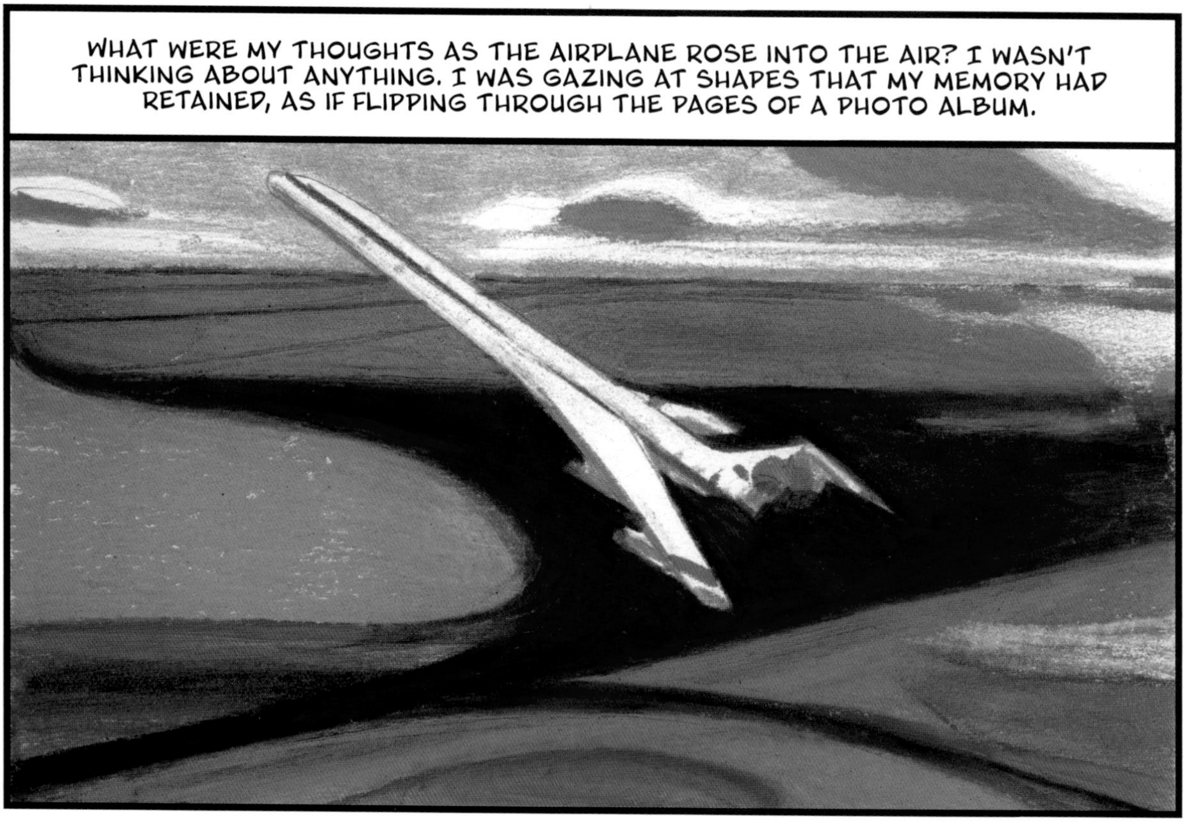
WHAT WERE MY THOUGHTS AS THE AIRPLANE ROSE INTO THE AIR? I WASN'T THINKING ABOUT ANYTHING. I WAS GAZING AT SHAPES THAT MY MEMORY HAD RETAINED, AS IF FLIPPING THROUGH THE PAGES OF A PHOTO ALBUM.

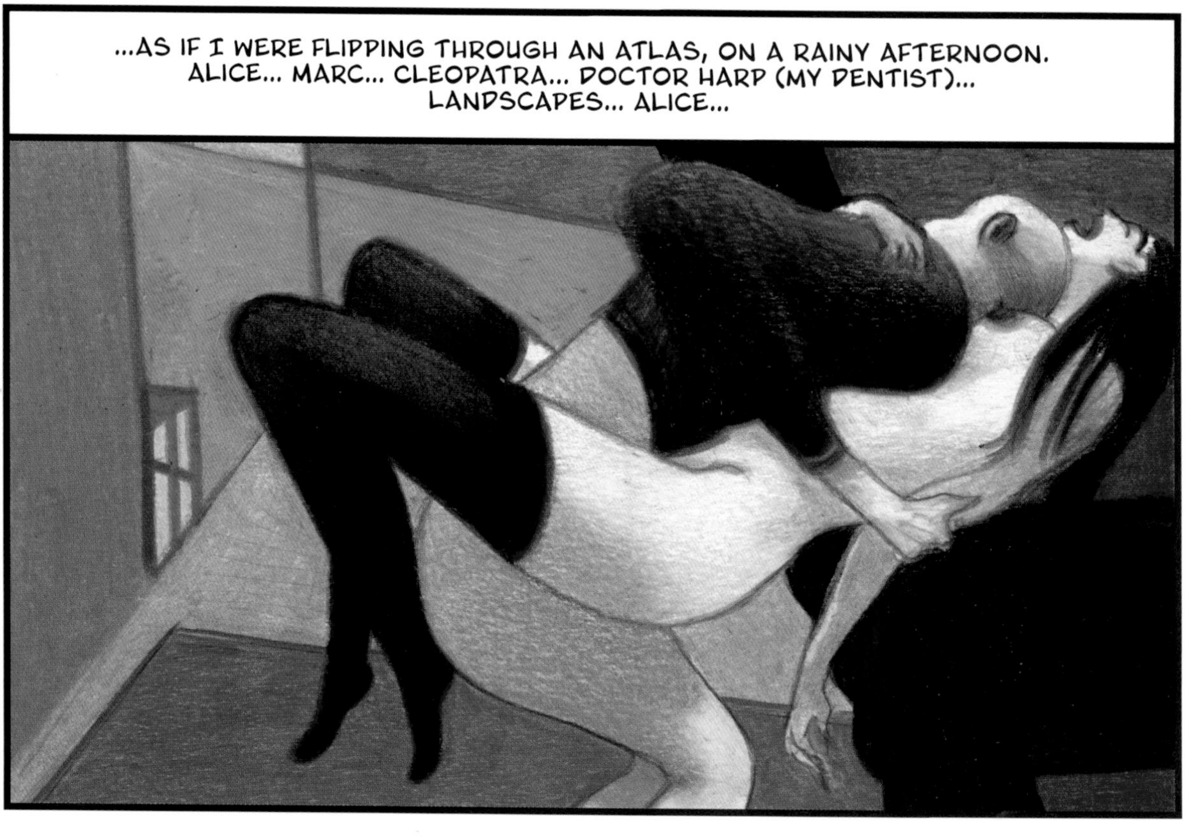
...AS IF I WERE FLIPPING THROUGH AN ATLAS, ON A RAINY AFTERNOON. ALICE... MARC... CLEOPATRA... DOCTOR HARP (MY DENTIST)... LANDSCAPES... ALICE...

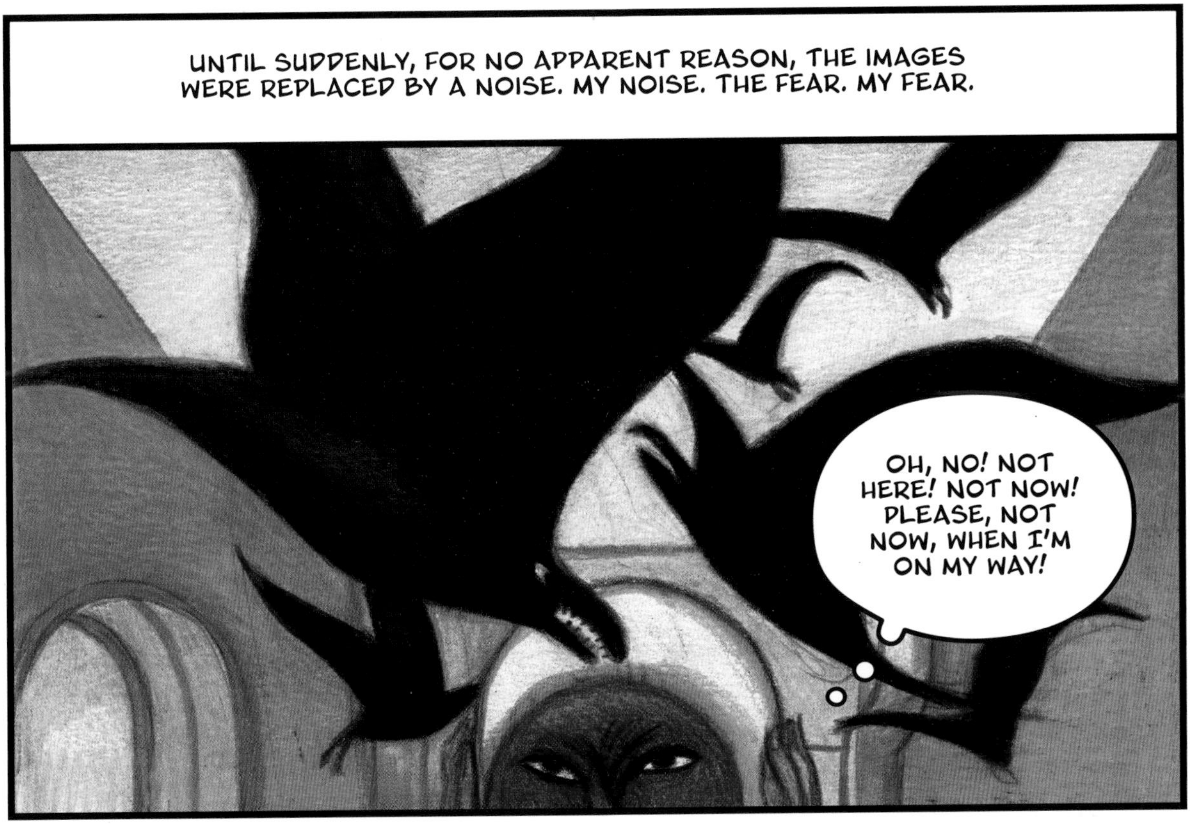
UNTIL SUDDENLY, FOR NO APPARENT REASON, THE IMAGES WERE REPLACED BY A NOISE. MY NOISE. THE FEAR. MY FEAR.
OH, NO! NOT HERE! NOT NOW! PLEASE, NOT NOW, WHEN I'M ON MY WAY!

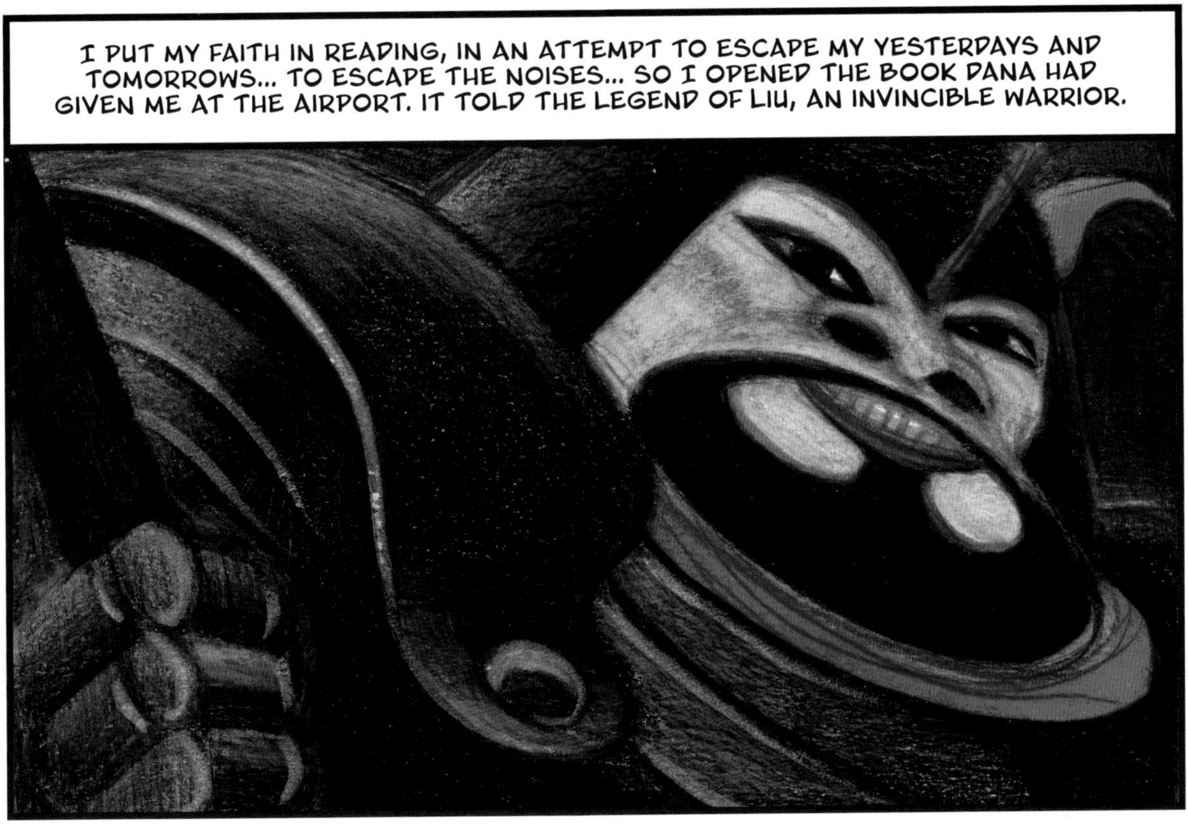
I PUT MY FAITH IN READING, IN AN ATTEMPT TO ESCAPE MY YESTERDAYS AND TOMORROWS... TO ESCAPE THE NOISES... SO I OPENED THE BOOK DANA HAD GIVEN ME AT THE AIRPORT. IT TOLD THE LEGEND OF LIU, AN INVINCIBLE WARRIOR.

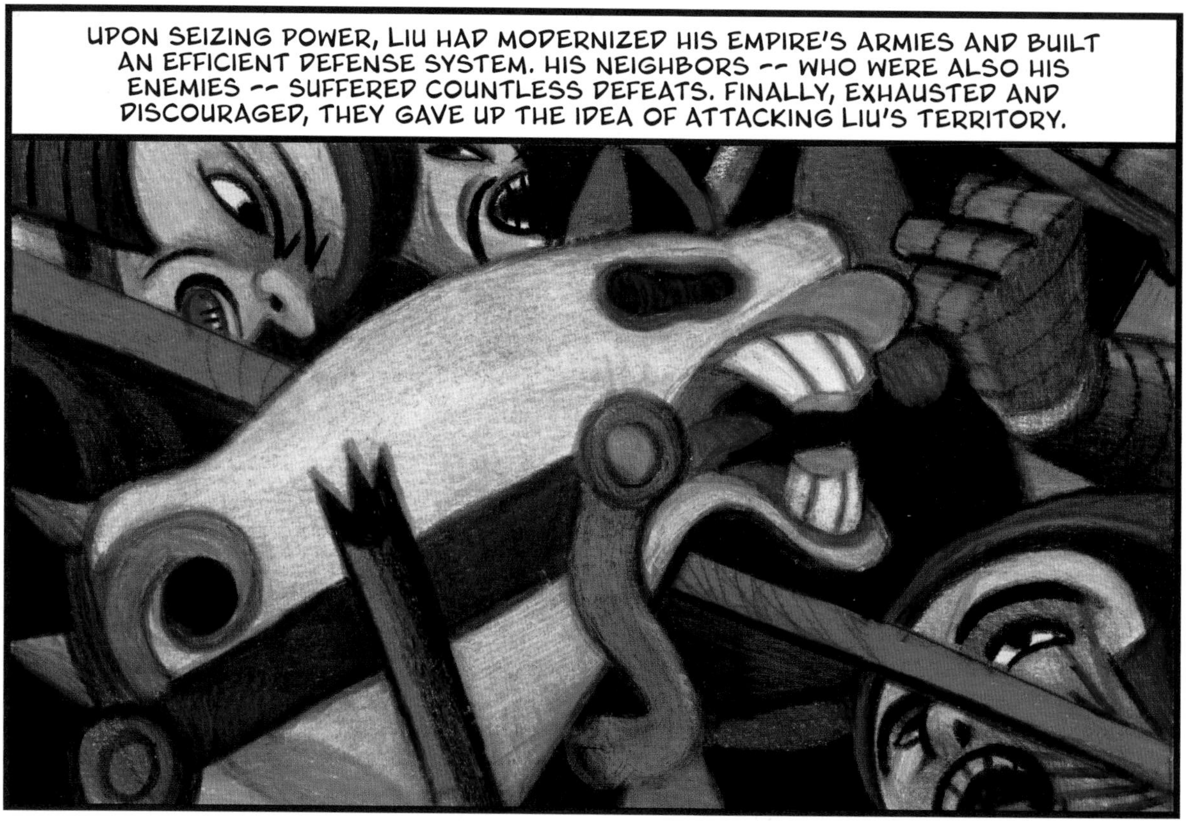
UPON SEIZING POWER, LIU HAD MODERNIZED HIS EMPIRE'S ARMIES AND BUILT AN EFFICIENT DEFENSE SYSTEM. HIS NEIGHBORS -- WHO WERE ALSO HIS ENEMIES -- SUFFERED COUNTLESS DEFEATS. FINALLY, EXHAUSTED AND DISCOURAGED, THEY GAVE UP THE IDEA OF ATTACKING LIU'S TERRITORY.

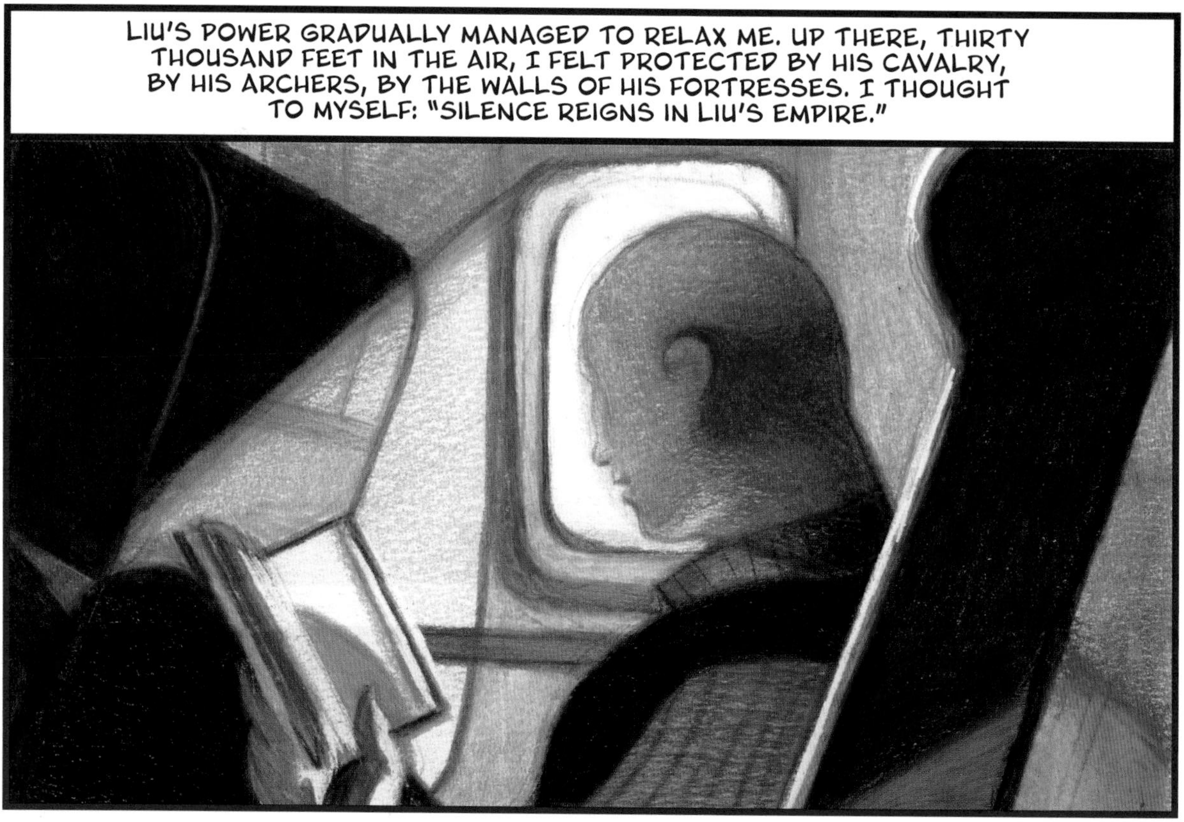
LIU'S POWER GRADUALLY MANAGED TO RELAX ME. UP THERE, THIRTY THOUSAND FEET IN THE AIR, I FELT PROTECTED BY HIS CAVALRY, BY HIS ARCHERS, BY THE WALLS OF HIS FORTRESSES. I THOUGHT TO MYSELF: "SILENCE REIGNS IN LIU'S EMPIRE."

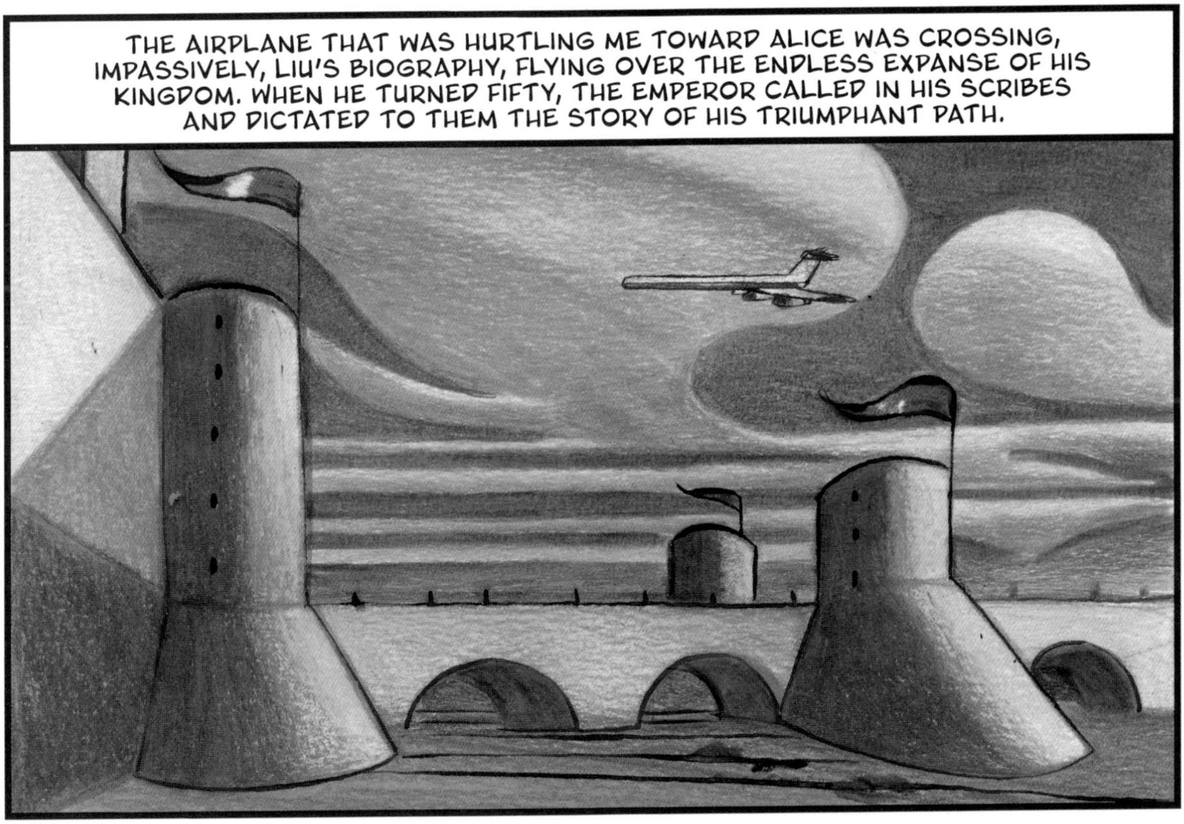
THE AIRPLANE THAT WAS HURTLING ME TOWARD ALICE WAS CROSSING, IMPASSIVELY, LIU'S BIOGRAPHY, FLYING OVER THE ENDLESS EXPANSE OF HIS KINGDOM. WHEN HE TURNED FIFTY, THE EMPEROR CALLED IN HIS SCRIBES AND DICTATED TO THEM THE STORY OF HIS TRIUMPHANT PATH.

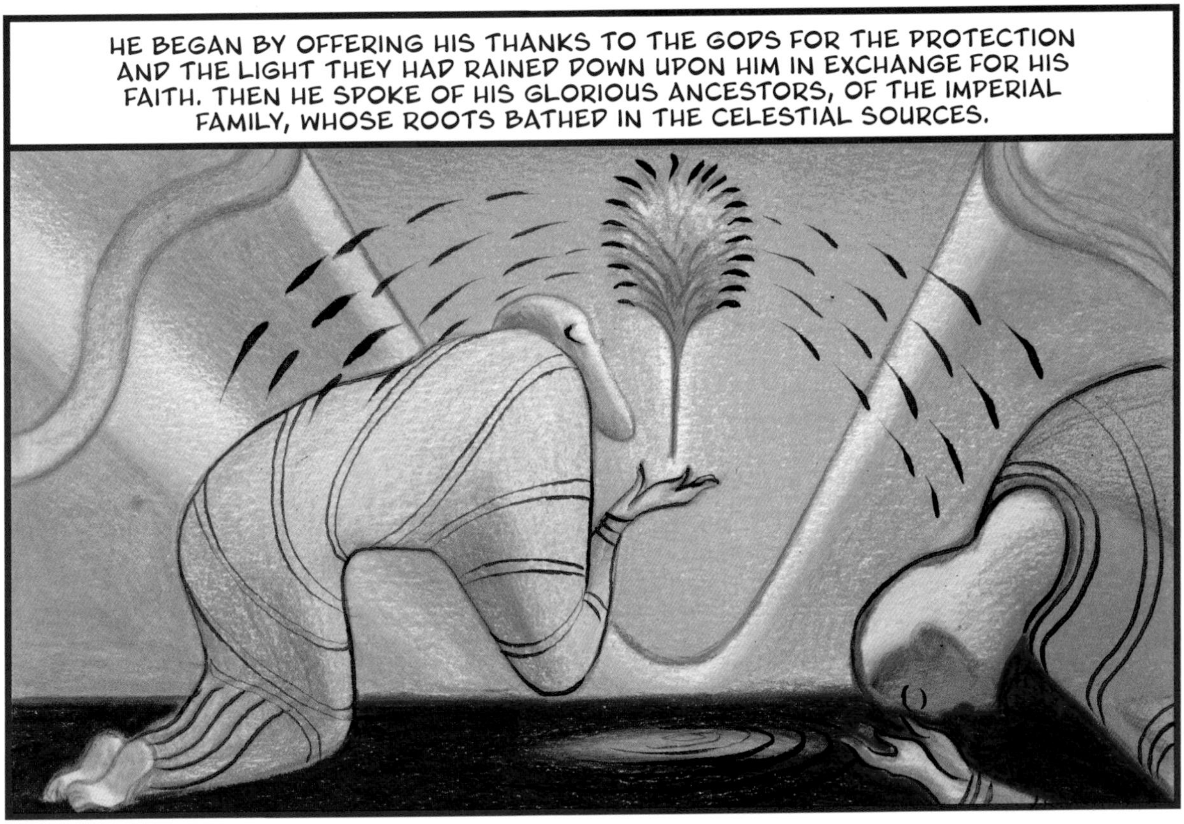
HE BEGAN BY OFFERING HIS THANKS TO THE GODS FOR THE PROTECTION AND THE LIGHT THEY HAD RAINED DOWN UPON HIM IN EXCHANGE FOR HIS FAITH. THEN HE SPOKE OF HIS GLORIOUS ANCESTORS, OF THE IMPERIAL FAMILY, WHOSE ROOTS BATHED IN THE CELESTIAL SOURCES.

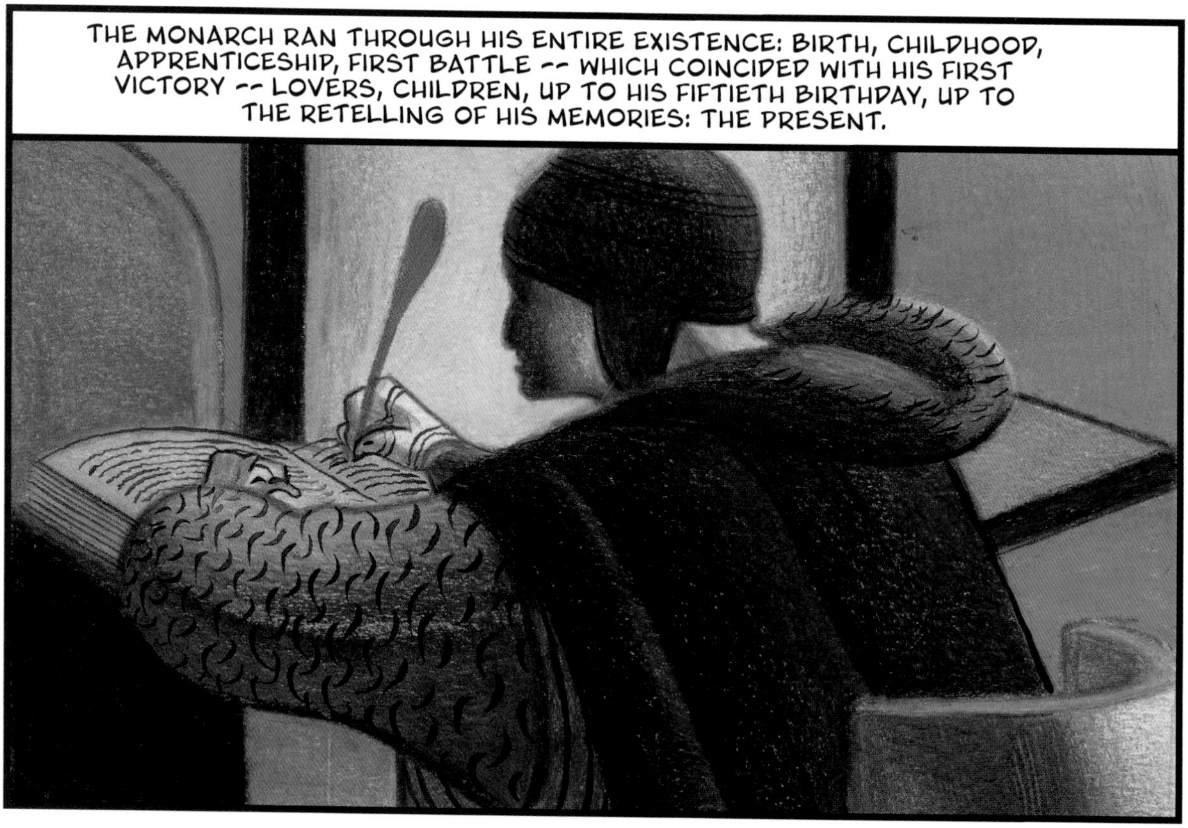
THE MONARCH RAN THROUGH HIS ENTIRE EXISTENCE: BIRTH, CHILDHOOD, APPRENTICESHIP, FIRST BATTLE -- WHICH COINCIDED WITH HIS FIRST VICTORY -- LOVERS, CHILDREN, UP TO HIS FIFTIETH BIRTHDAY, UP TO THE RETELLING OF HIS MEMORIES: THE PRESENT.

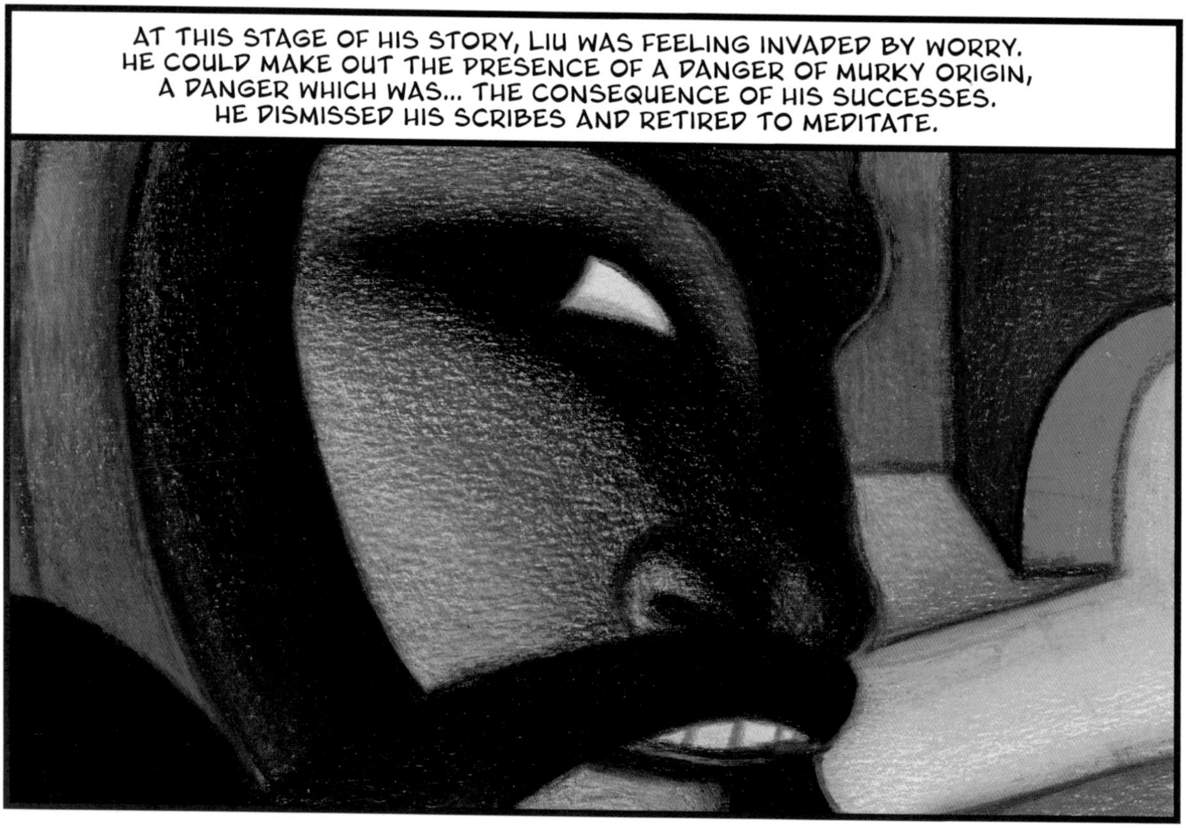
AT THIS STAGE OF HIS STORY, LIU WAS FEELING INVADED BY WORRY. HE COULD MAKE OUT THE PRESENCE OF A DANGER OF MURKY ORIGIN, A DANGER WHICH WAS... THE CONSEQUENCE OF HIS SUCCESSES. HE DISMISSED HIS SCRIBES AND RETIRED TO MEDITATE.

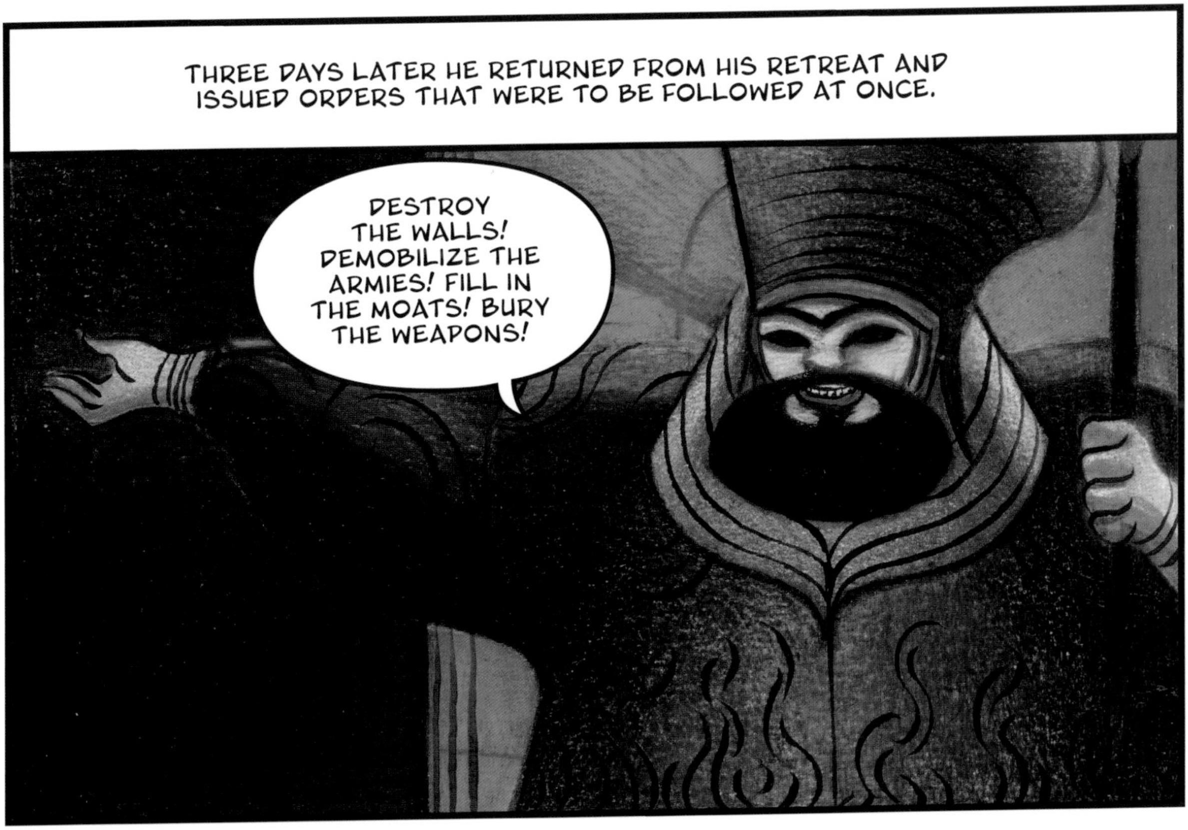
THREE DAYS LATER HE RETURNED FROM HIS RETREAT AND ISSUED ORDERS THAT WERE TO BE FOLLOWED AT ONCE.
DESTROY THE WALLS! DEMOBILIZE THE ARMIES! FILL IN THE MOATS! BURY THE WEAPONS!

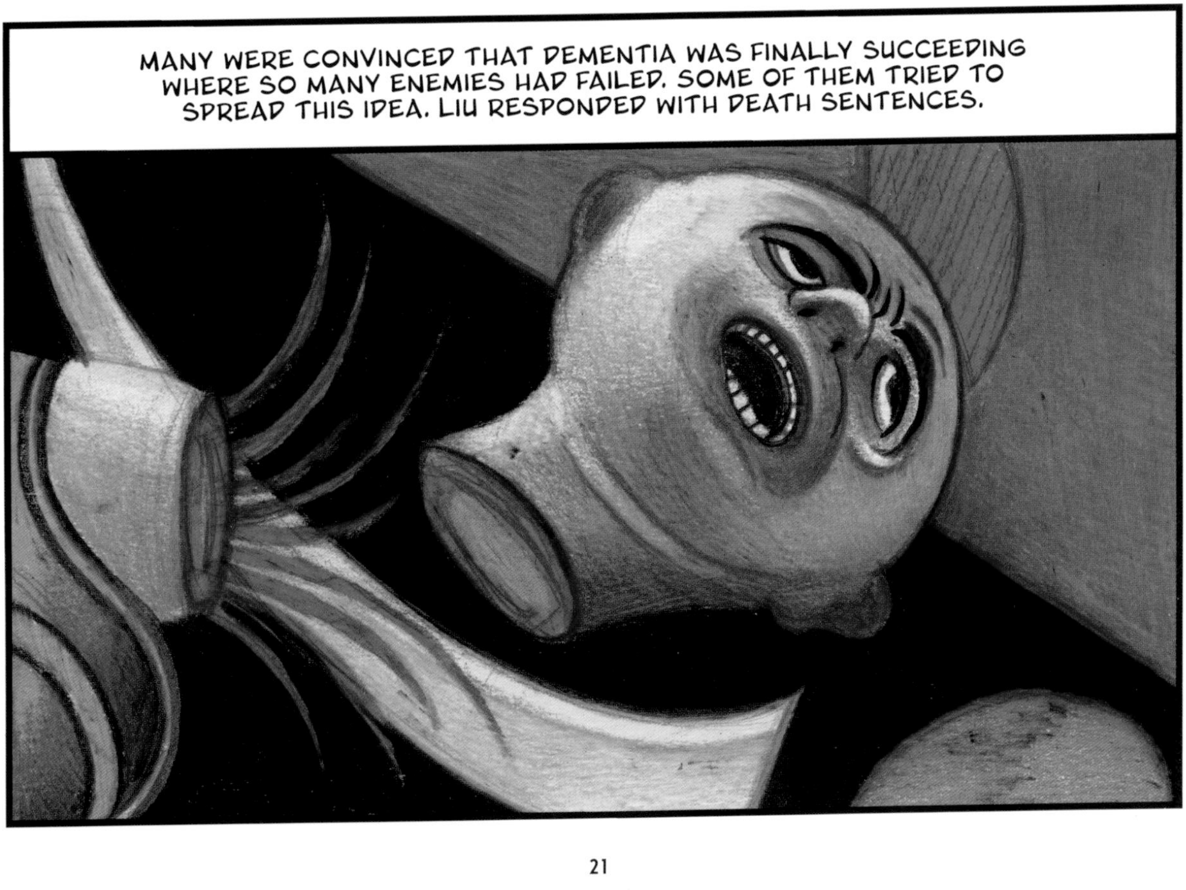
MANY WERE CONVINCED THAT DEMENTIA WAS FINALLY SUCCEEDING WHERE SO MANY ENEMIES HAD FAILED. SOME OF THEM TRIED TO SPREAD THIS IDEA. LIU RESPONDED WITH DEATH SENTENCES.

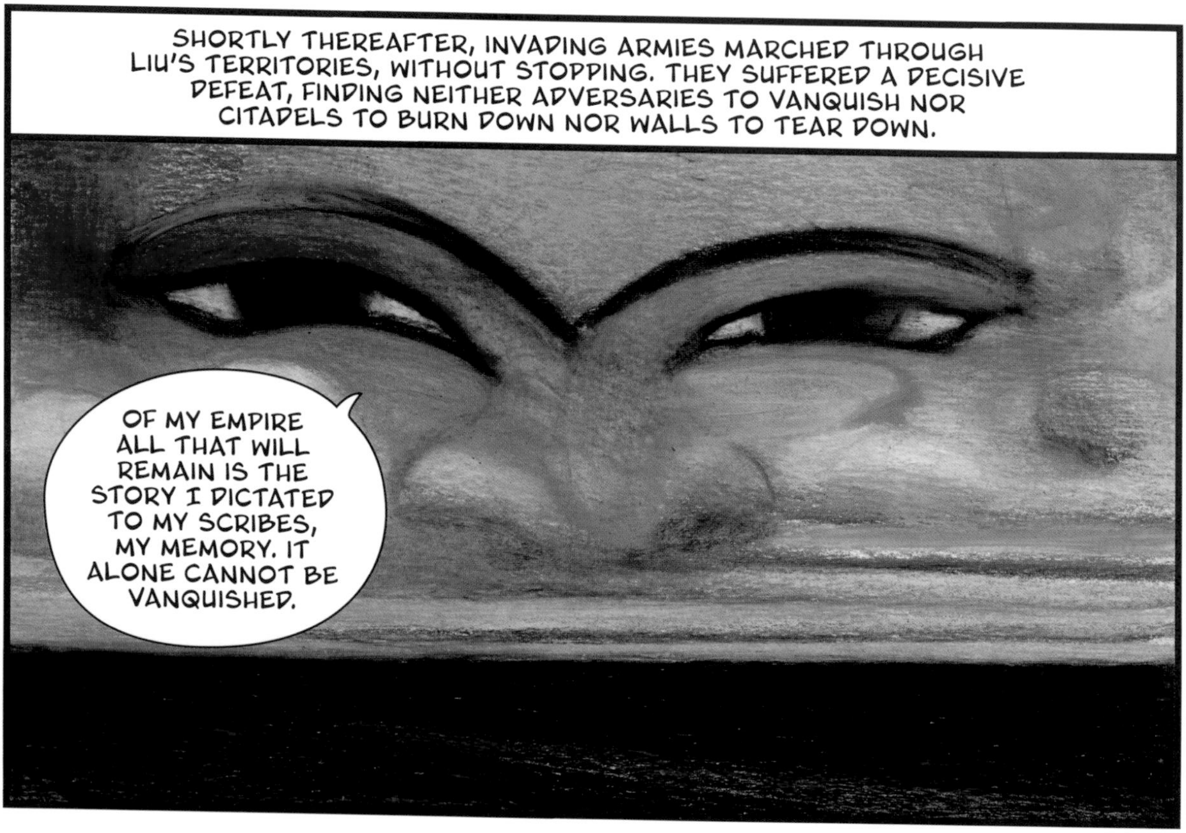
SHORTLY THEREAFTER, INVADING ARMIES MARCHED THROUGH LIU'S TERRITORIES, WITHOUT STOPPING. THEY SUFFERED A DECISIVE DEFEAT, FINDING NEITHER ADVERSARIES TO VANQUISH NOR CITADELS TO BURN DOWN NOR WALLS TO TEAR DOWN.
OF MY EMPIRE ALL THAT WILL REMAIN IS THE STORY I DICTATED TO MY SCRIBES, MY MEMORY. IT ALONE CANNOT BE VANQUISHED.

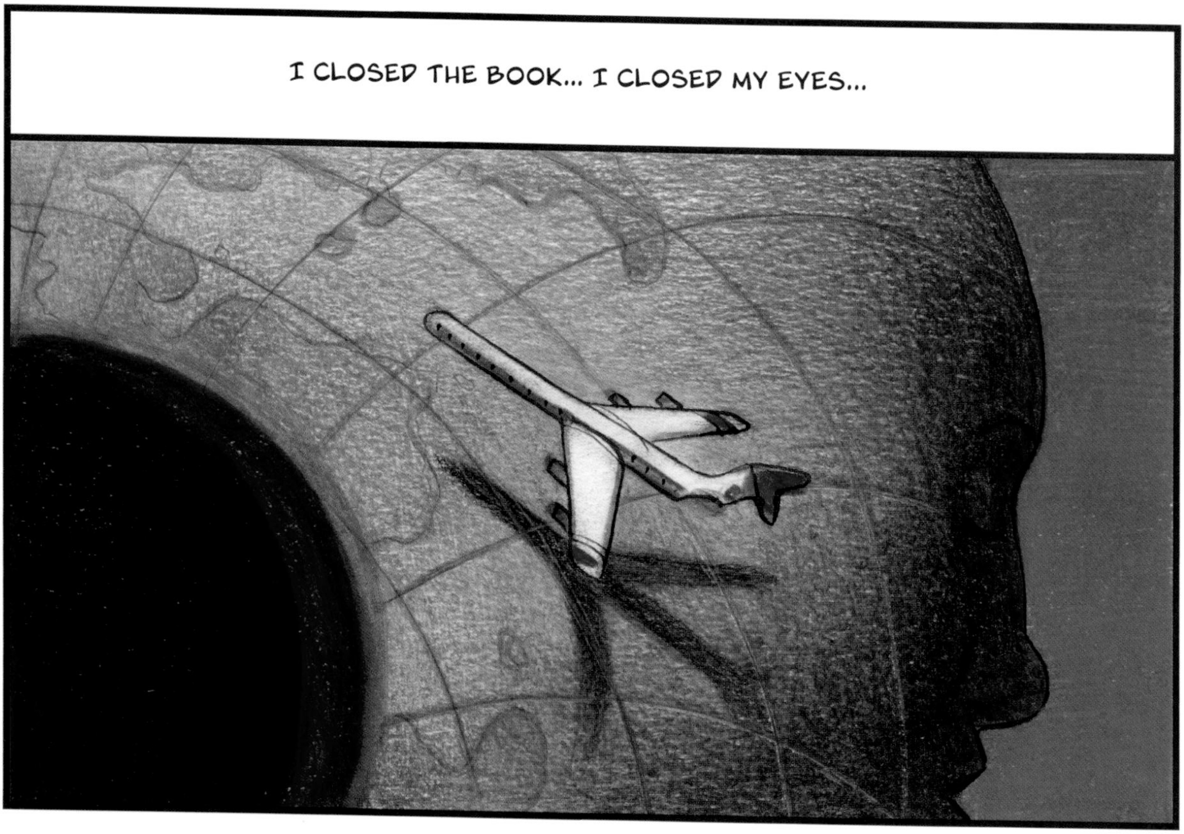
I CLOSED THE BOOK... I CLOSED MY EYES...

2

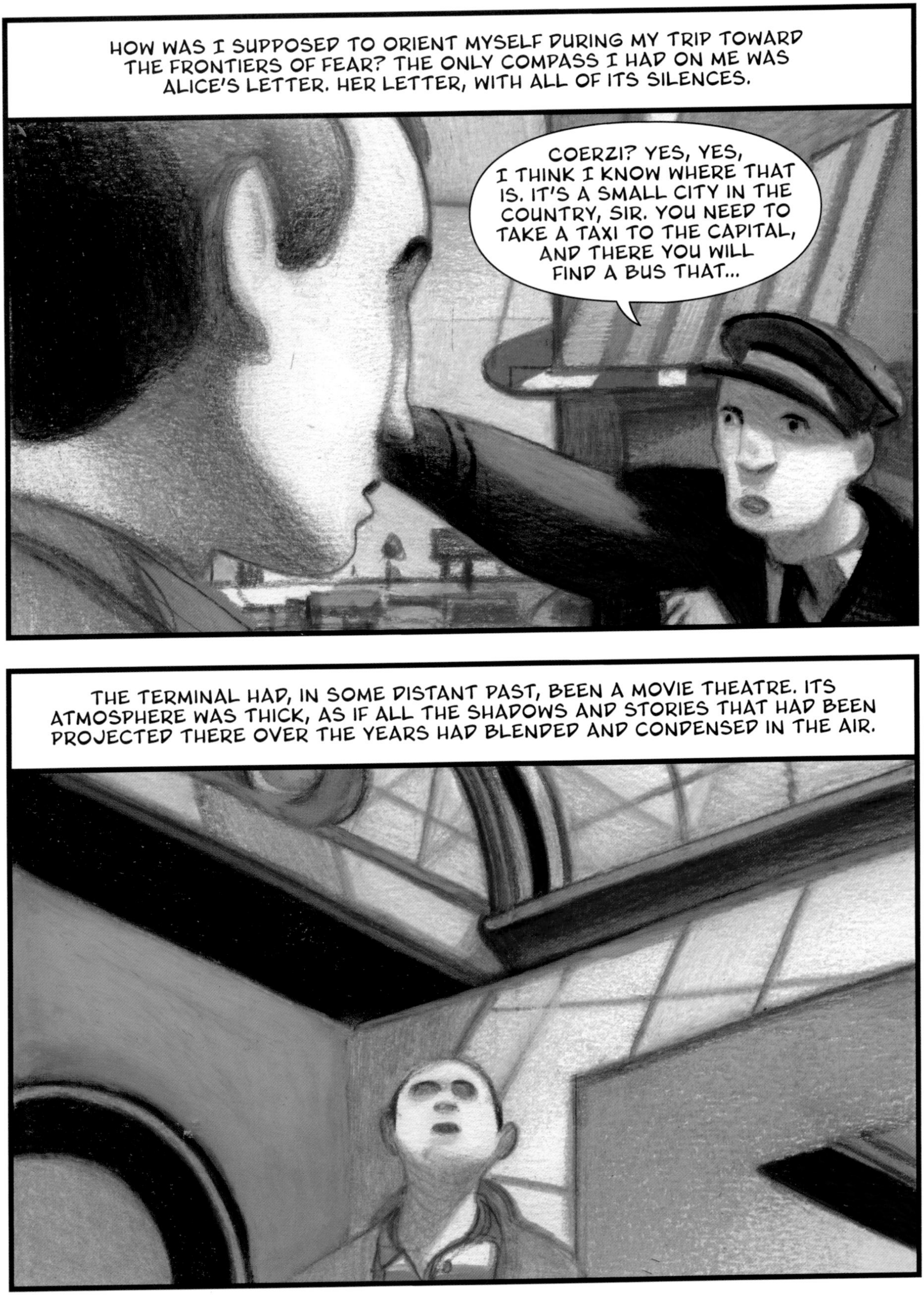
HOW WAS I SUPPOSED TO ORIENT MYSELF DURING MY TRIP TOWARD THE FRONTIERS OF FEAR? THE ONLY COMPASS I HAD ON ME WAS ALICE'S LETTER. HER LETTER, WITH ALL OF ITS SILENCES.
COERZI? YES, YES, I THINK I KNOW WHERE THAT IS. IT'S A SMALL CITY IN THE COUNTRY, SIR. YOU NEED TO TAKE A TAXI TO THE CAPITAL, AND THERE YOU WILL FIND A BUS THAT...
THE TERMINAL HAD, IN SOME DISTANT PAST, BEEN A MOVIE THEATRE. ITS ATMOSPHERE WAS THICK, AS IF ALL THE SHADOWS AND STORIES THAT HAD BEEN PROJECTED THERE OVER THE YEARS HAD BLENDED AND CONDENSED IN THE AIR.

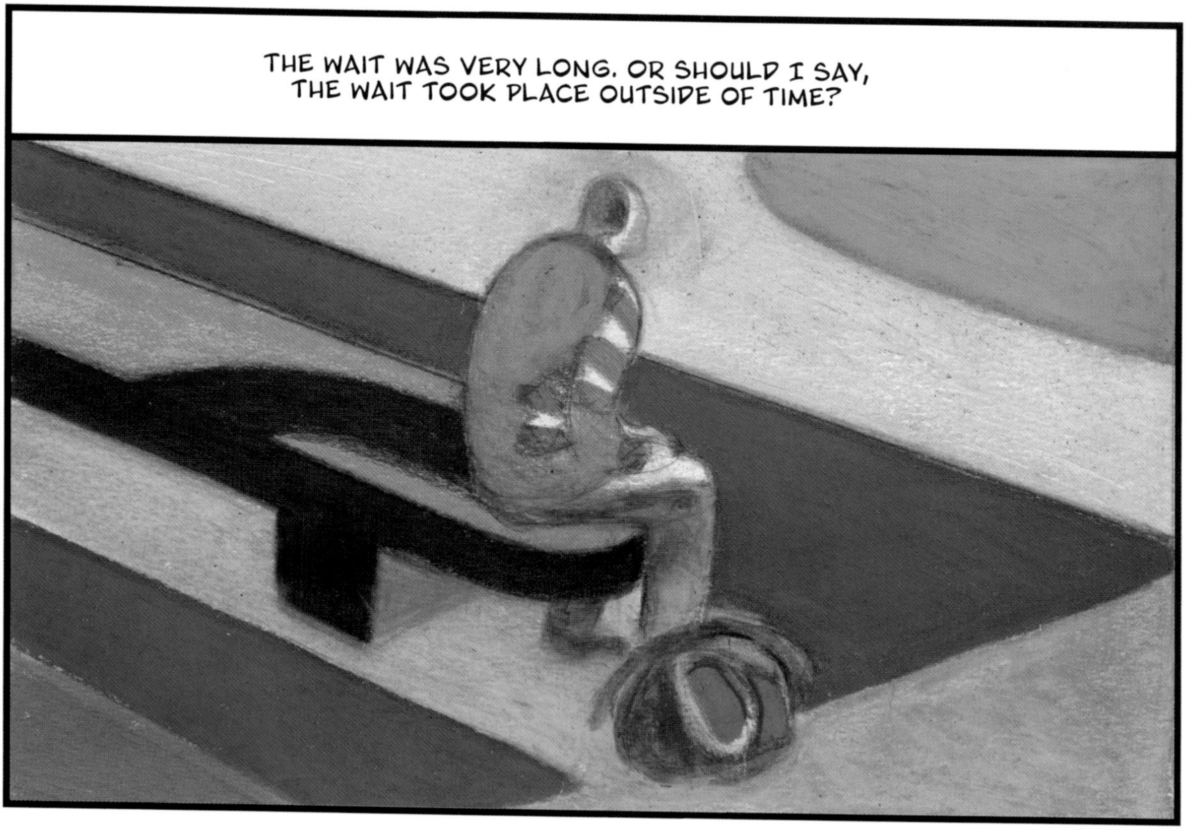
THE WAIT WAS VERY LONG. OR SHOULD I SAY, THE WAIT TOOK PLACE OUTSIDE OF TIME?

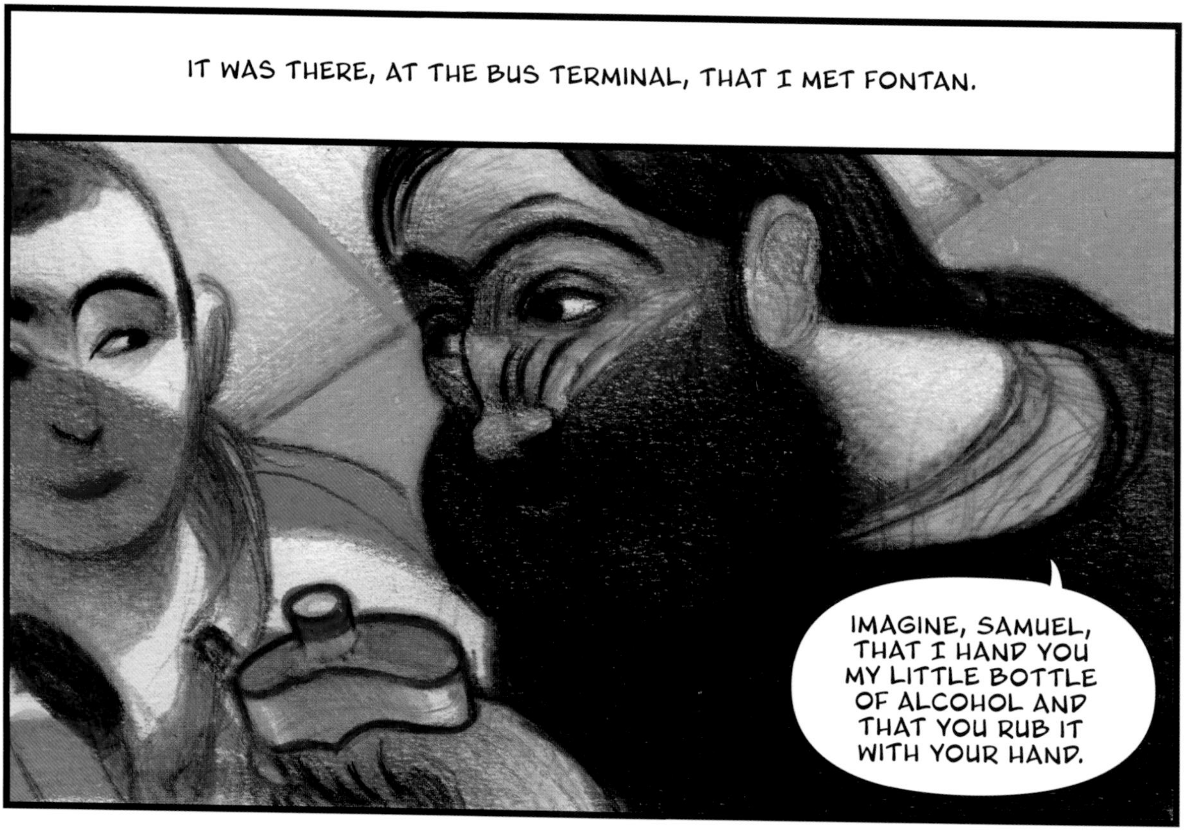
IT WAS THERE, AT THE BUS TERMINAL, THAT I MET FONTAN.
IMAGINE, SAMUEL, THAT I HAND YOU MY LITTLE BOTTLE OF ALCOHOL AND THAT YOU RUB IT WITH YOUR HAND.

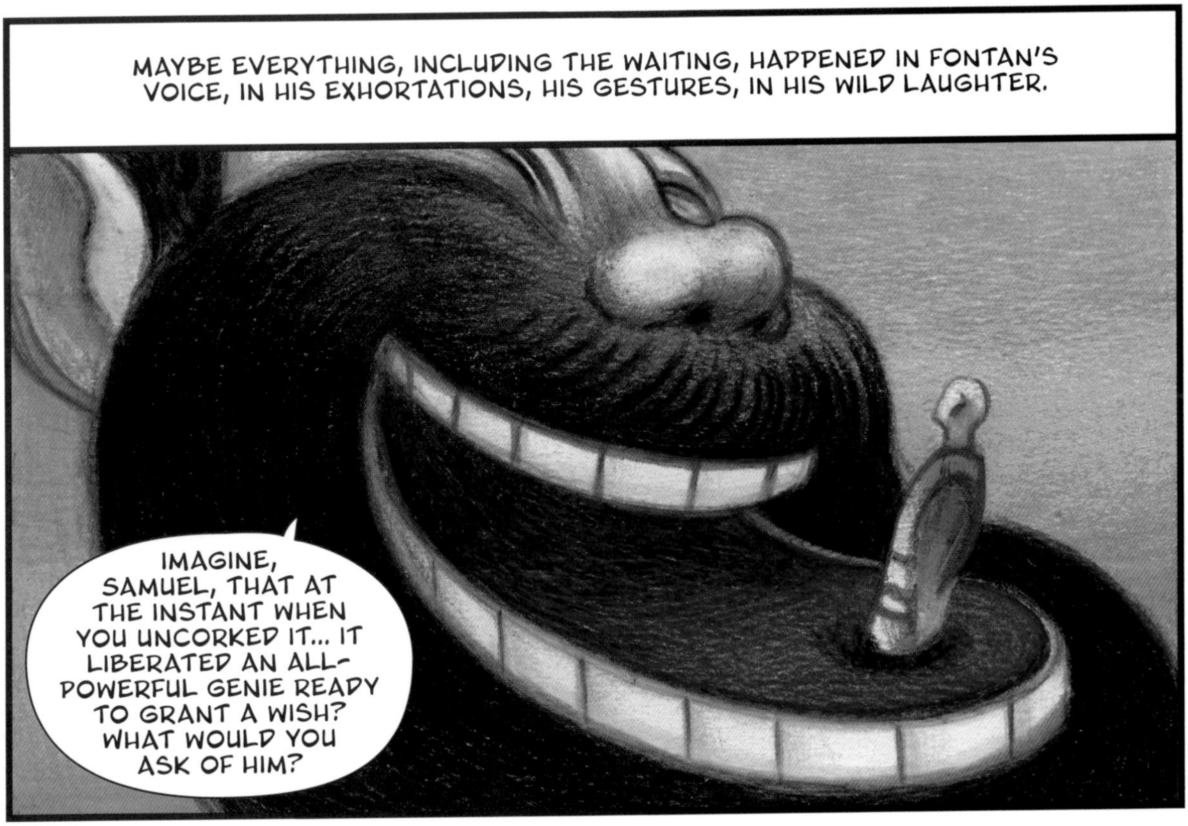
MAYBE EVERYTHING, INCLUDING THE WAITING, HAPPENED IN FONTAN'S VOICE, IN HIS EXHORTATIONS, HIS GESTURES, IN HIS WILD LAUGHTER.
IMAGINE, SAMUEL, THAT AT THE INSTANT WHEN YOU UNCORKED IT... IT LIBERATED AN ALL-POWERFUL GENIE READY TO GRANT A WISH? WHAT WOULD YOU ASK OF HIM?

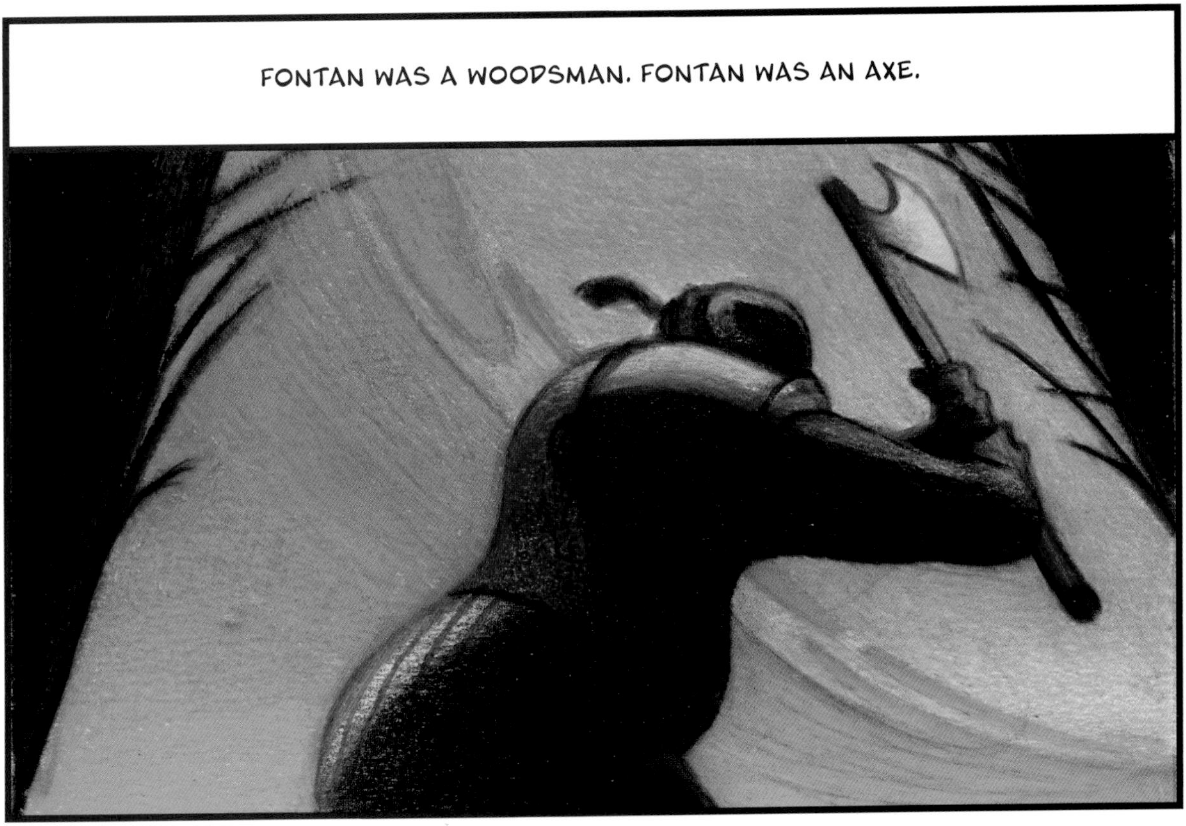
FONTAN WAS A WOODSMAN. FONTAN WAS AN AXE.

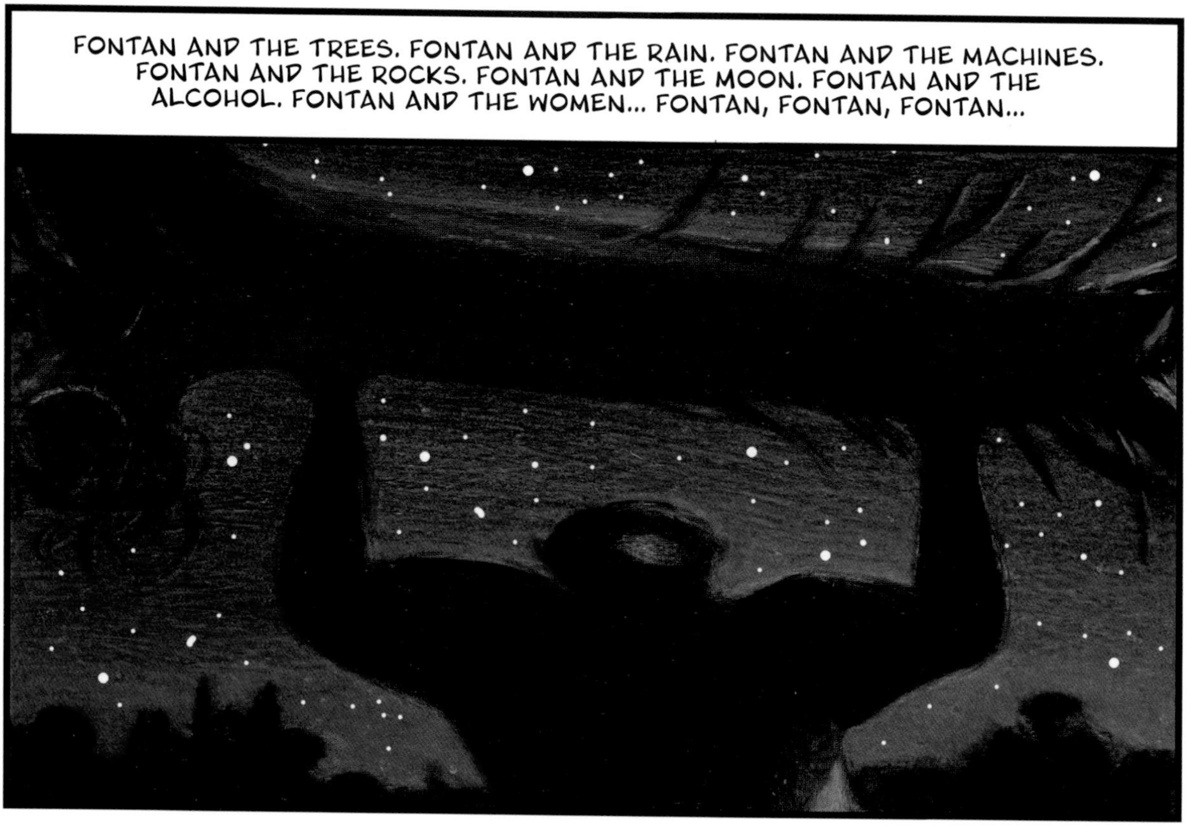
FONTAN AND THE TREES. FONTAN AND THE RAIN. FONTAN AND THE MACHINES. FONTAN AND THE ROCKS. FONTAN AND THE MOON. FONTAN AND THE ALCOHOL. FONTAN AND THE WOMEN... FONTAN, FONTAN, FONTAN...

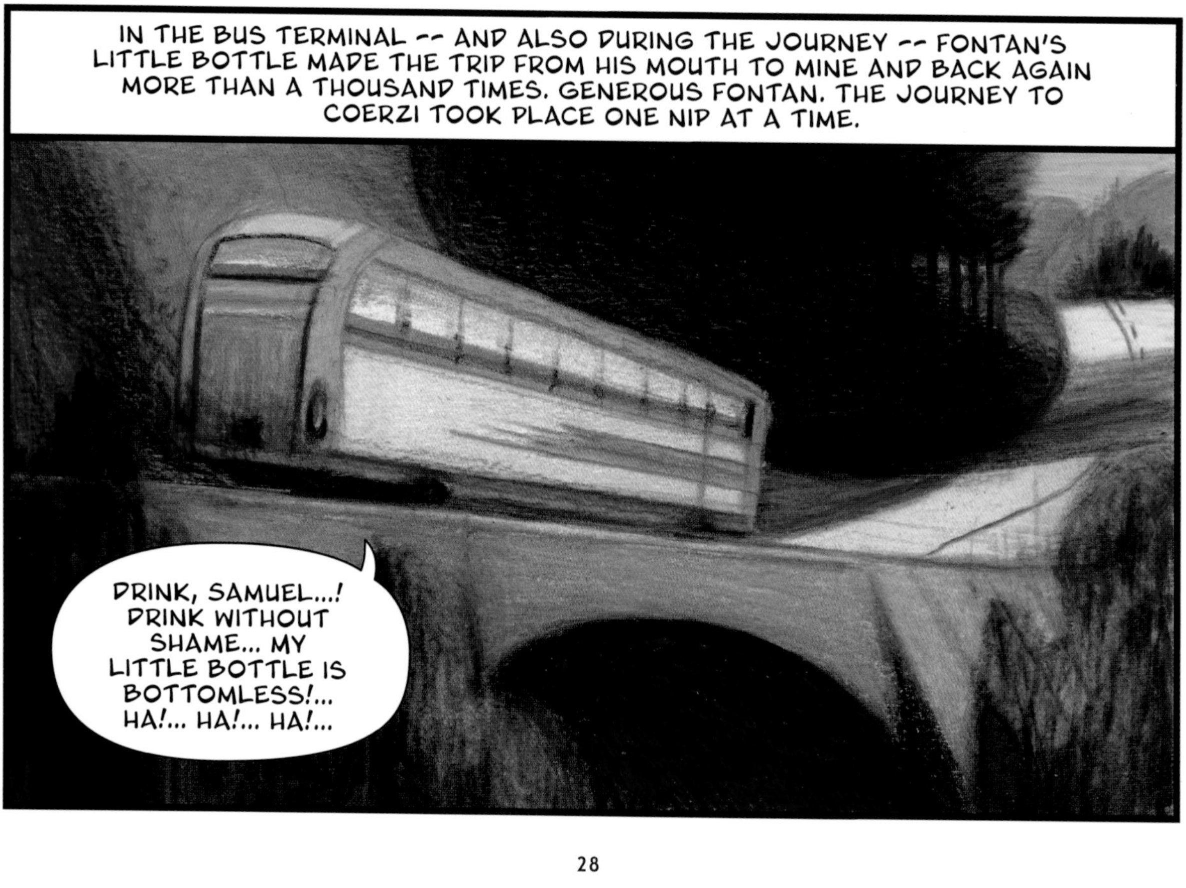
IN THE BUS TERMINAL -- AND ALSO DURING THE JOURNEY -- FONTAN'S LITTLE BOTTLE MADE THE TRIP FROM HIS MOUTH TO MINE AND BACK AGAIN MORE THAN A THOUSAND TIMES. GENEROUS FONTAN. THE JOURNEY TO COERZI TOOK PLACE ONE NIP AT A TIME.
DRINK, SAMUEL...! DRINK WITHOUT SHAME... MY LITTLE BOTTLE IS BOTTOMLESS!... HA!... HA!... HA!...

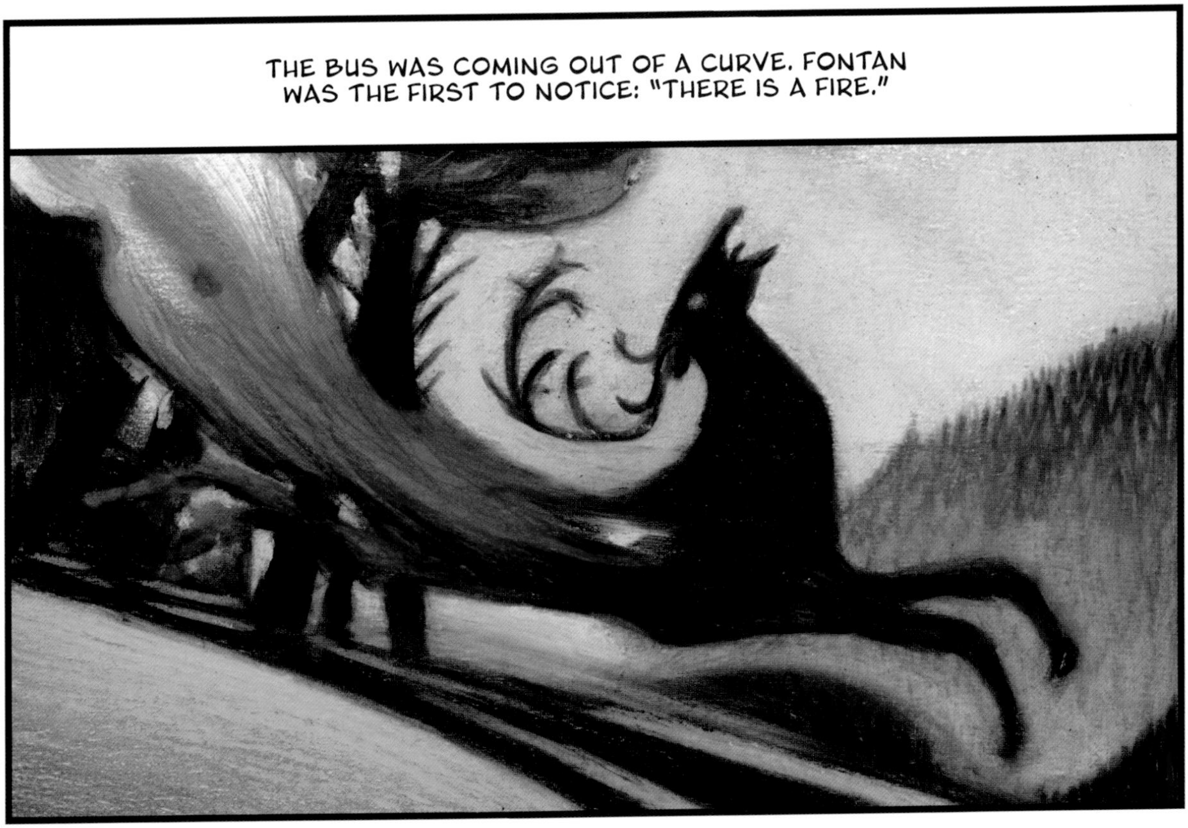
THE BUS WAS COMING OUT OF A CURVE. FONTAN WAS THE FIRST TO NOTICE: "THERE IS A FIRE."

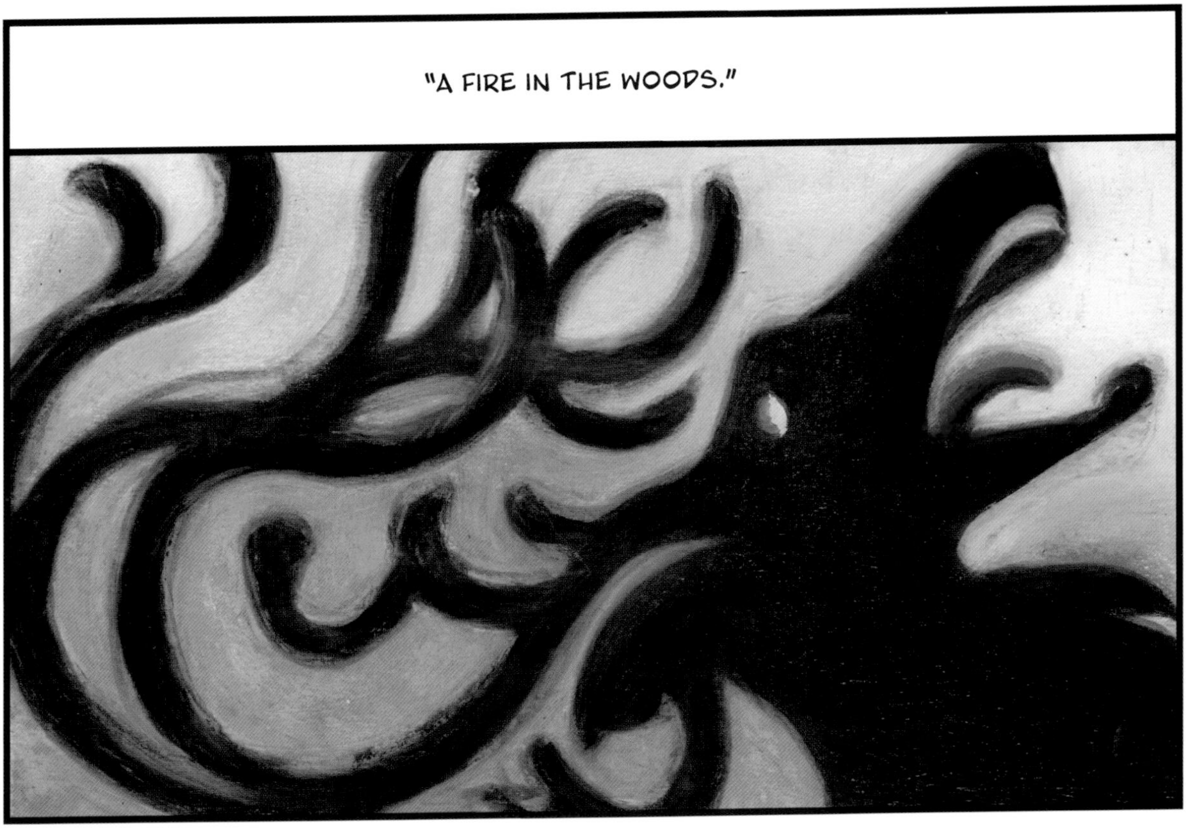
"A FIRE IN THE WOODS."

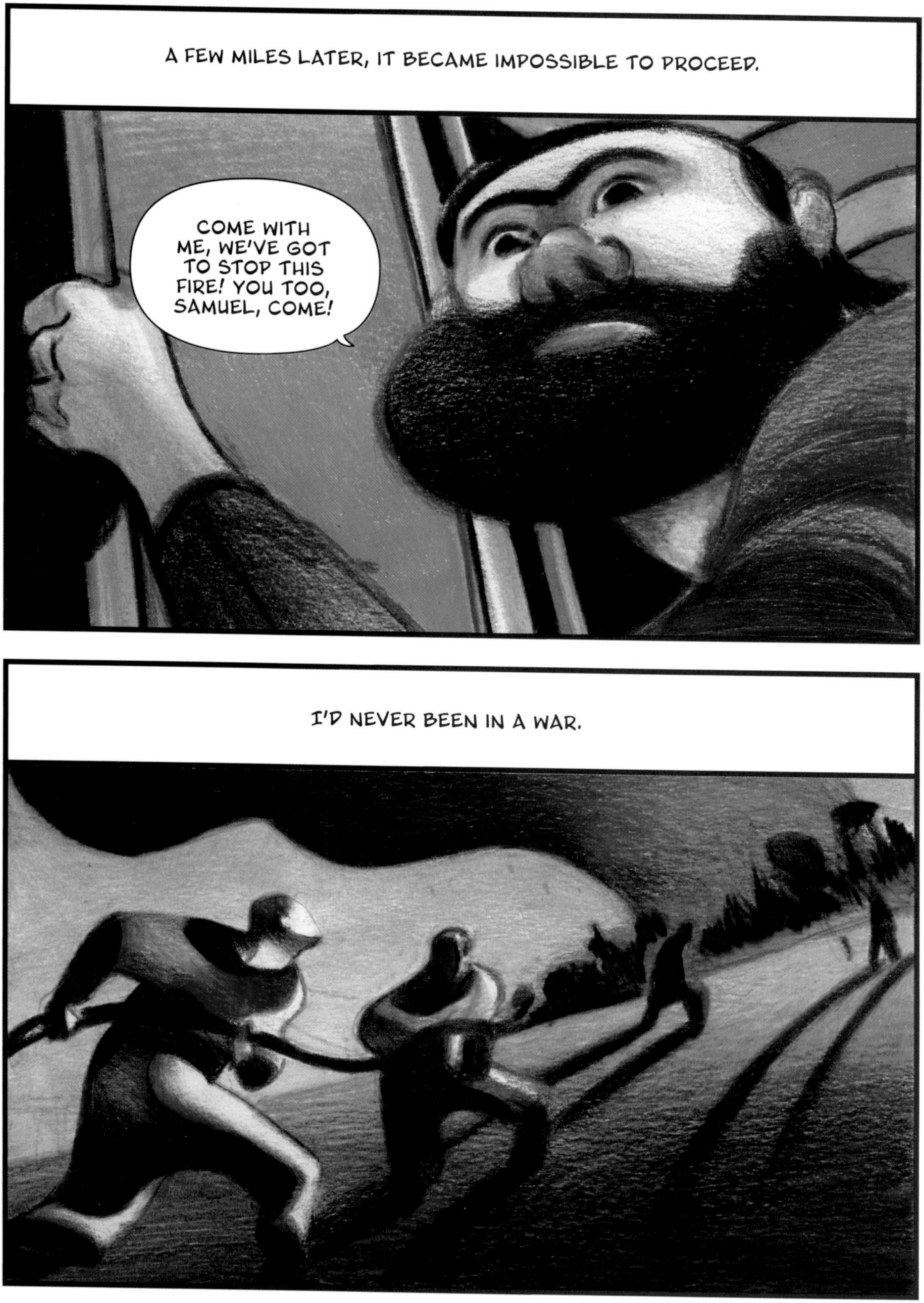
A FEW MILES LATER, IT BECAME IMPOSSIBLE TO PROCEED.
COME WITH ME, WE'VE GOT TO STOP THIS FIRE! YOU TOO, SAMUEL, COME!
I'D NEVER BEEN IN A WAR.

ALL THE HELLS I'D KNOWN WERE THOSE OF SOUNDS... ALICE'S MATERNAL DESIRES... THE HELLS ENGENDERED BY A FEAR OF LIFE.

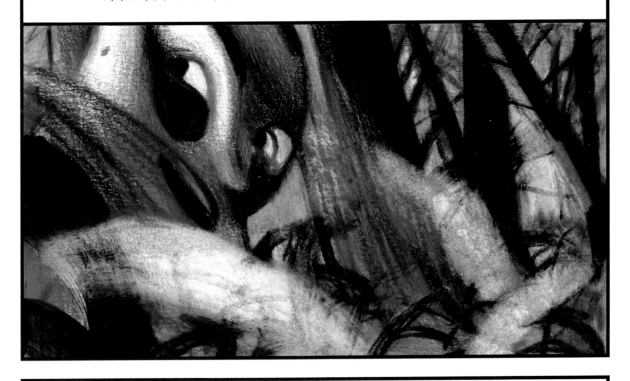

BUT THE FLAMING FOREST WAS DRENCHED IN DEATH: THERE WAS NO ROOM FOR FEAR. AT LEAST, NOT THAT KIND OF FEAR.

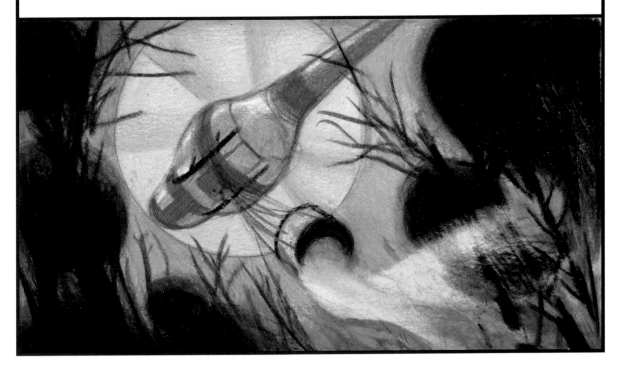

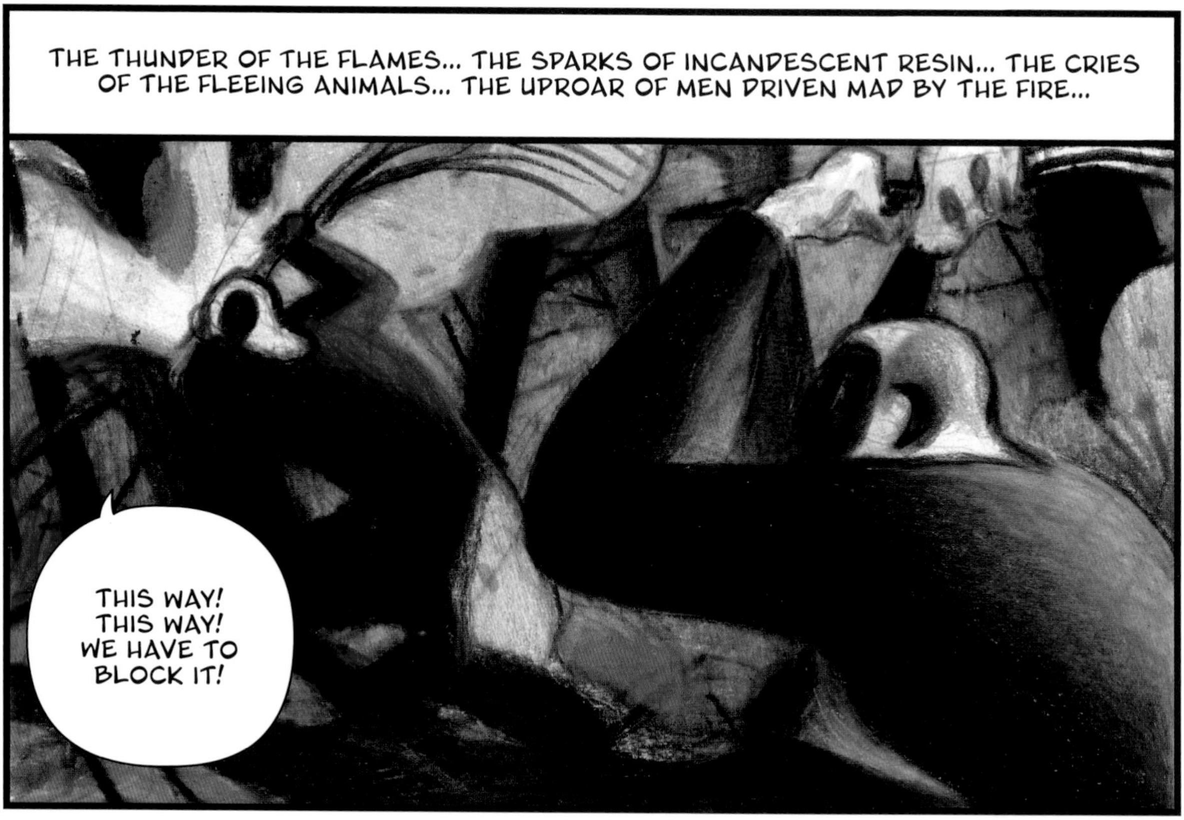
THE THUNDER OF THE FLAMES... THE SPARKS OF INCANDESCENT RESIN... THE CRIES OF THE FLEEING ANIMALS... THE UPROAR OF MEN DRIVEN MAD BY THE FIRE...
THIS WAY! THIS WAY! WE HAVE TO BLOCK IT!

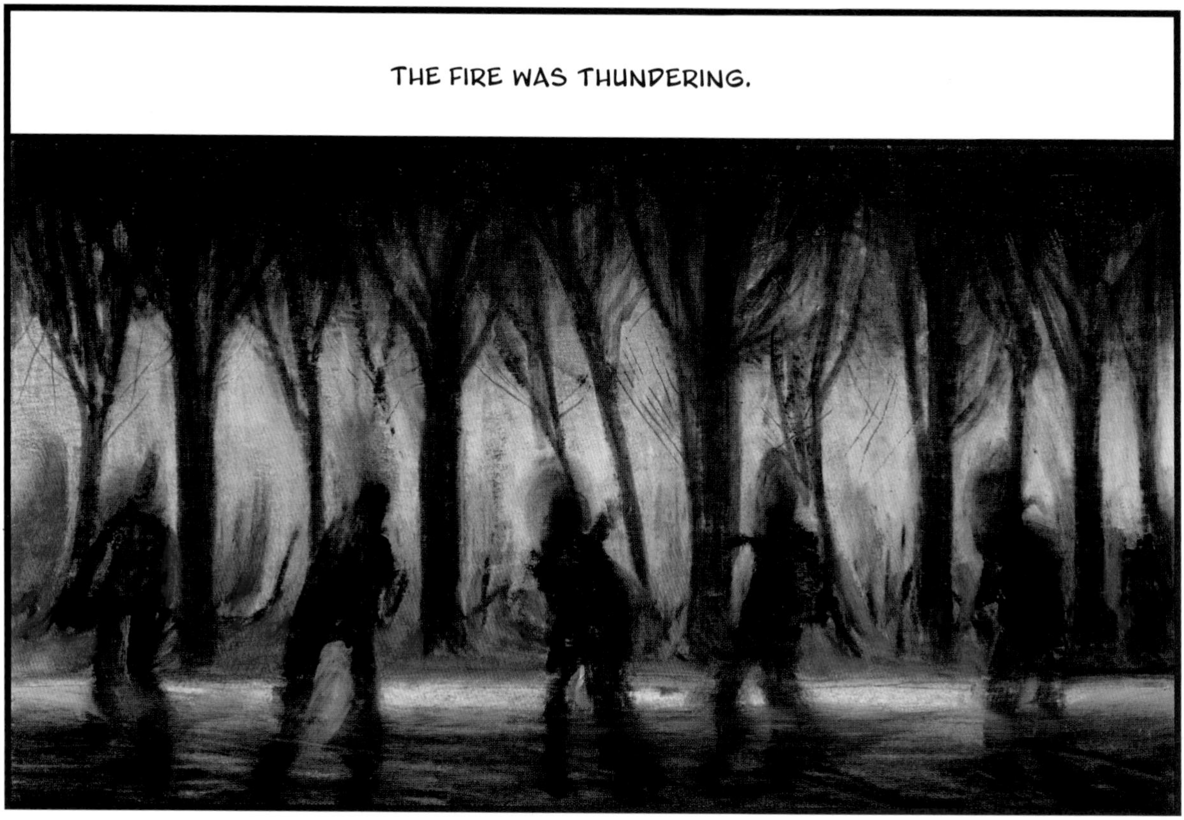
THE FIRE WAS THUNDERING.

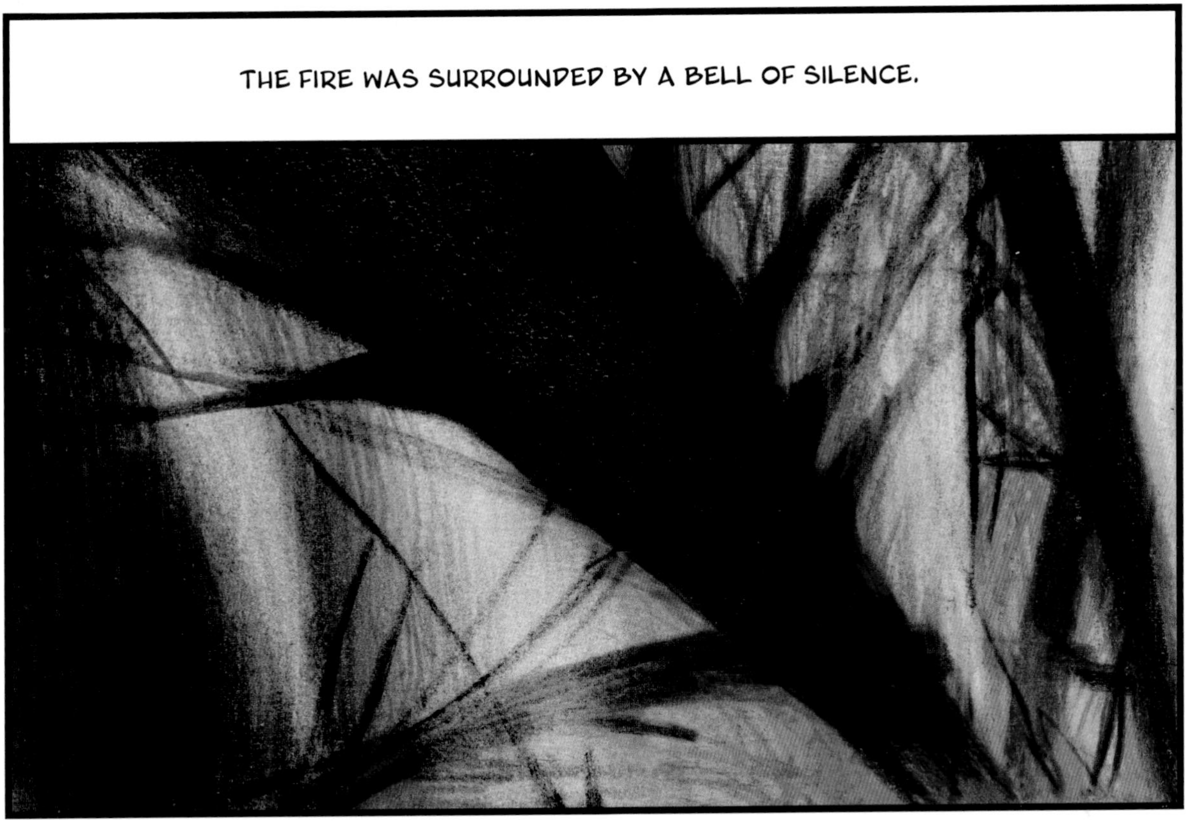
THE FIRE WAS SURROUNDED BY A BELL OF SILENCE.

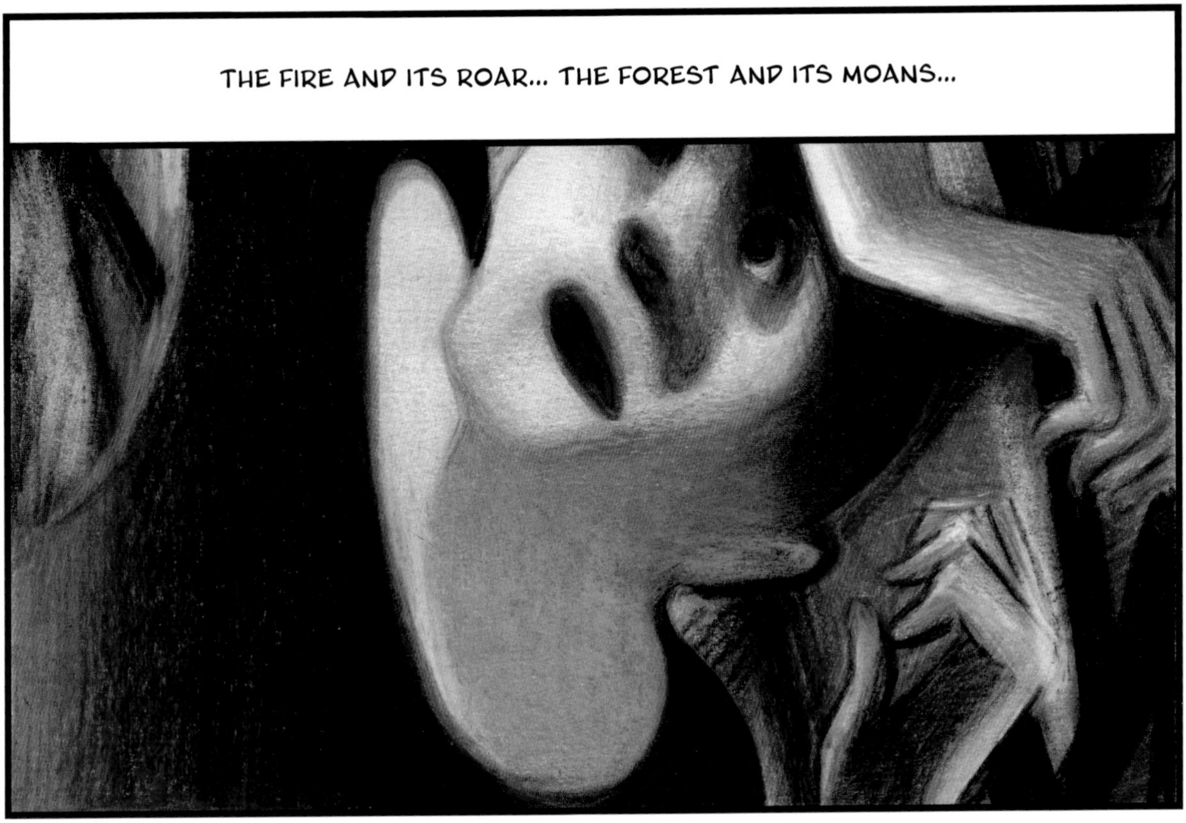
THE FIRE AND ITS ROAR... THE FOREST AND ITS MOANS...

WHAT COULD WE DO, WE HUMANS, WHEN FACED WITH THIS BATTLE OF GIANTS?

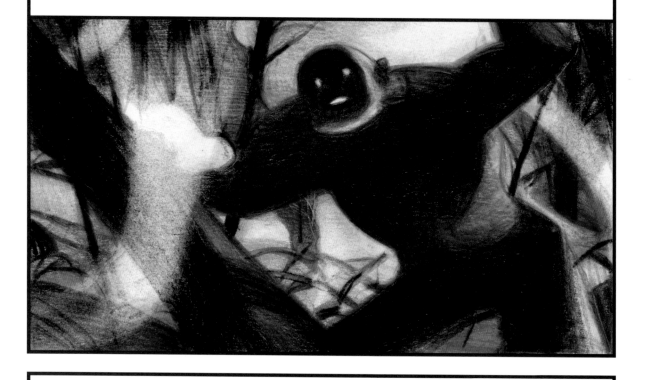

ALL I REMEMBER IS BLACK SMOKE.

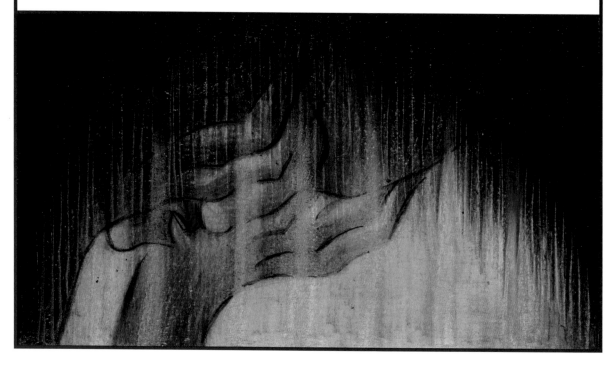

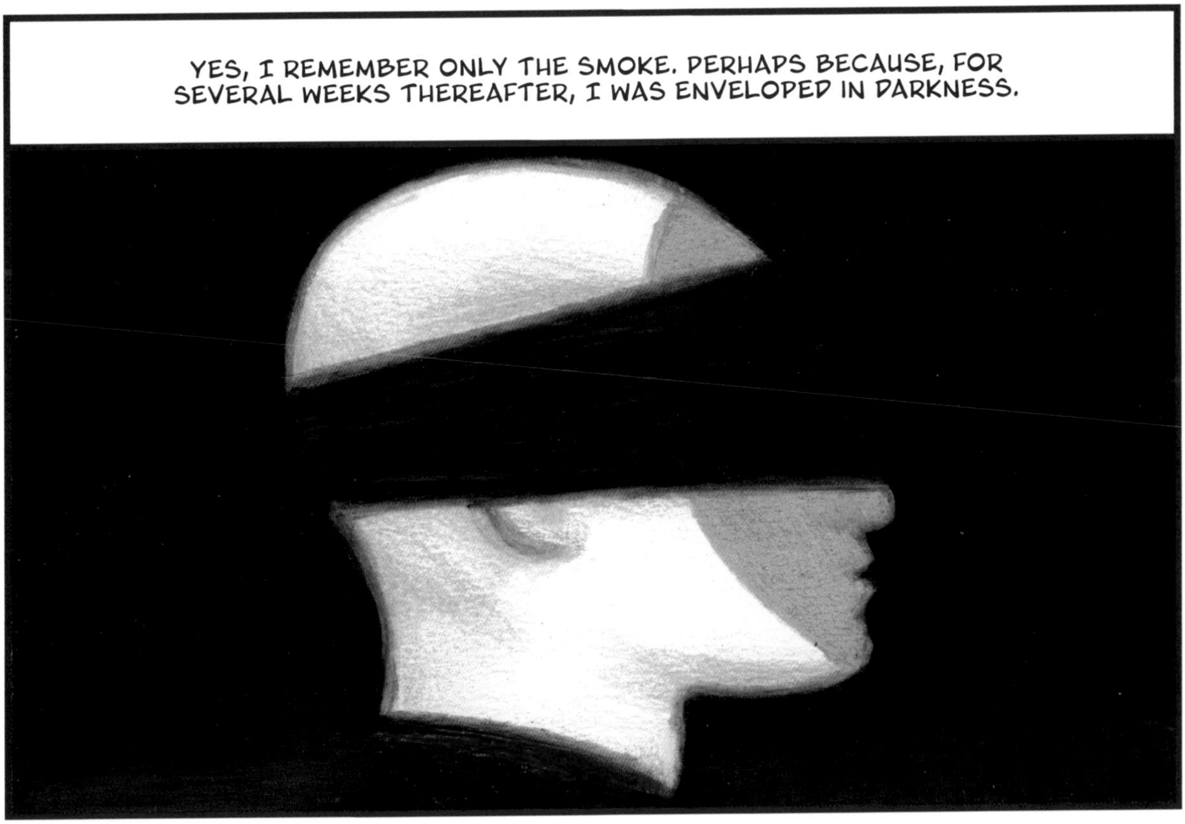
YES, I REMEMBER ONLY THE SMOKE. PERHAPS BECAUSE, FOR SEVERAL WEEKS THEREAFTER, I WAS ENVELOPED IN DARKNESS.

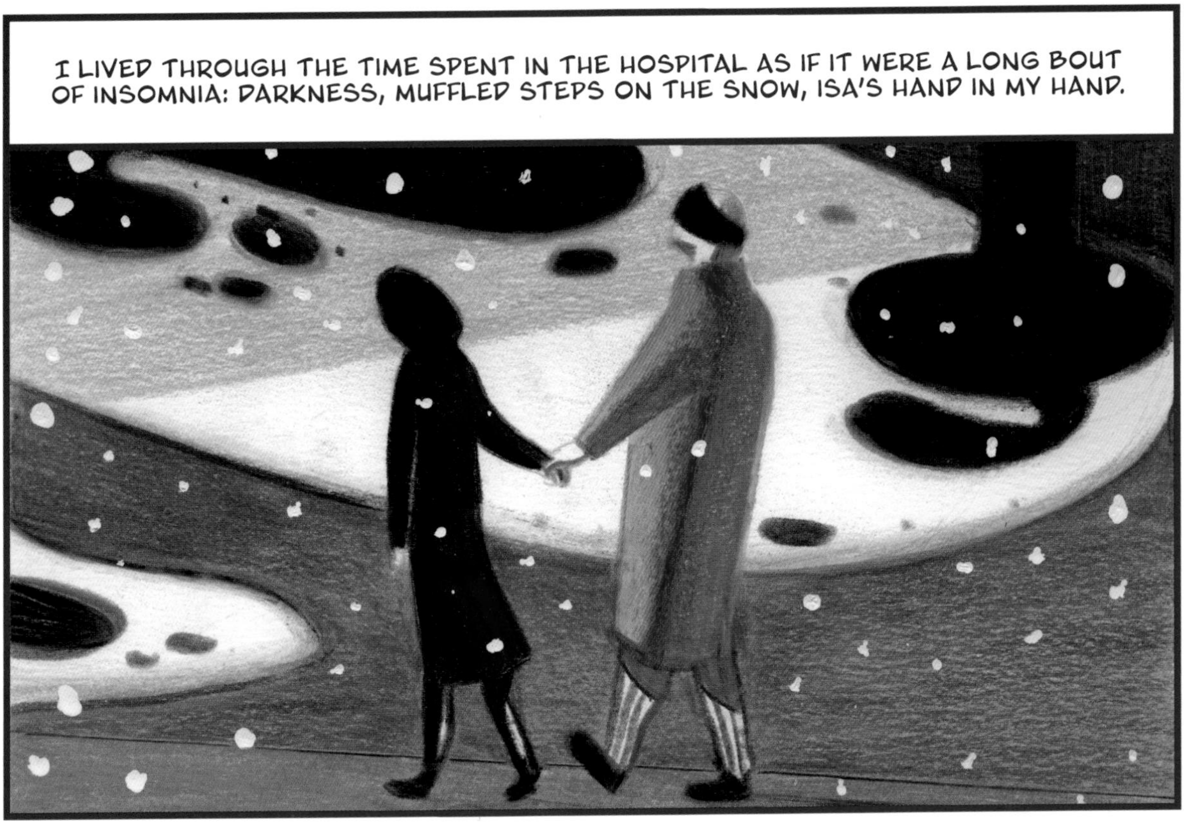
I LIVED THROUGH THE TIME SPENT IN THE HOSPITAL AS IF IT WERE A LONG BOUT OF INSOMNIA: DARKNESS, MUFFLED STEPS ON THE SNOW, ISA'S HAND IN MY HAND.

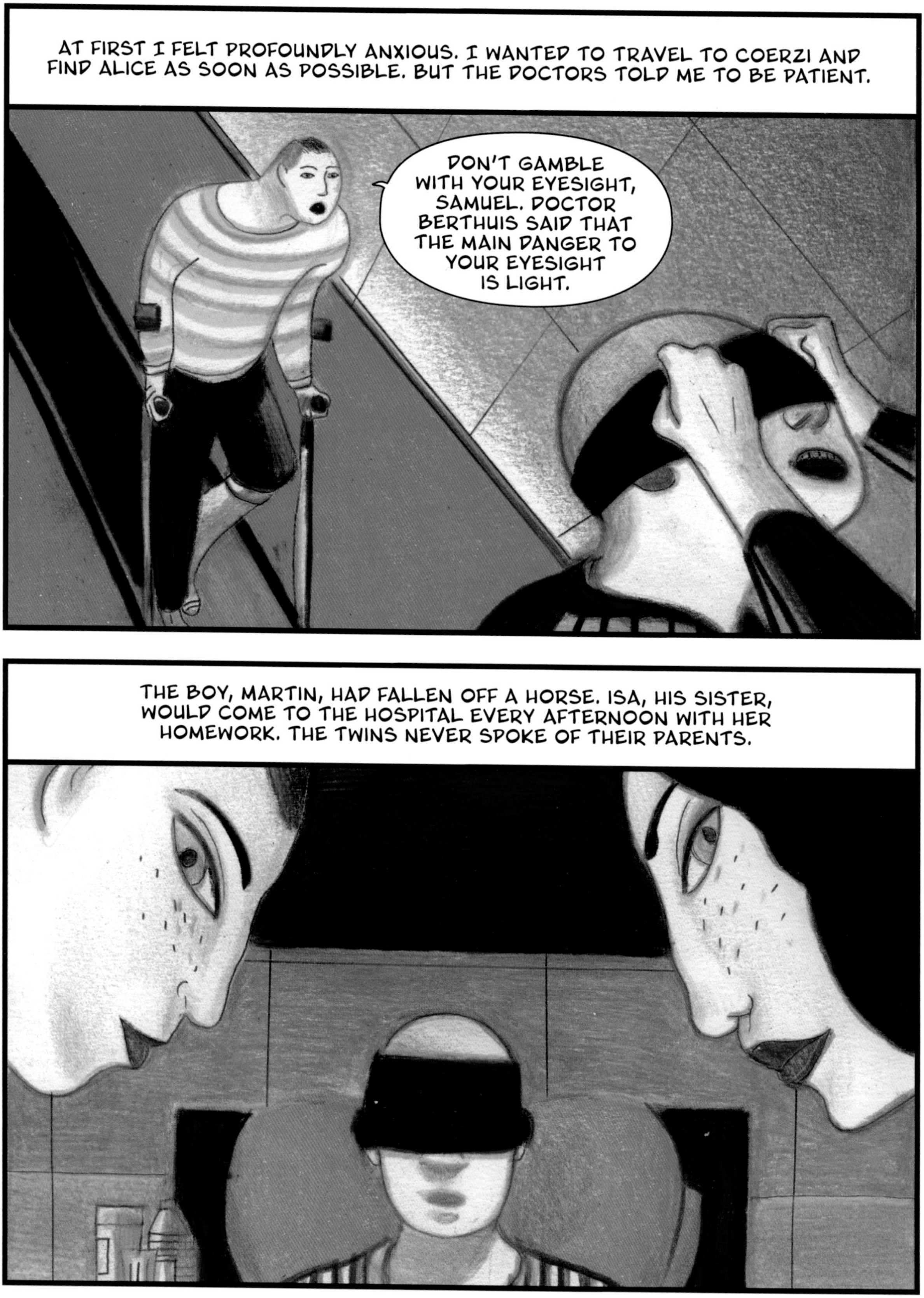
AT FIRST I FELT PROFOUNDLY ANXIOUS. I WANTED TO TRAVEL TO COERZI AND FIND ALICE AS SOON AS POSSIBLE. BUT THE DOCTORS TOLD ME TO BE PATIENT.
DON'T GAMBLE WITH YOUR EYESIGHT, SAMUEL. DOCTOR BERTHUIS SAID THAT THE MAIN DANGER TO YOUR EYESIGHT IS LIGHT.
THE BOY, MARTIN, HAD FALLEN OFF A HORSE. ISA, HIS SISTER, WOULD COME TO THE HOSPITAL EVERY AFTERNOON WITH HER HOMEWORK. THE TWINS NEVER SPOKE OF THEIR PARENTS.

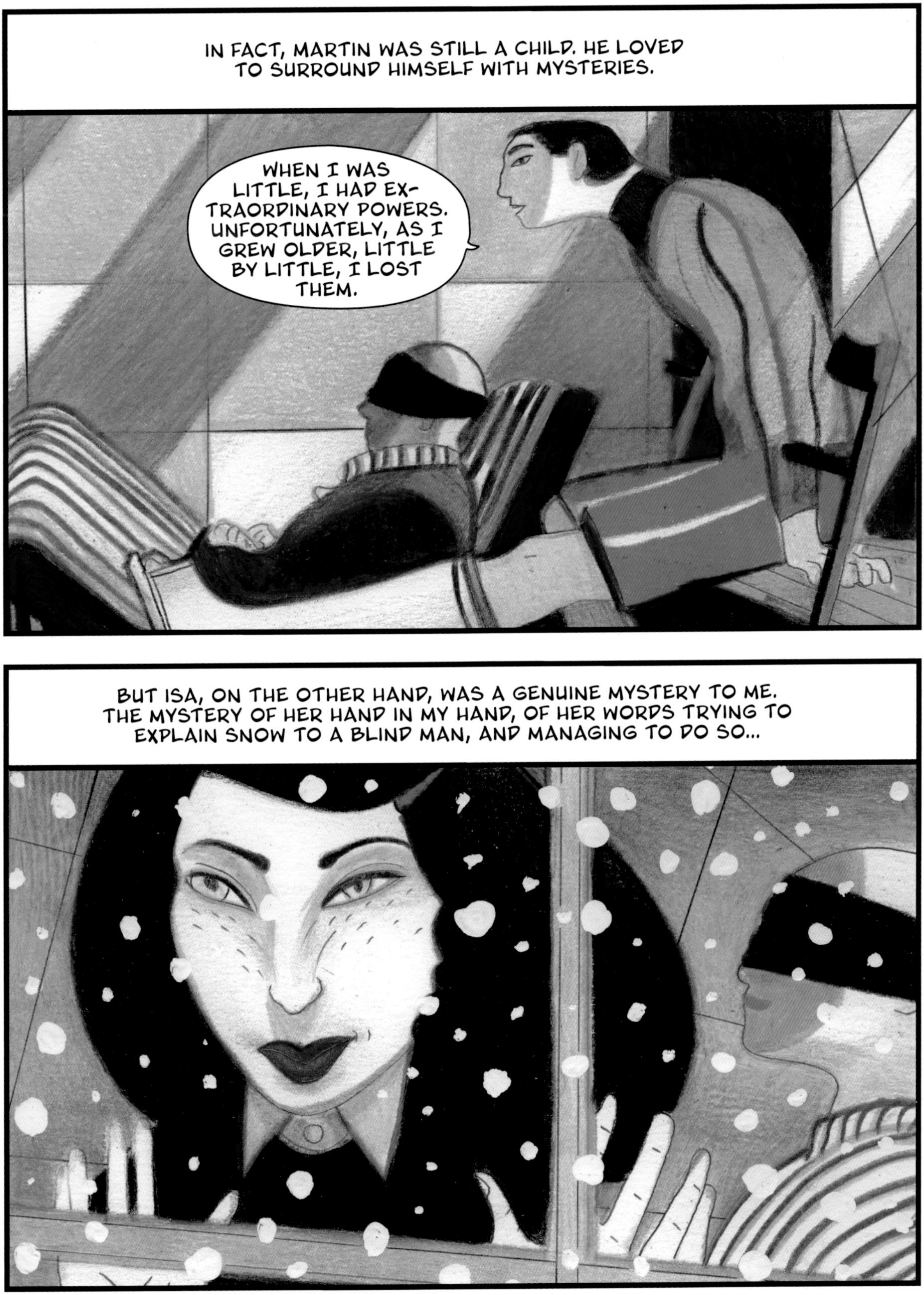
IN FACT, MARTIN WAS STILL A CHILD. HE LOVED TO SURROUND HIMSELF WITH MYSTERIES.
WHEN I WAS LITTLE, I HAD EX-TRAORDINARY POWERS. UNFORTUNATELY, AS I GREW OLDER, LITTLE BY LITTLE, I LOST THEM.
BUT ISA, ON THE OTHER HAND, WAS A GENUINE MYSTERY TO ME. THE MYSTERY OF HER HAND IN MY HAND, OF HER WORDS TRYING TO EXPLAIN SNOW TO A BLIND MAN, AND MANAGING TO DO SO...

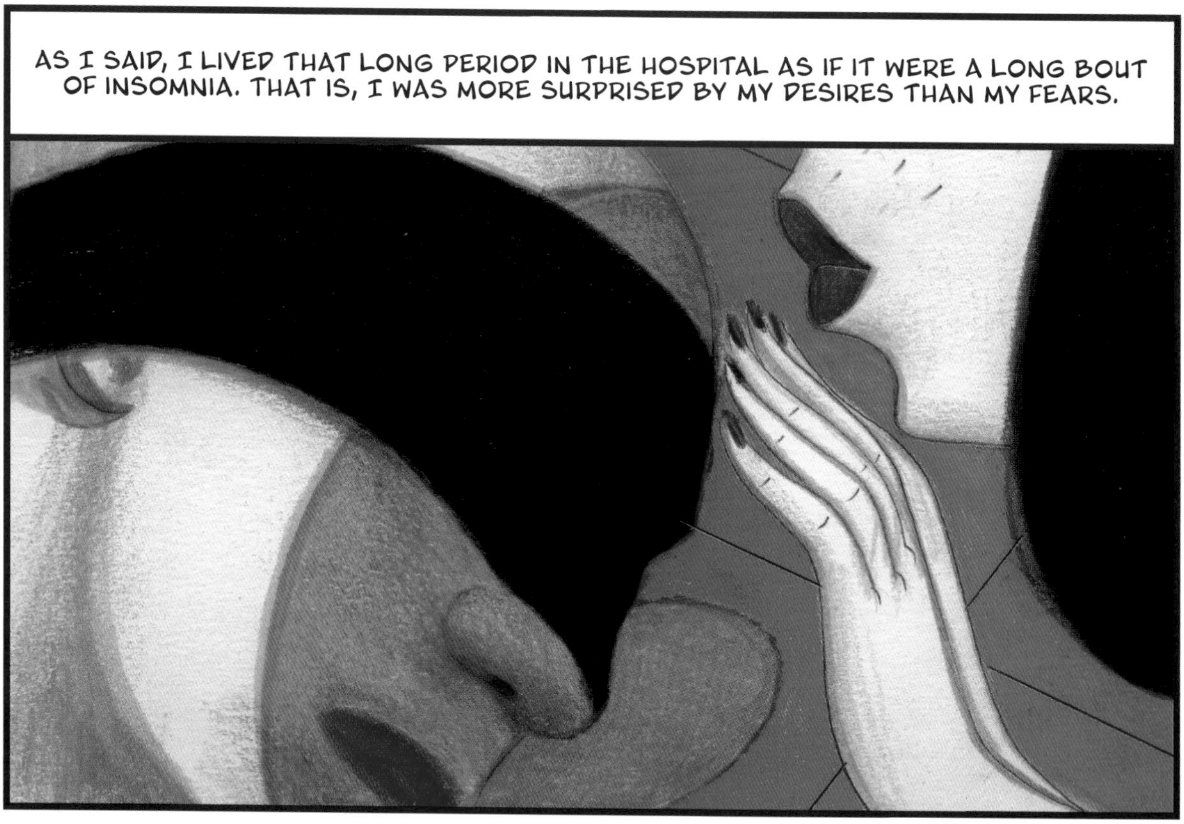
AS I SAID, I LIVED THAT LONG PERIOD IN THE HOSPITAL AS IF IT WERE A LONG BOUT OF INSOMNIA. THAT IS, I WAS MORE SURPRISED BY MY DESIRES THAN MY FEARS.

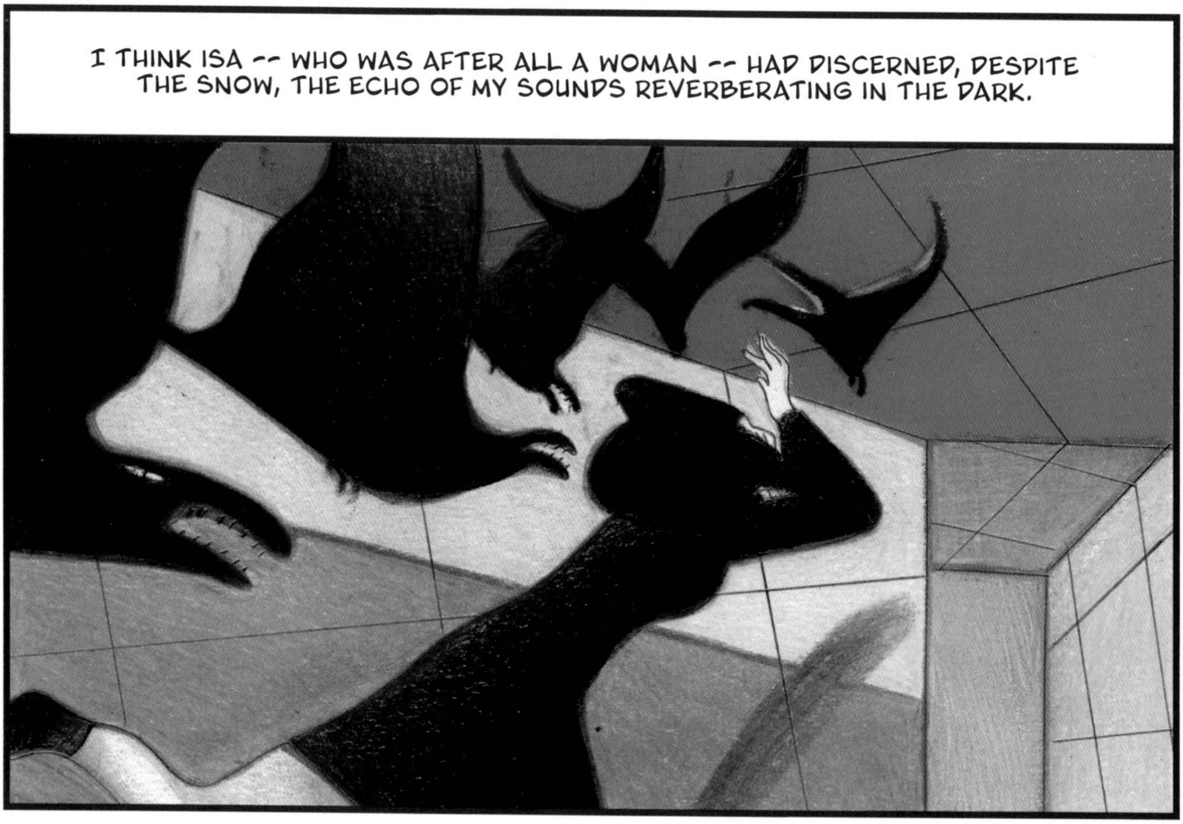
I THINK ISA -- WHO WAS AFTER ALL A WOMAN -- HAD DISCERNED, DESPITE THE SNOW, THE ECHO OF MY SOUNDS REVERBERATING IN THE DARK.

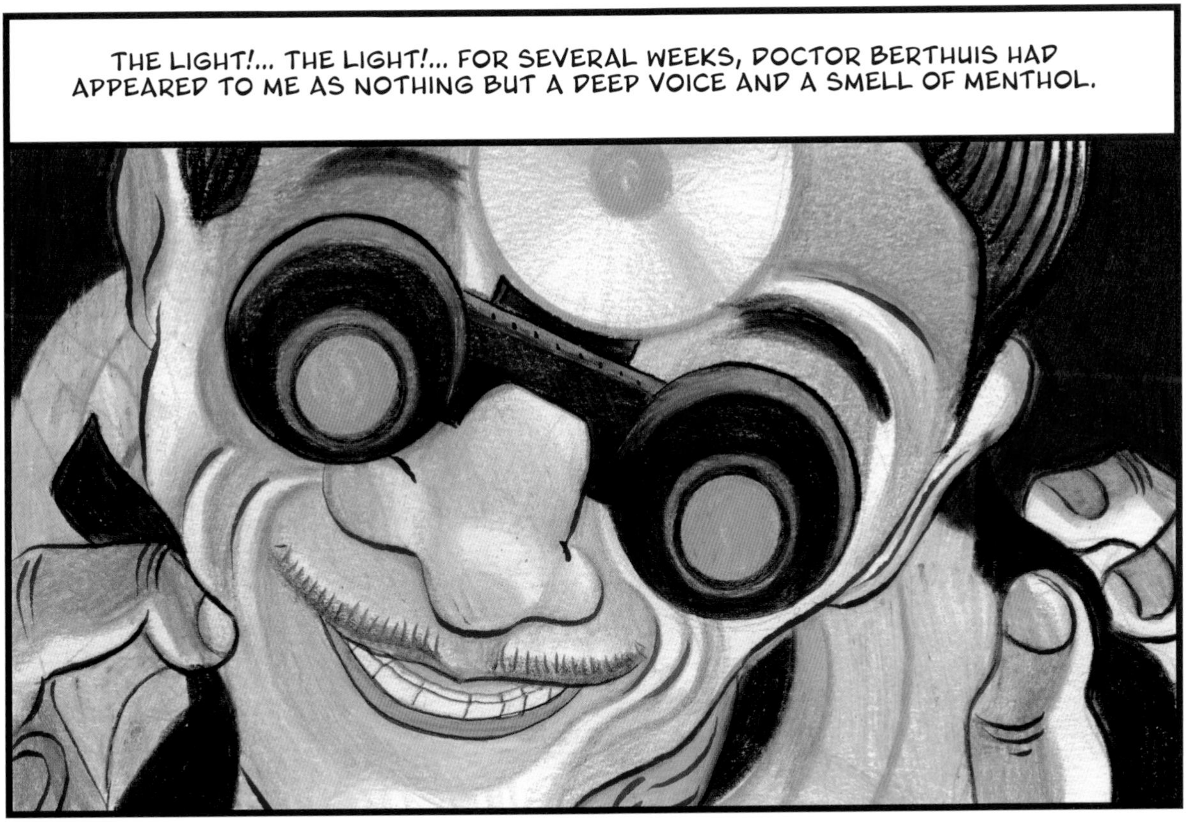
THE LIGHT!... THE LIGHT!... FOR SEVERAL WEEKS, DOCTOR BERTHUIS HAD APPEARED TO ME AS NOTHING BUT A DEEP VOICE AND A SMELL OF MENTHOL.

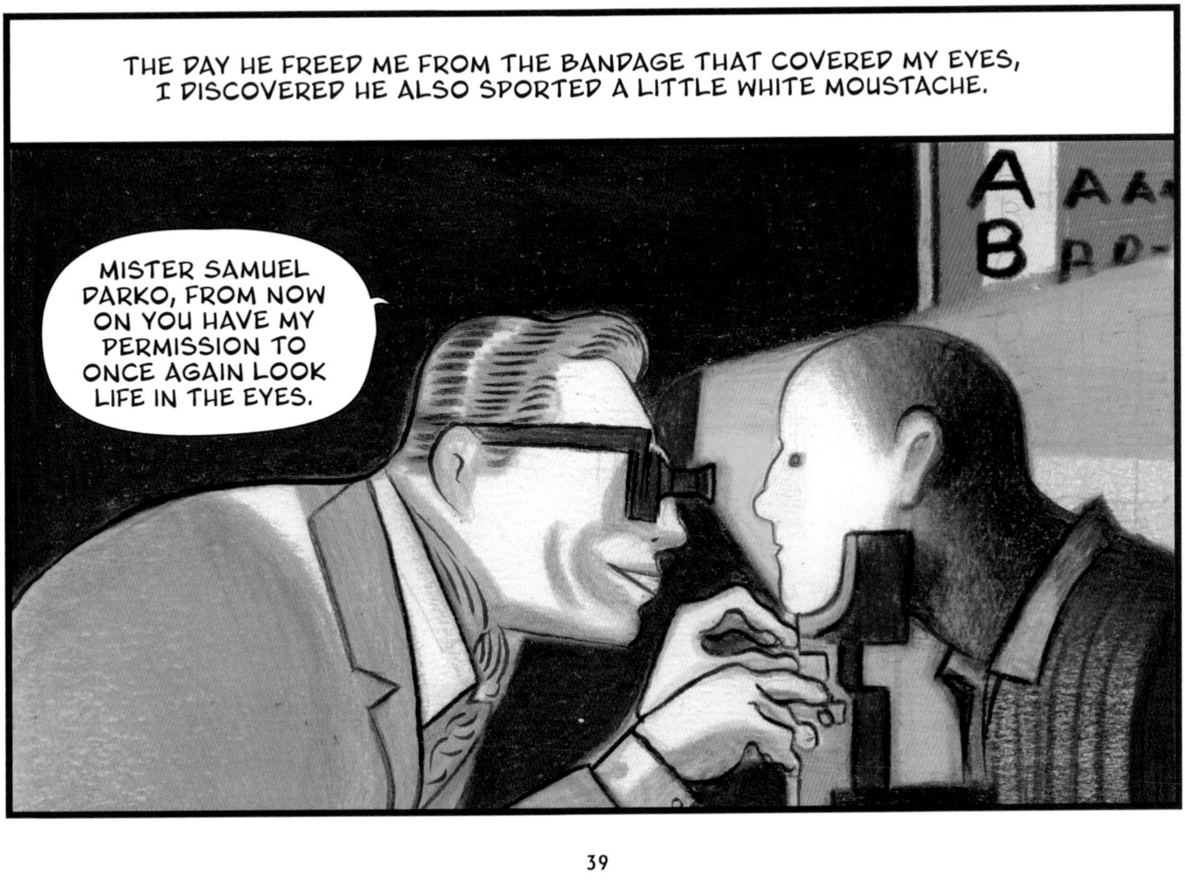
THE DAY HE FREED ME FROM THE BANDAGE THAT COVERED MY EYES, I DISCOVERED HE ALSO SPORTED A LITTLE WHITE MOUSTACHE.
MISTER SAMUEL DARKO, FROM NOW ON YOU HAVE MY PERMISSION TO ONCE AGAIN LOOK LIFE IN THE EYES.

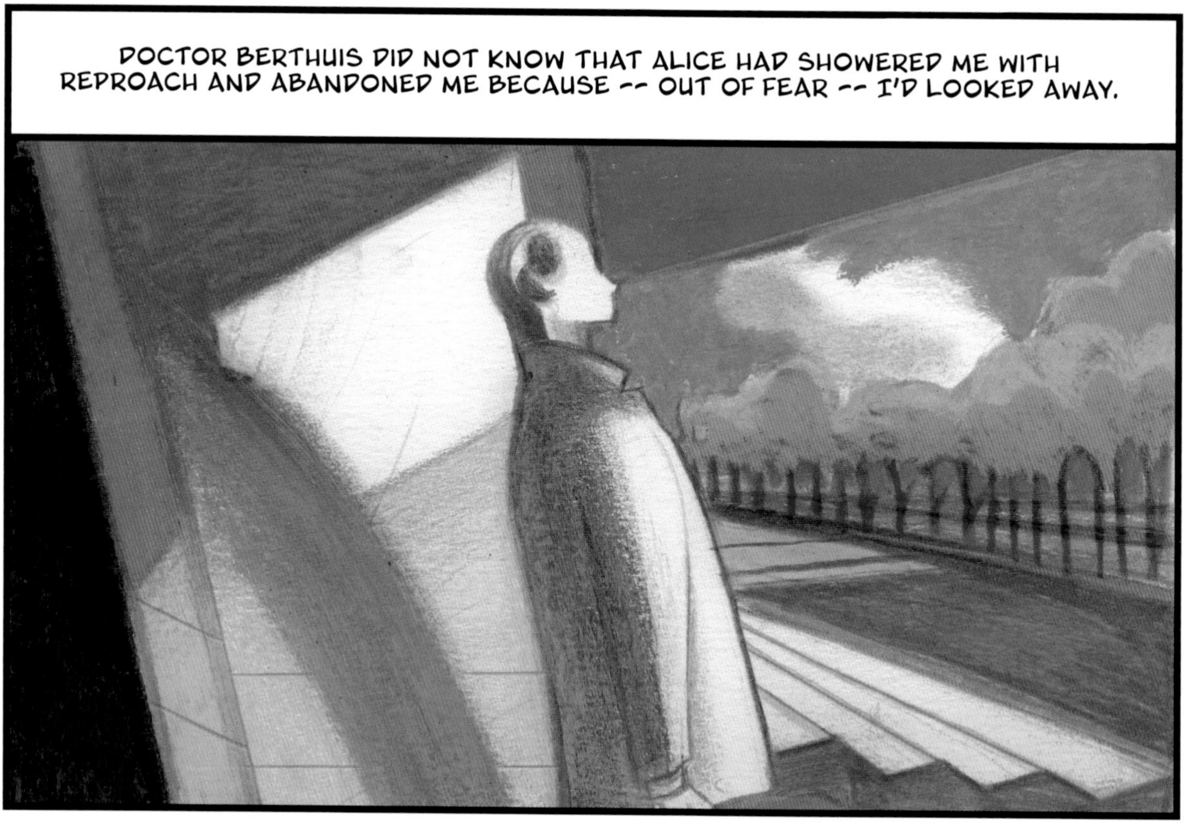
DOCTOR BERTHUIS DID NOT KNOW THAT ALICE HAD SHOWERED ME WITH REPROACH AND ABANDONED ME BECAUSE -- OUT OF FEAR -- I'D LOOKED AWAY.

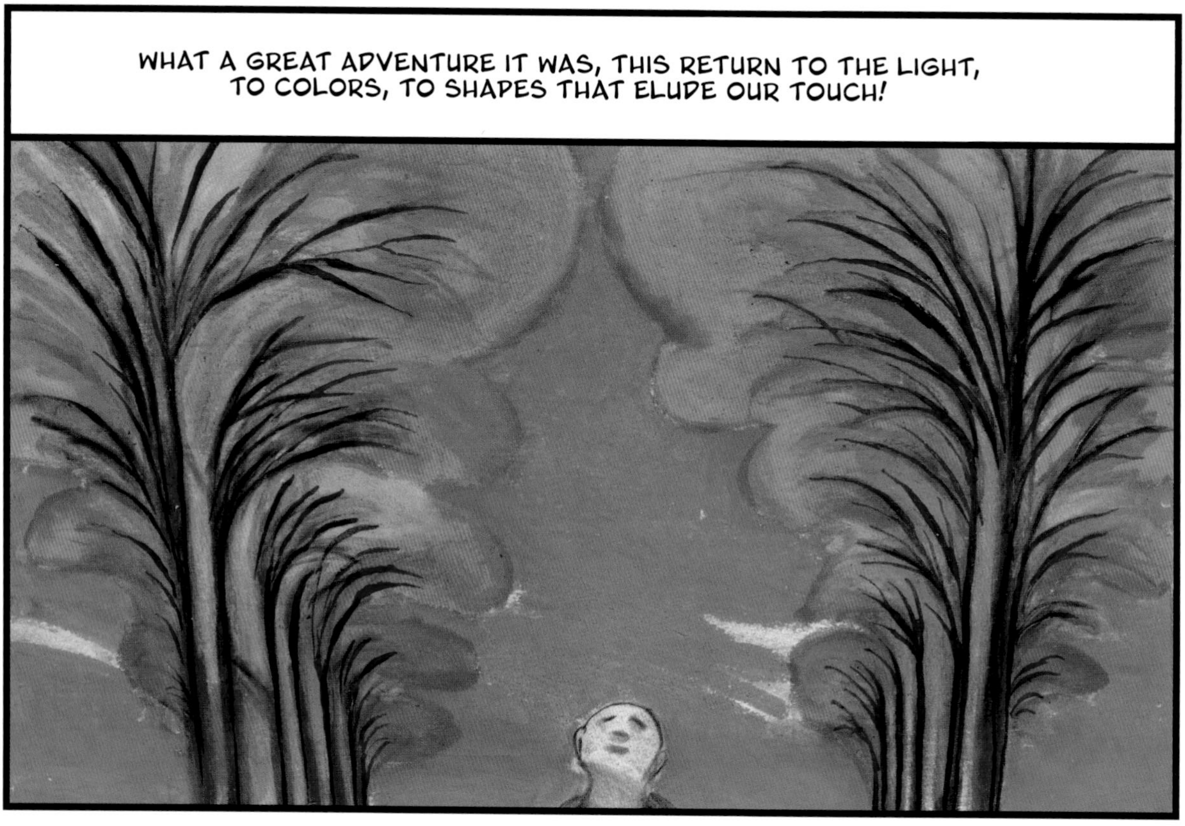
WHAT A GREAT ADVENTURE IT WAS, THIS RETURN TO THE LIGHT, TO COLORS, TO SHAPES THAT ELUDE OUR TOUCH!

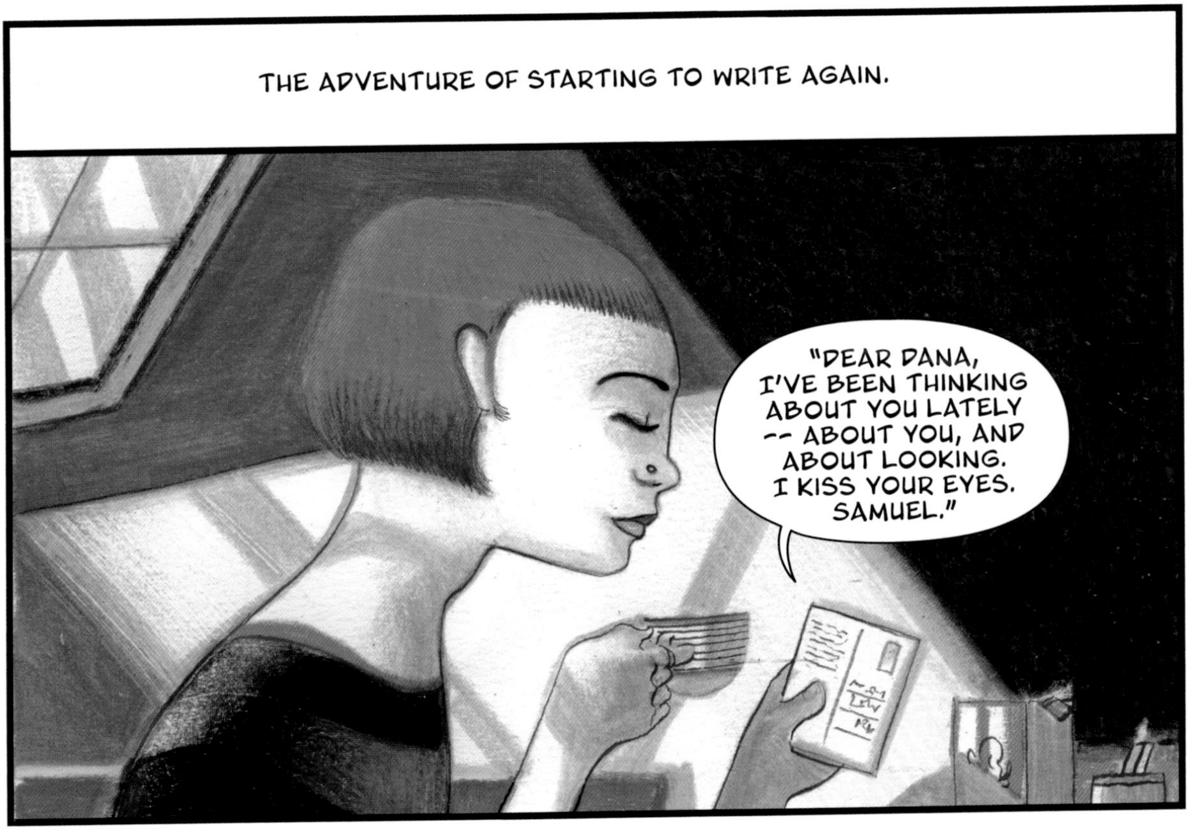
THE ADVENTURE OF STARTING TO WRITE AGAIN.
"DEAR DANA, I'VE BEEN THINKING ABOUT YOU LATELY -- ABOUT YOU, AND ABOUT LOOKING. I KISS YOUR EYES. SAMUEL."

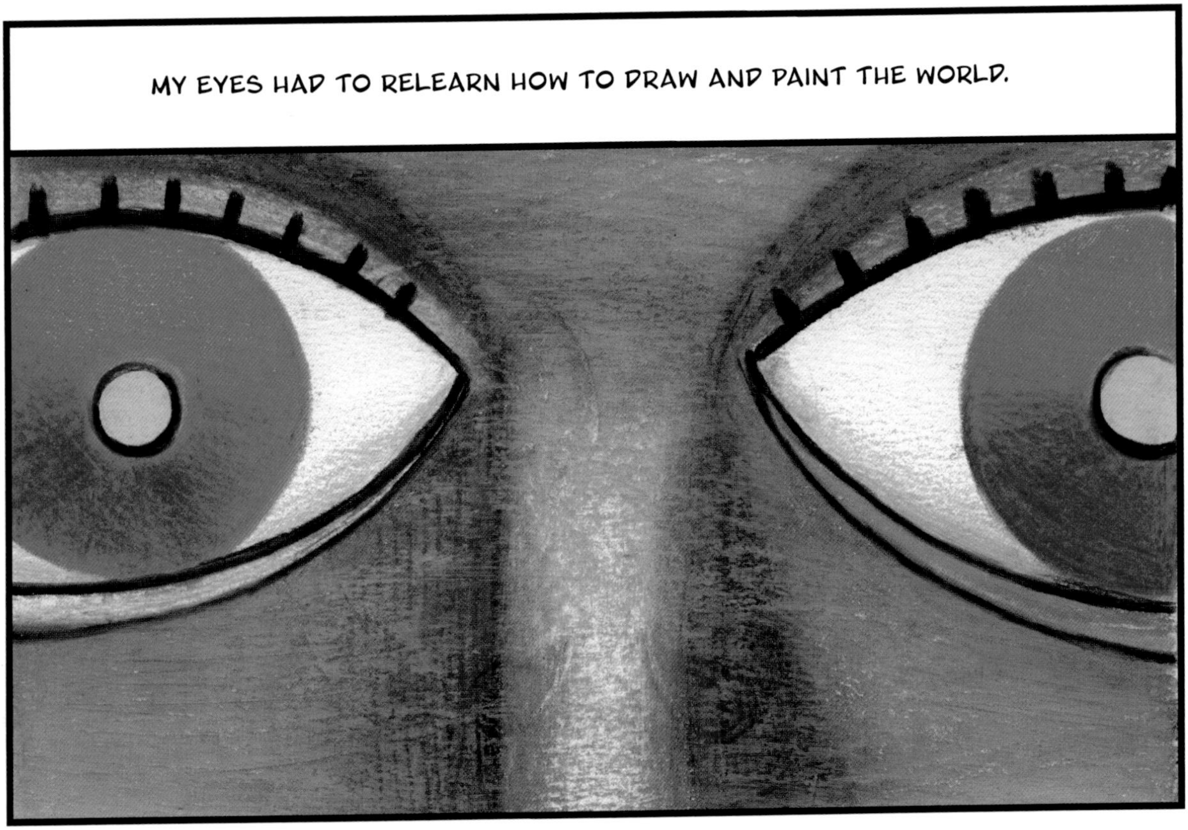
MY EYES HAD TO RELEARN HOW TO DRAW AND PAINT THE WORLD.

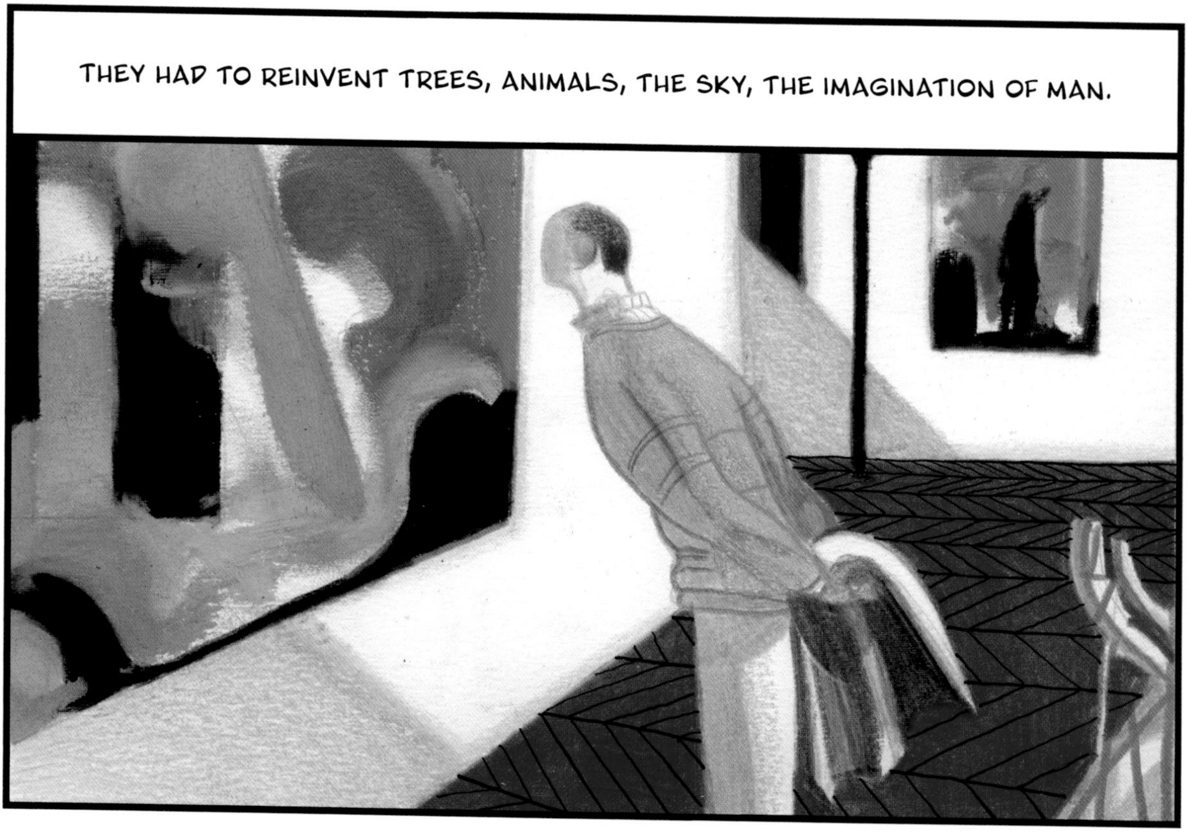
THEY HAD TO REINVENT TREES, ANIMALS, THE SKY, THE IMAGINATION OF MAN.

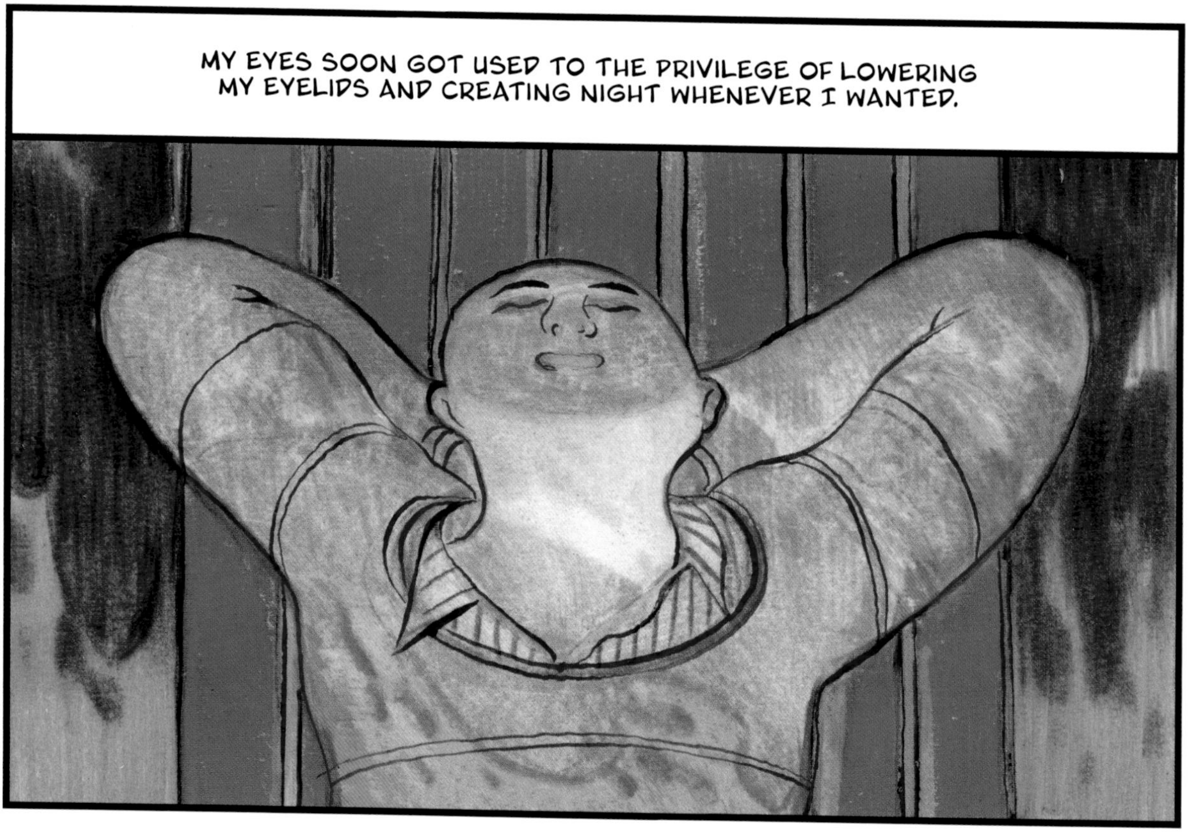
MY EYES SOON GOT USED TO THE PRIVILEGE OF LOWERING MY EYELIDS AND CREATING NIGHT WHENEVER I WANTED.

3

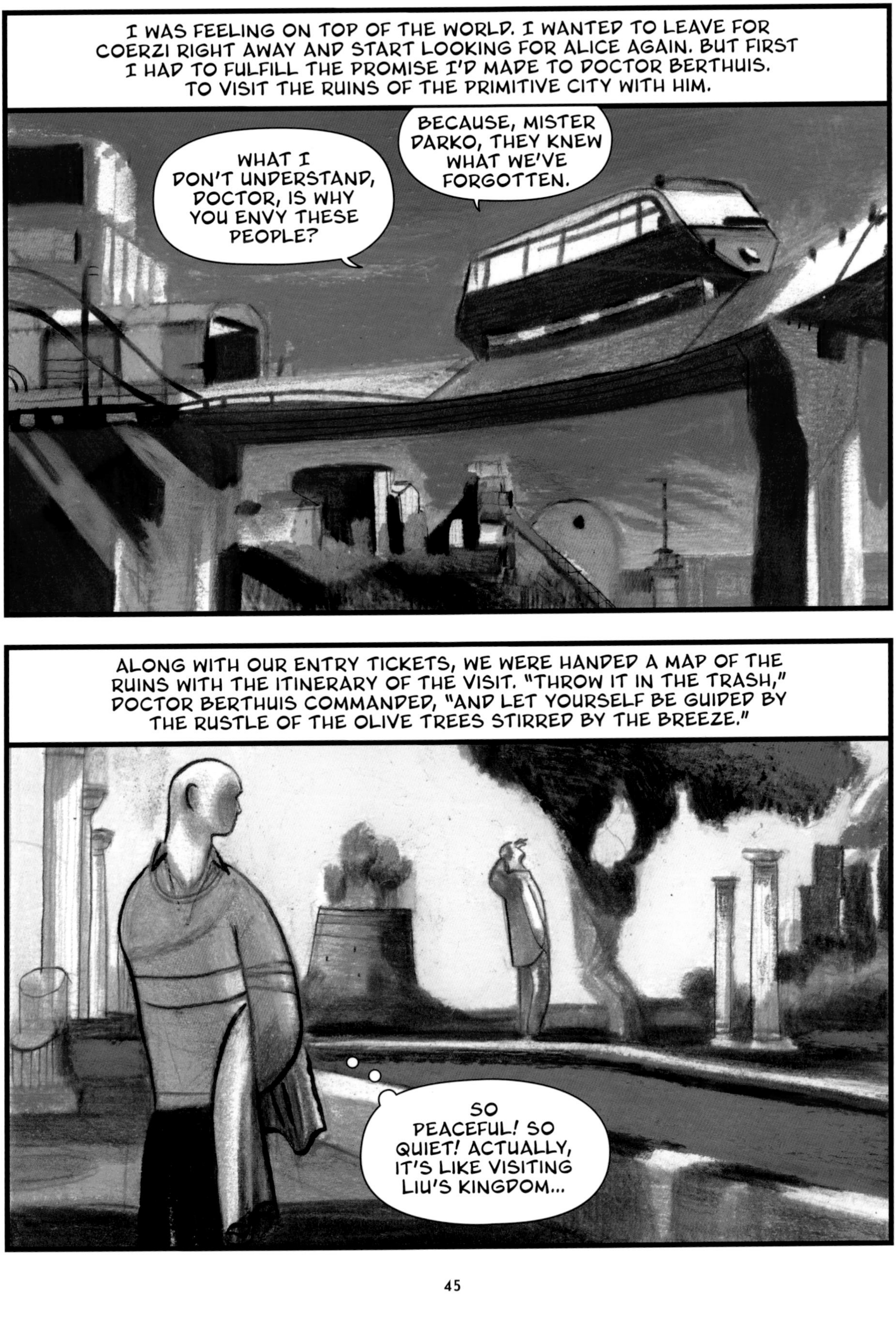
I WAS FEELING ON TOP OF THE WORLD. I WANTED TO LEAVE FOR COERZI RIGHT AWAY AND START LOOKING FOR ALICE AGAIN. BUT FIRST I HAD TO FULFILL THE PROMISE I'D MADE TO DOCTOR BERTHUIS. TO VISIT THE RUINS OF THE PRIMITIVE CITY WITH HIM.
WHAT I DON'T UNDERSTAND, DOCTOR, IS WHY YOU ENVY THESE PEOPLE?
BECAUSE, MISTER DARKO, THEY KNEW WHAT WE'VE FORGOTTEN.
ALONG WITH OUR ENTRY TICKETS, WE WERE HANDED A MAP OF THE RUINS WITH THE ITINERARY OF THE VISIT. "THROW IT IN THE TRASH," DOCTOR BERTHUIS COMMANDED, "AND LET YOURSELF BE GUIDED BY THE RUSTLE OF THE OLIVE TREES STIRRED BY THE BREEZE."
SO PEACEFUL! SO QUIET! ACTUALLY, IT'S LIKE VISITING LIU'S KINGDOM...

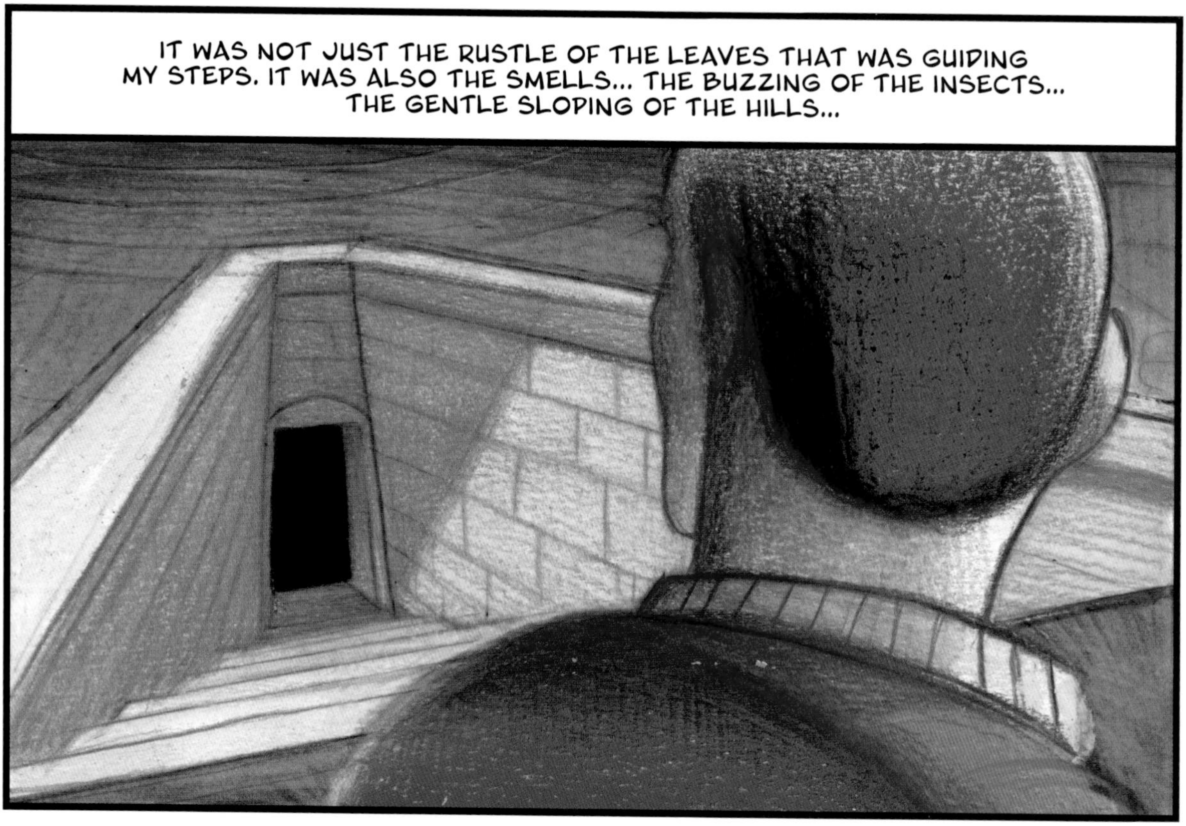
IT WAS NOT JUST THE RUSTLE OF THE LEAVES THAT WAS GUIDING MY STEPS. IT WAS ALSO THE SMELLS... THE BUZZING OF THE INSECTS... THE GENTLE SLOPING OF THE HILLS...

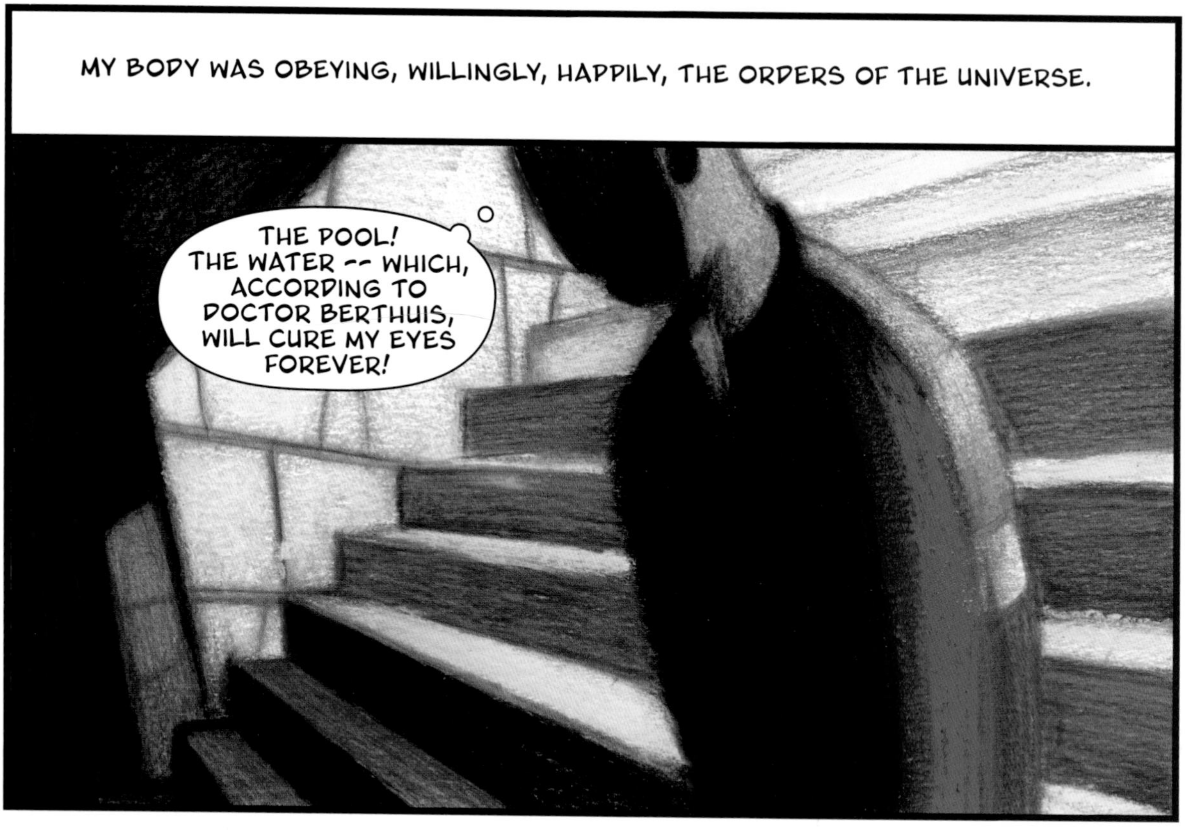
MY BODY WAS OBEYING, WILLINGLY, HAPPILY, THE ORDERS OF THE UNIVERSE.
THE POOL! THE WATER -- WHICH, ACCORDING TO DOCTOR BERTHUIS, WILL CURE MY EYES FOREVER!

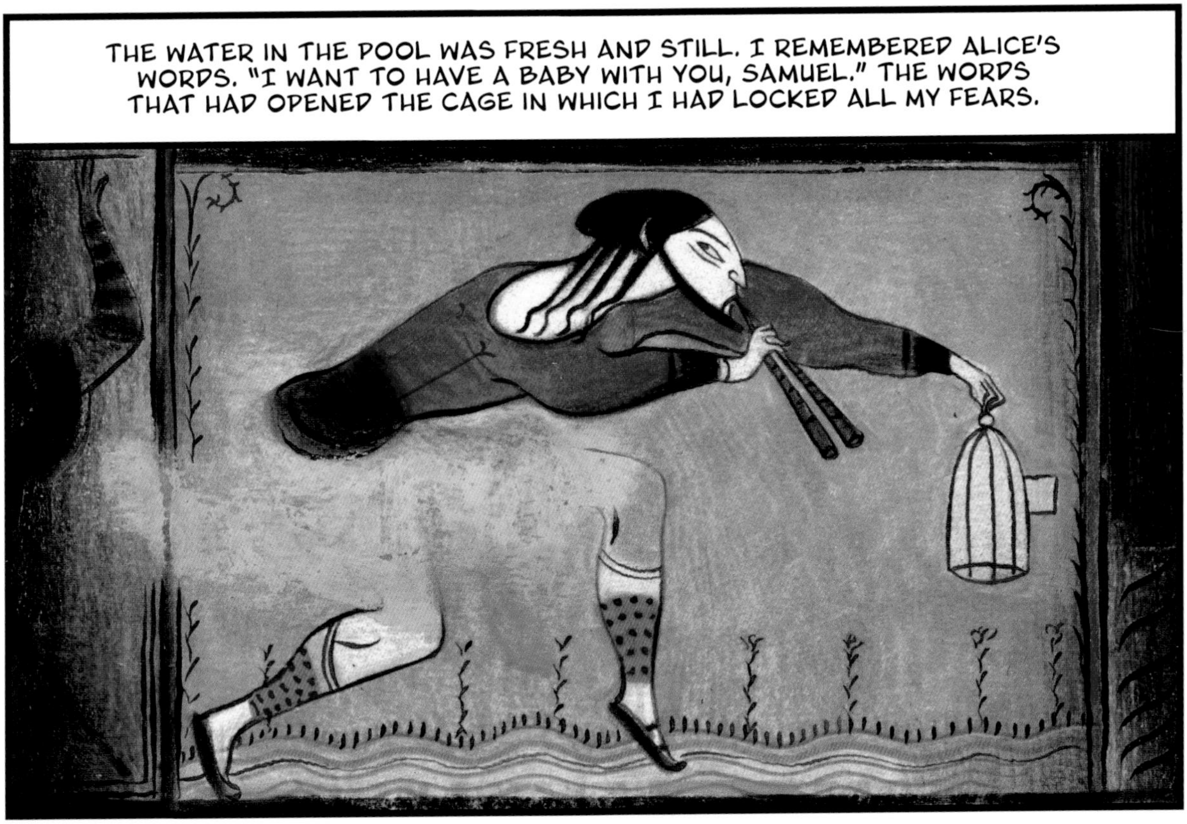
THE WATER IN THE POOL WAS FRESH AND STILL. I REMEMBERED ALICE'S WORDS. "I WANT TO HAVE A BABY WITH YOU, SAMUEL." THE WORDS THAT HAD OPENED THE CAGE IN WHICH I HAD LOCKED ALL MY FEARS.

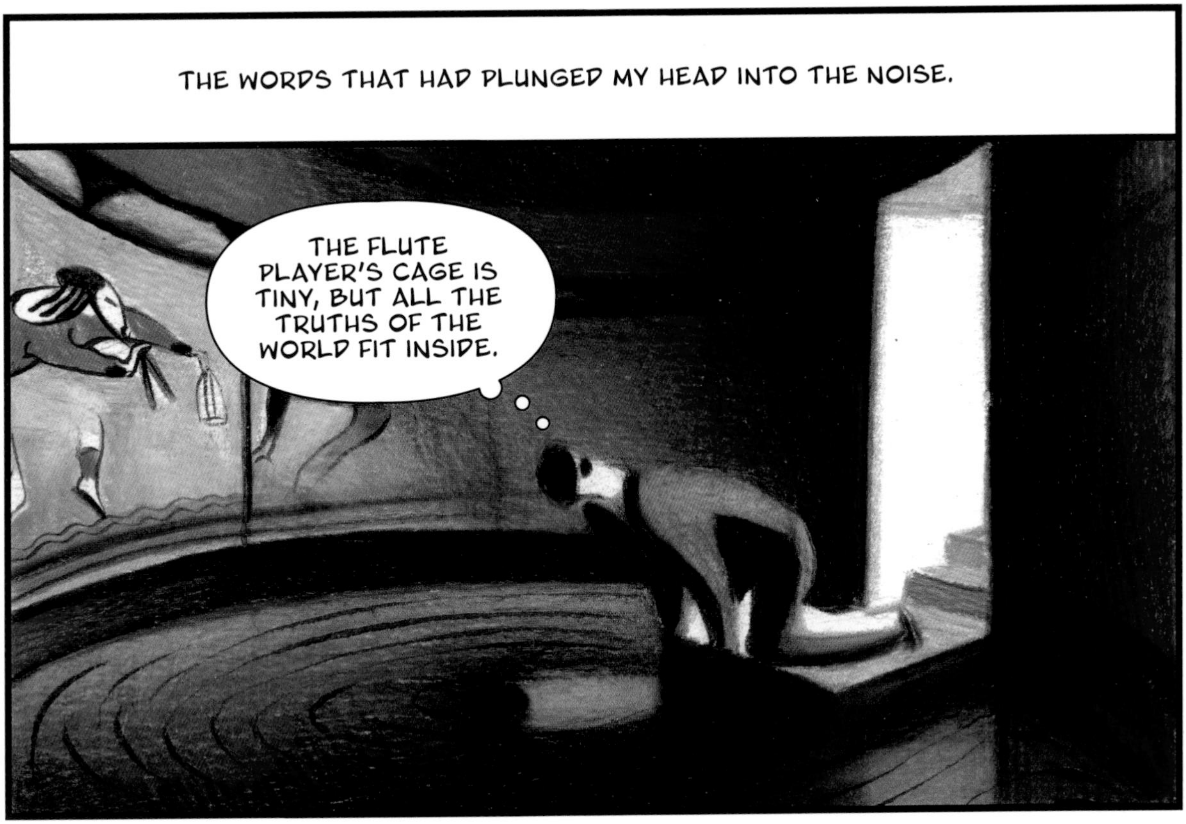
THE WORDS THAT HAD PLUNGED MY HEAD INTO THE NOISE.
THE FLUTE PLAYER'S CAGE IS TINY, BUT ALL THE TRUTHS OF THE WORLD FIT INSIDE.

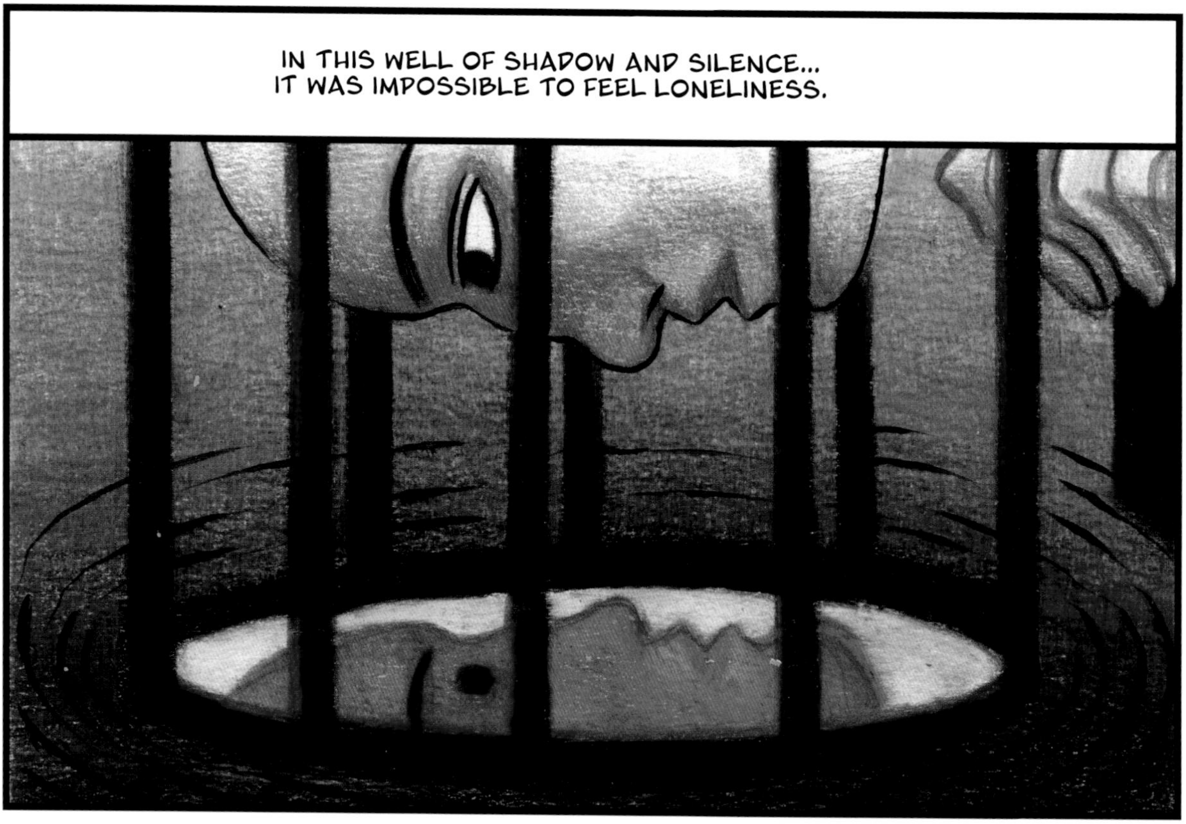
IN THIS WELL OF SHADOW AND SILENCE... IT WAS IMPOSSIBLE TO FEEL LONELINESS.

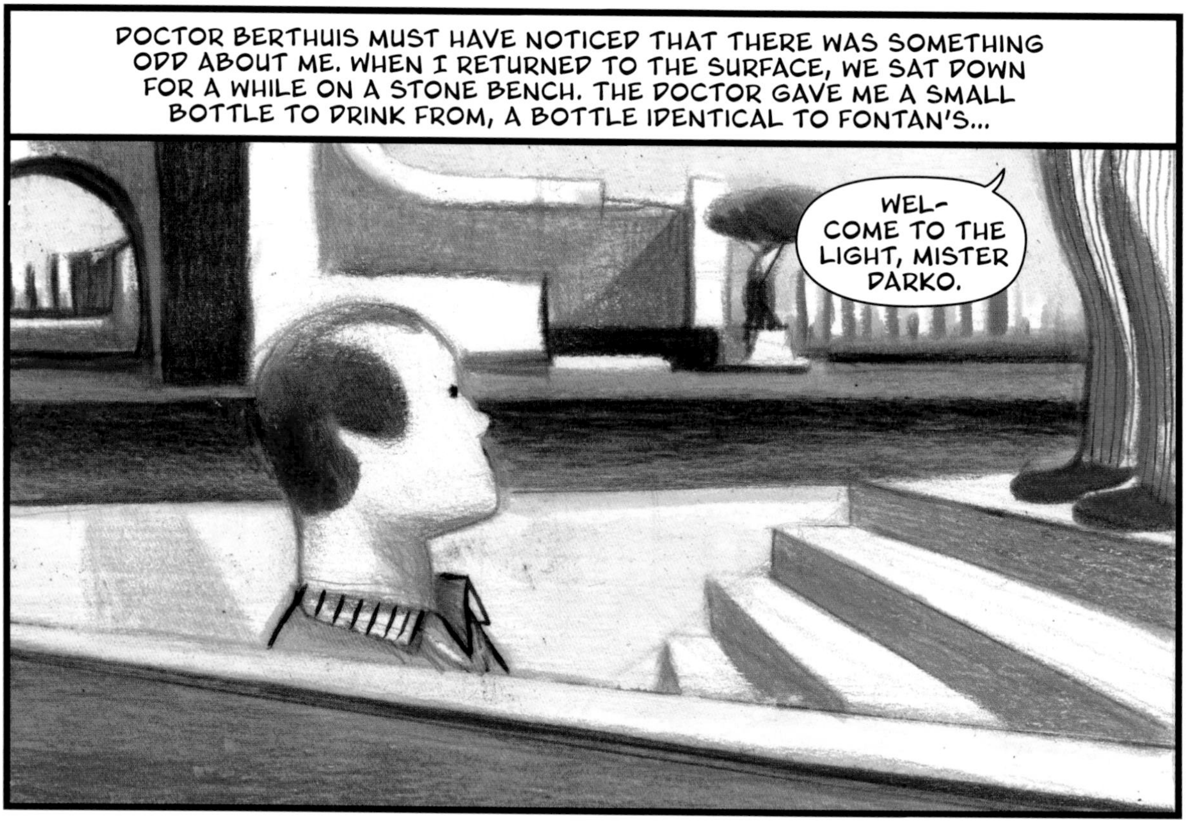
DOCTOR BERTHUIS MUST HAVE NOTICED THAT THERE WAS SOMETHING ODD ABOUT ME. WHEN I RETURNED TO THE SURFACE, WE SAT DOWN FOR A WHILE ON A STONE BENCH. THE DOCTOR GAVE ME A SMALL BOTTLE TO DRINK FROM, A BOTTLE IDENTICAL TO FONTAN'S...
WEL-COME TO THE LIGHT, MISTER DARKO.

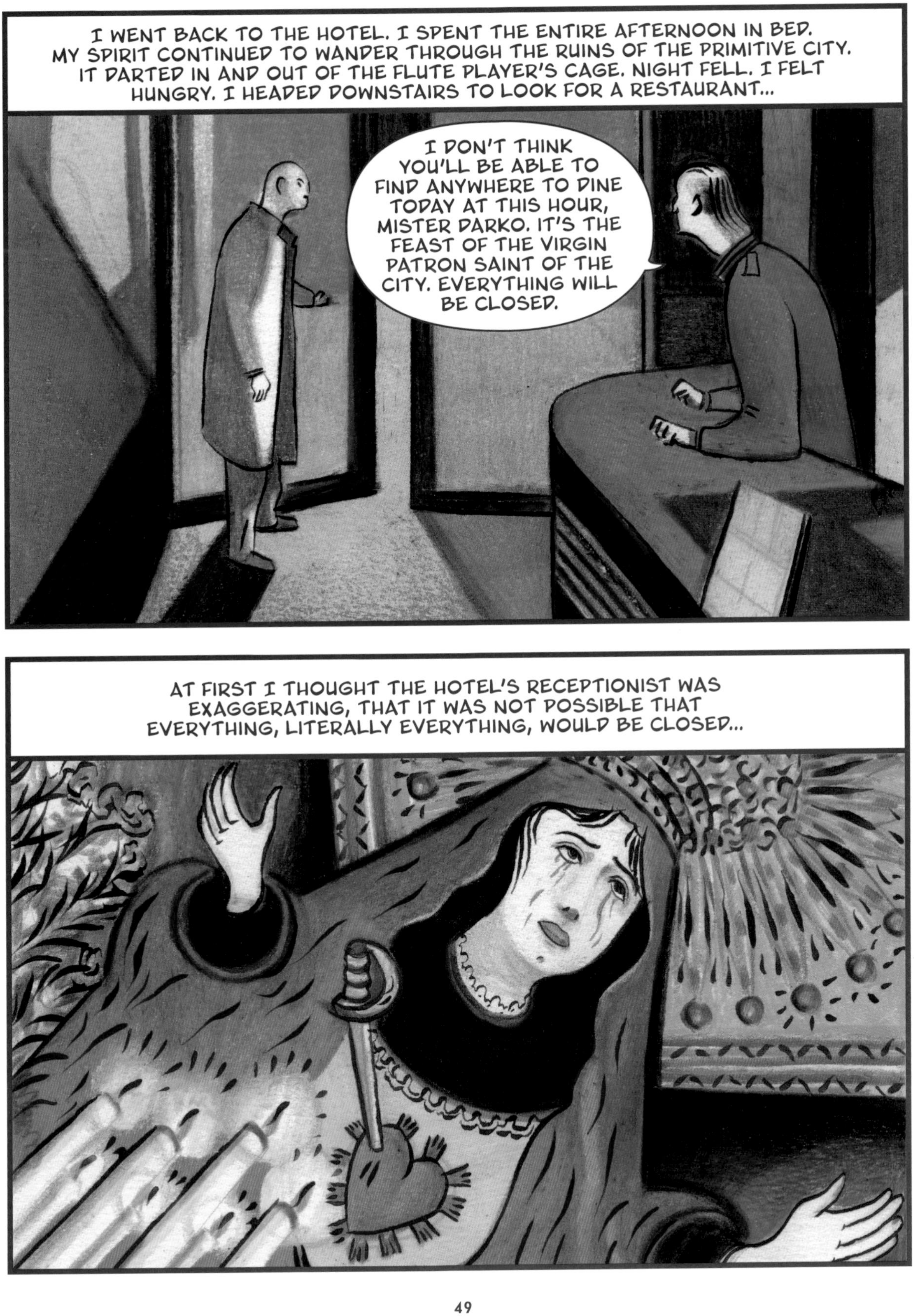
I WENT BACK TO THE HOTEL. I SPENT THE ENTIRE AFTERNOON IN BED. MY SPIRIT CONTINUED TO WANDER THROUGH THE RUINS OF THE PRIMITIVE CITY. IT DARTED IN AND OUT OF THE FLUTE PLAYER'S CAGE. NIGHT FELL. I FELT HUNGRY. I HEADED DOWNSTAIRS TO LOOK FOR A RESTAURANT...
I DON'T THINK YOU'LL BE ABLE TO FIND ANYWHERE TO DINE TODAY AT THIS HOUR, MISTER DARKO. IT'S THE FEAST OF THE VIRGIN PATRON SAINT OF THE CITY. EVERYTHING WILL BE CLOSED.
AT FIRST I THOUGHT THE HOTEL'S RECEPTIONIST WAS EXAGGERATING, THAT IT WAS NOT POSSIBLE THAT EVERYTHING, LITERALLY EVERYTHING, WOULD BE CLOSED...

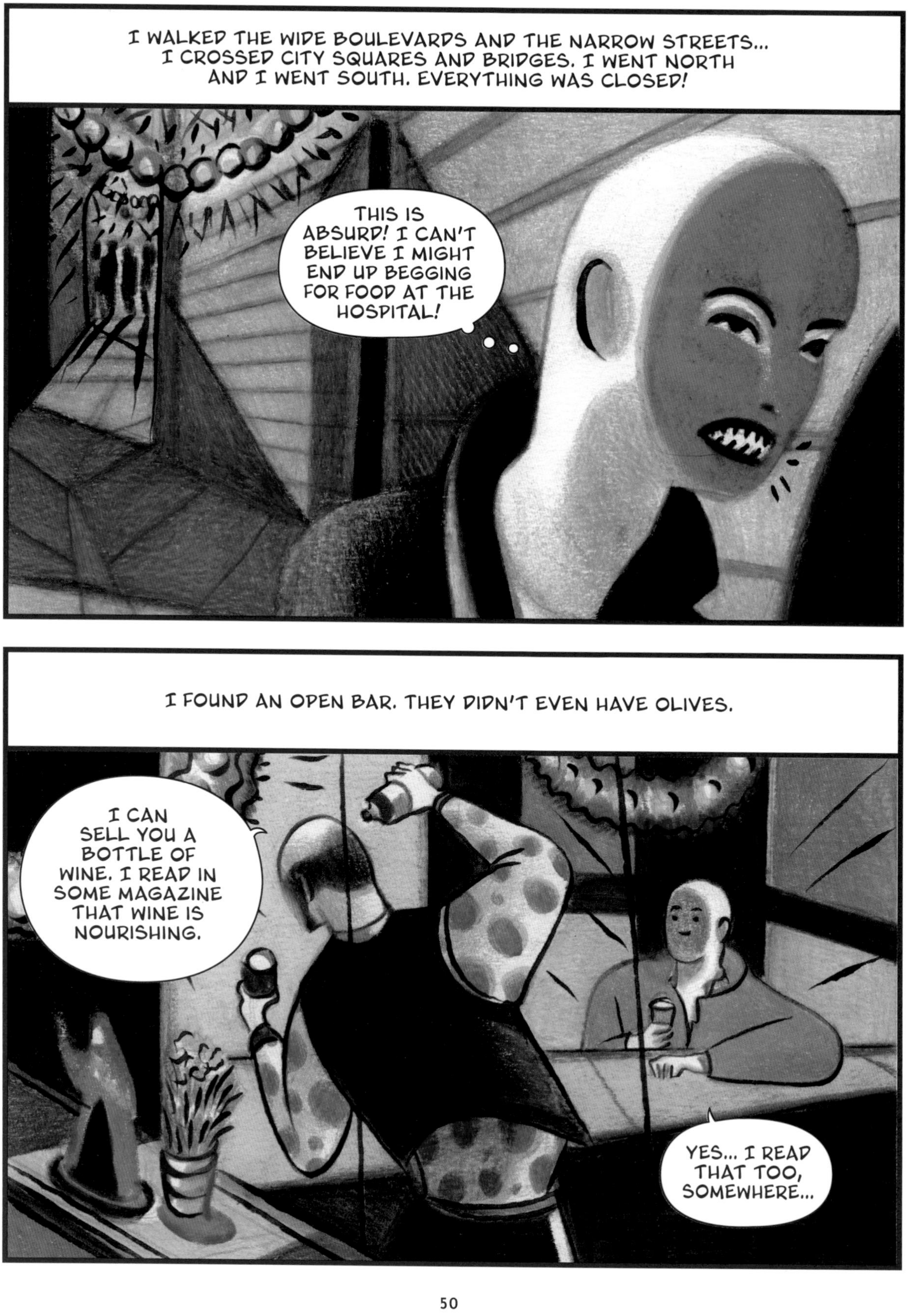
I WALKED THE WIDE BOULEVARDS AND THE NARROW STREETS... I CROSSED CITY SQUARES AND BRIDGES. I WENT NORTH AND I WENT SOUTH. EVERYTHING WAS CLOSED!
THIS IS ABSURD! I CAN'T BELIEVE I MIGHT END UP BEGGING FOR FOOD AT THE HOSPITAL!
I FOUND AN OPEN BAR. THEY DIDN'T EVEN HAVE OLIVES.
I CAN SELL YOU A BOTTLE OF WINE. I READ IN SOME MAGAZINE THAT WINE IS NOURISHING.
YES... I READ THAT TOO, SOMEWHERE...

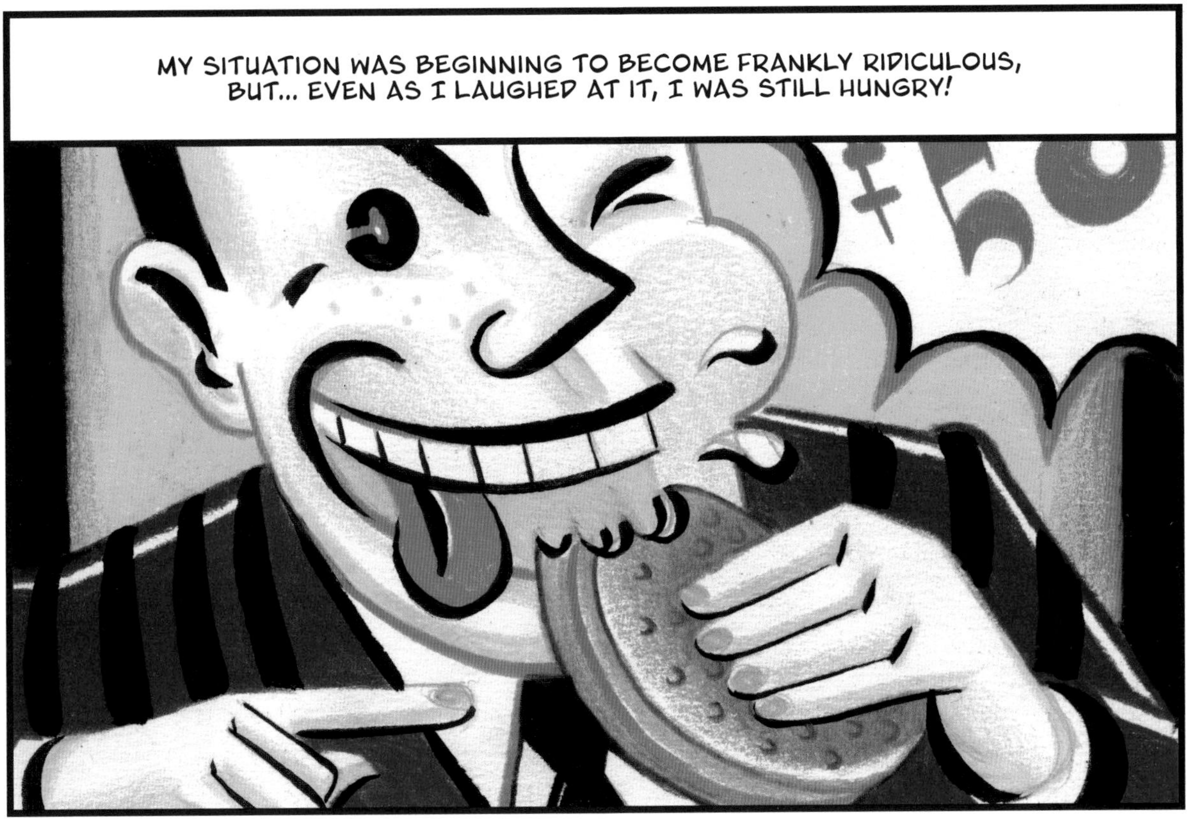
MY SITUATION WAS BEGINNING TO BECOME FRANKLY RIDICULOUS, BUT... EVEN AS I LAUGHED AT IT, I WAS STILL HUNGRY!

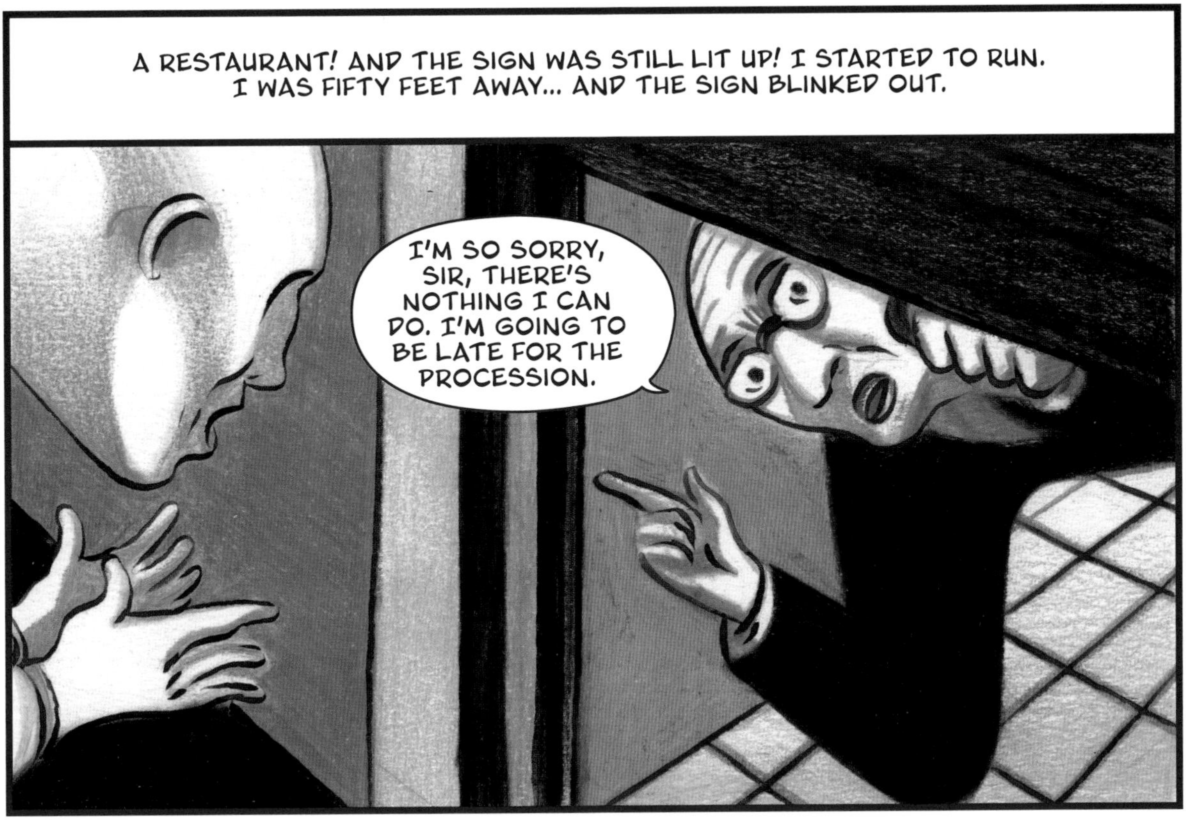
A RESTAURANT! AND THE SIGN WAS STILL LIT UP! I STARTED TO RUN. I WAS FIFTY FEET AWAY... AND THE SIGN BLINKED OUT.
I'M SO SORRY, SIR, THERE'S NOTHING I CAN DO. I'M GOING TO BE LATE FOR THE PROCESSION.

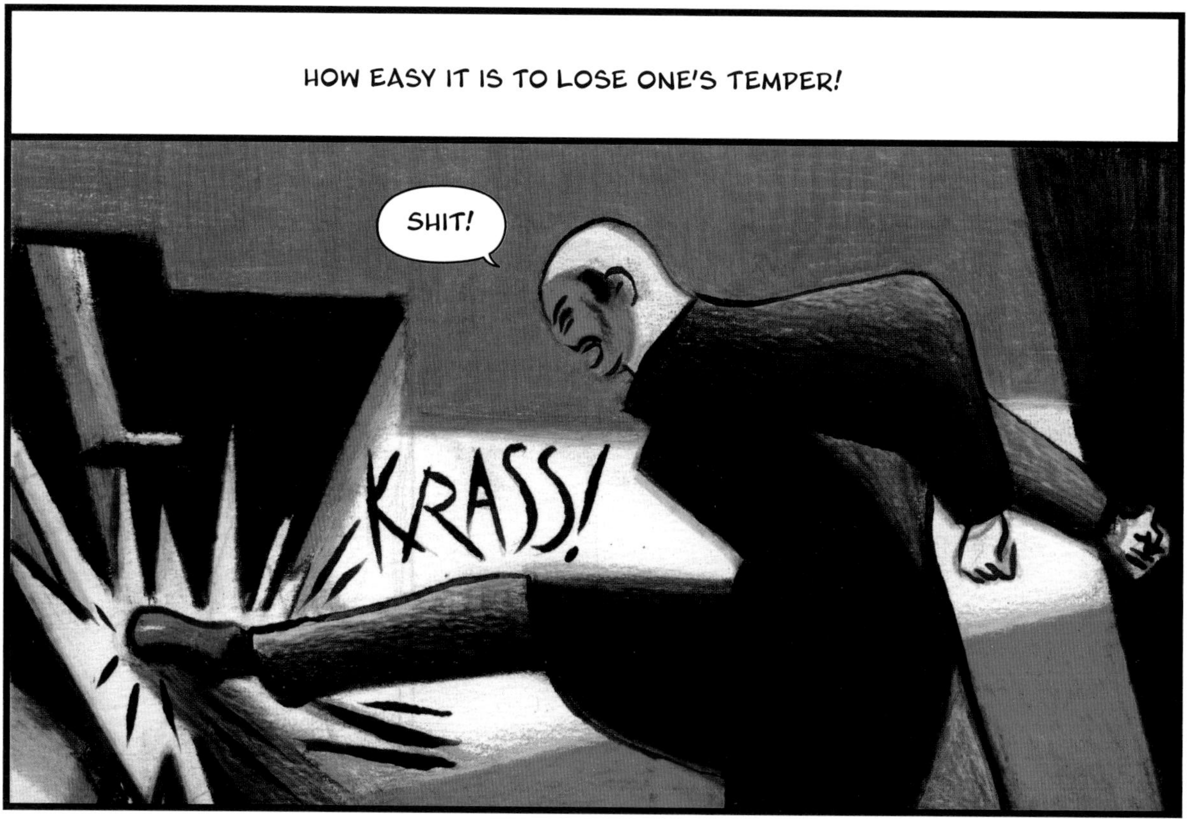
HOW EASY IT IS TO LOSE ONE'S TEMPER!
SHIT!
KRASS!

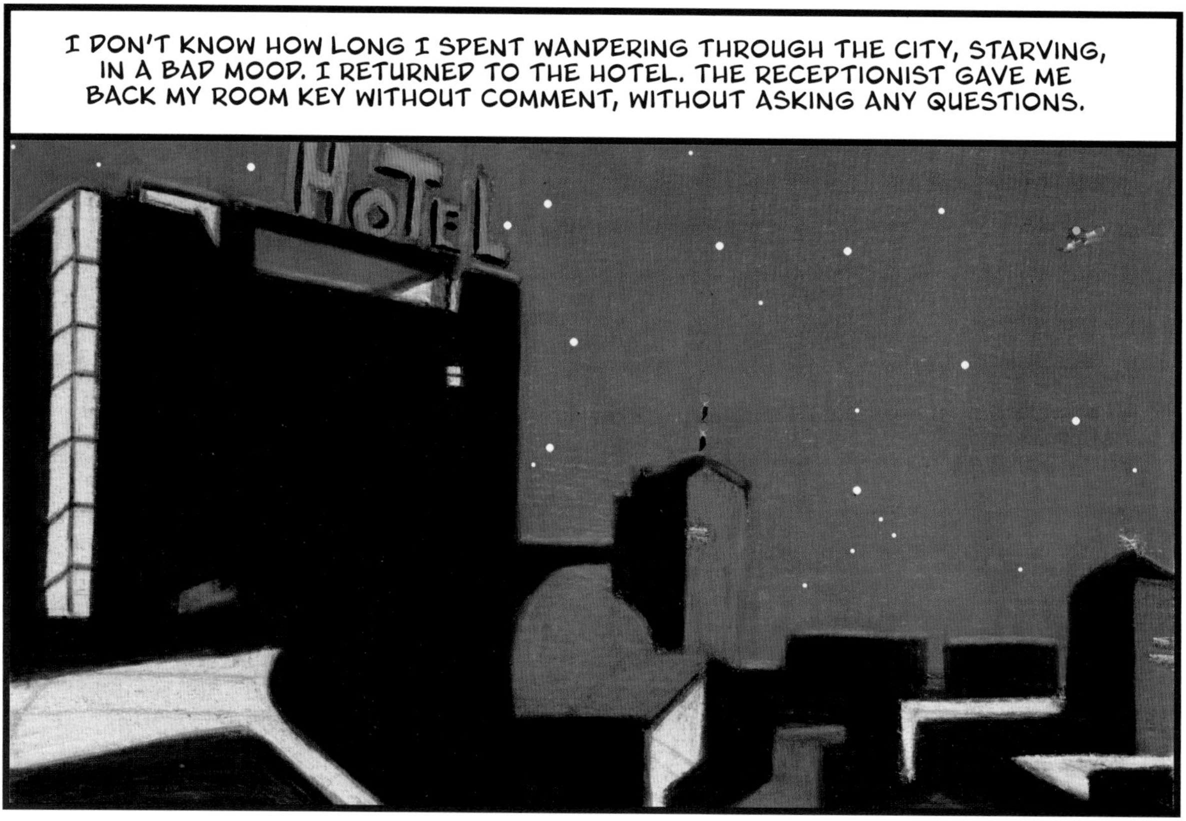
I DON'T KNOW HOW LONG I SPENT WANDERING THROUGH THE CITY, STARVING, IN A BAD MOOD. I RETURNED TO THE HOTEL. THE RECEPTIONIST GAVE ME BACK MY ROOM KEY WITHOUT COMMENT, WITHOUT ASKING ANY QUESTIONS.
HOTEL

THAT NIGHT WAS THE WORST AND THE BEST NIGHT OF MY LIFE.

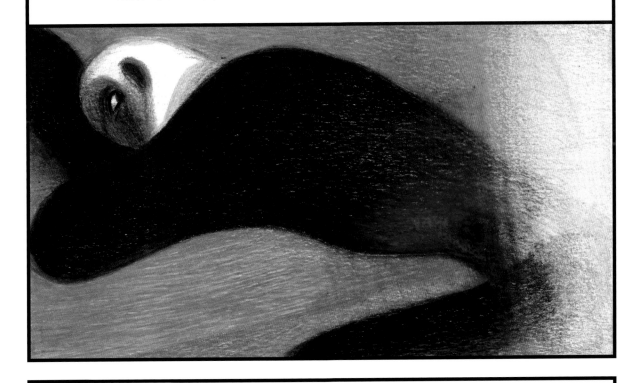

I FOUND MYSELF BACK IN THE FOREST FIRE,
SURROUNDED BY FLAMES, DEATH, FEAR.

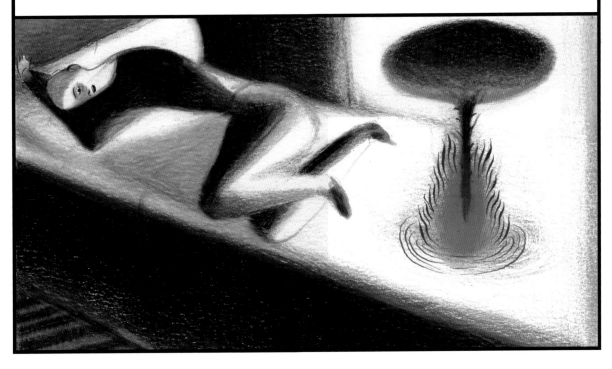

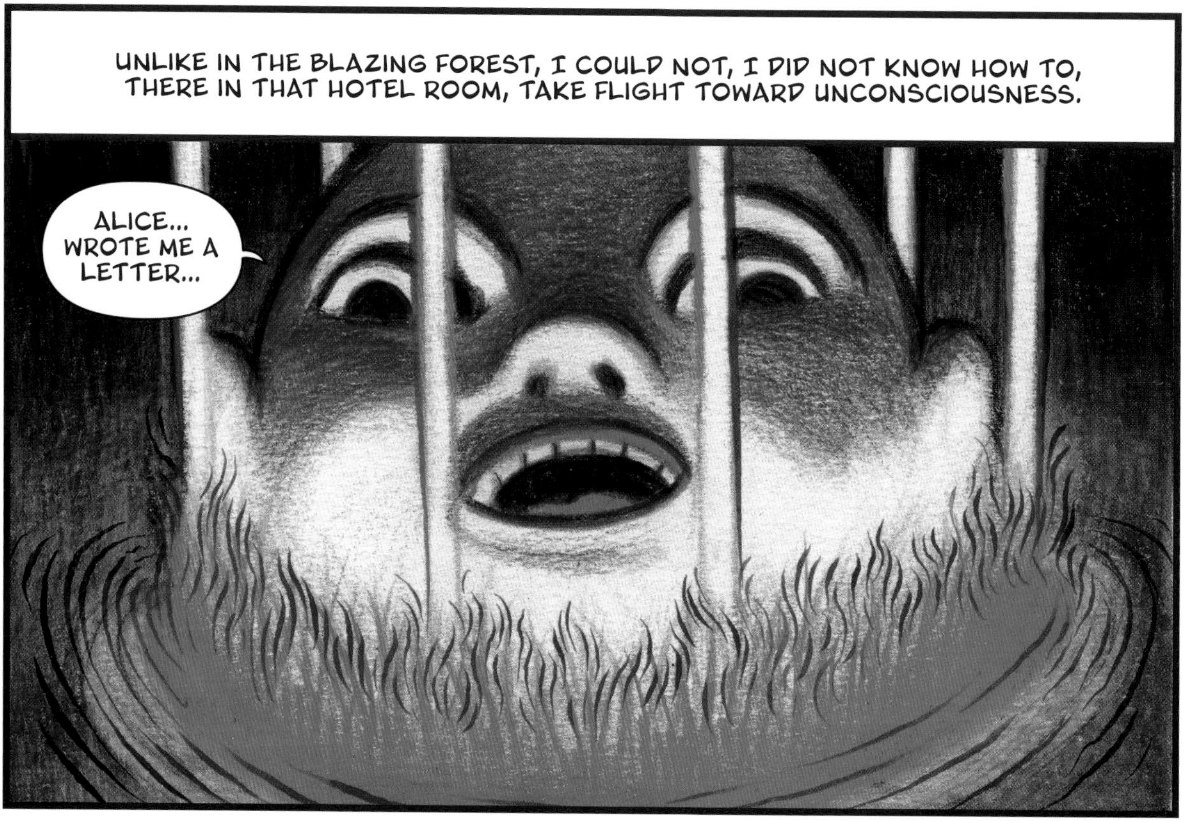
UNLIKE IN THE BLAZING FOREST, I COULD NOT, I DID NOT KNOW HOW TO, THERE IN THAT HOTEL ROOM, TAKE FLIGHT TOWARD UNCONSCIOUSNESS.
ALICE... WROTE ME A LETTER...

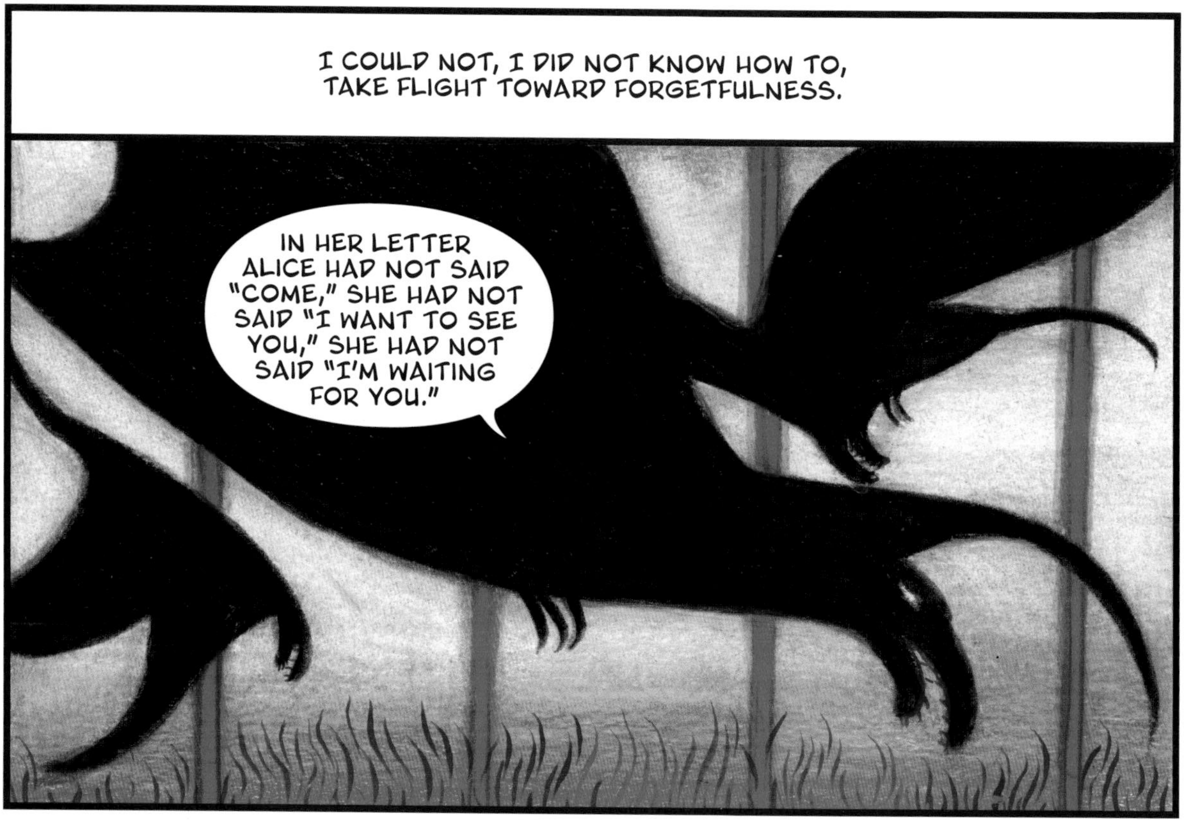
I COULD NOT, I DID NOT KNOW HOW TO, TAKE FLIGHT TOWARD FORGETFULNESS.
IN HER LETTER ALICE HAD NOT SAID "COME," SHE HAD NOT SAID "I WANT TO SEE YOU," SHE HAD NOT SAID "I'M WAITING FOR YOU."

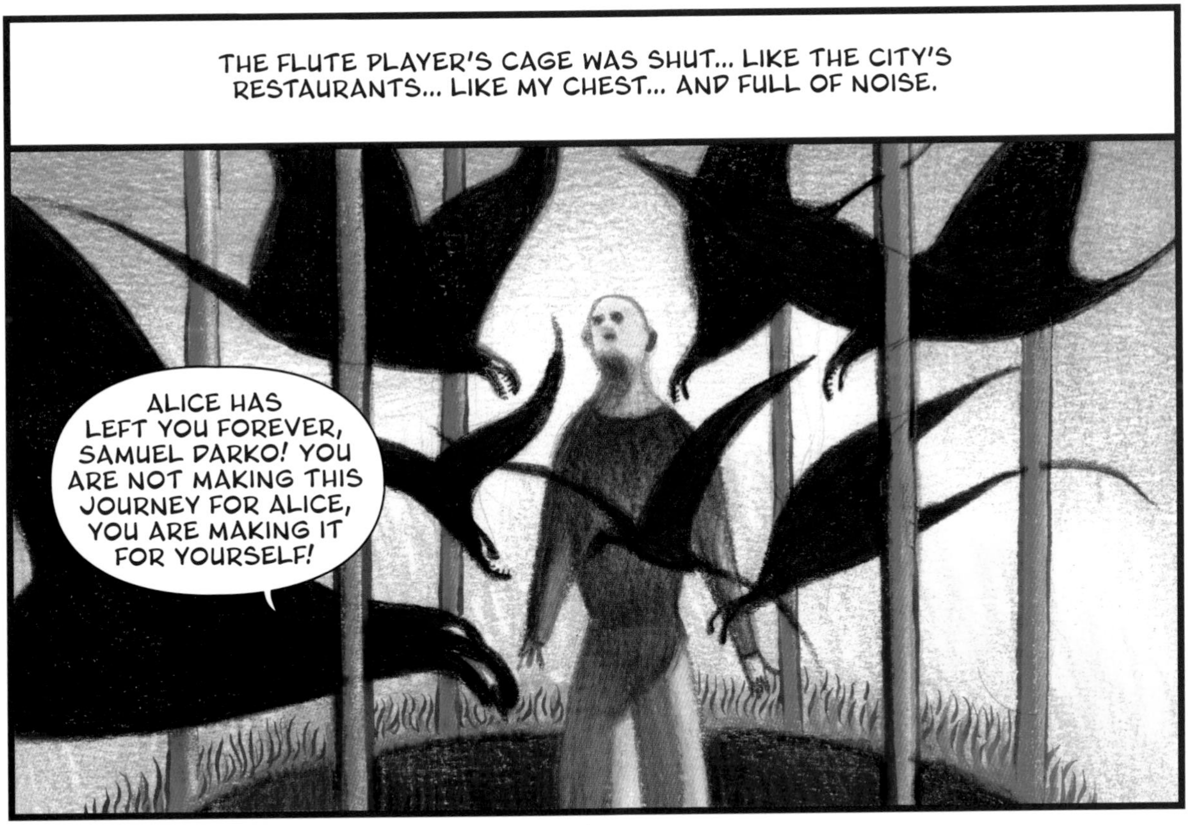
THE FLUTE PLAYER'S CAGE WAS SHUT... LIKE THE CITY'S RESTAURANTS... LIKE MY CHEST... AND FULL OF NOISE.
ALICE HAS LEFT YOU FOREVER, SAMUEL DARKO! YOU ARE NOT MAKING THIS JOURNEY FOR ALICE, YOU ARE MAKING IT FOR YOURSELF!

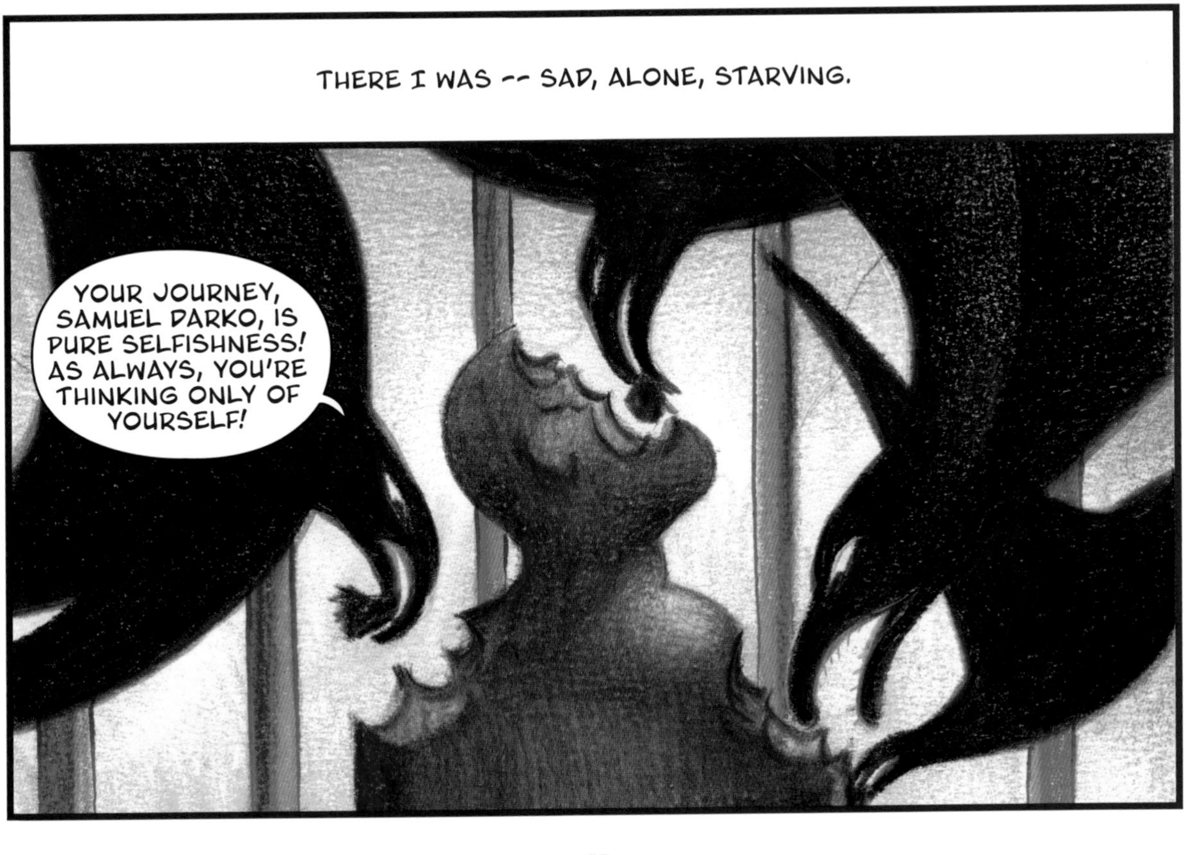
THERE I WAS -- SAD, ALONE, STARVING.
YOUR JOURNEY, SAMUEL DARKO, IS PURE SELFISHNESS! AS ALWAYS, YOU'RE THINKING ONLY OF YOURSELF!

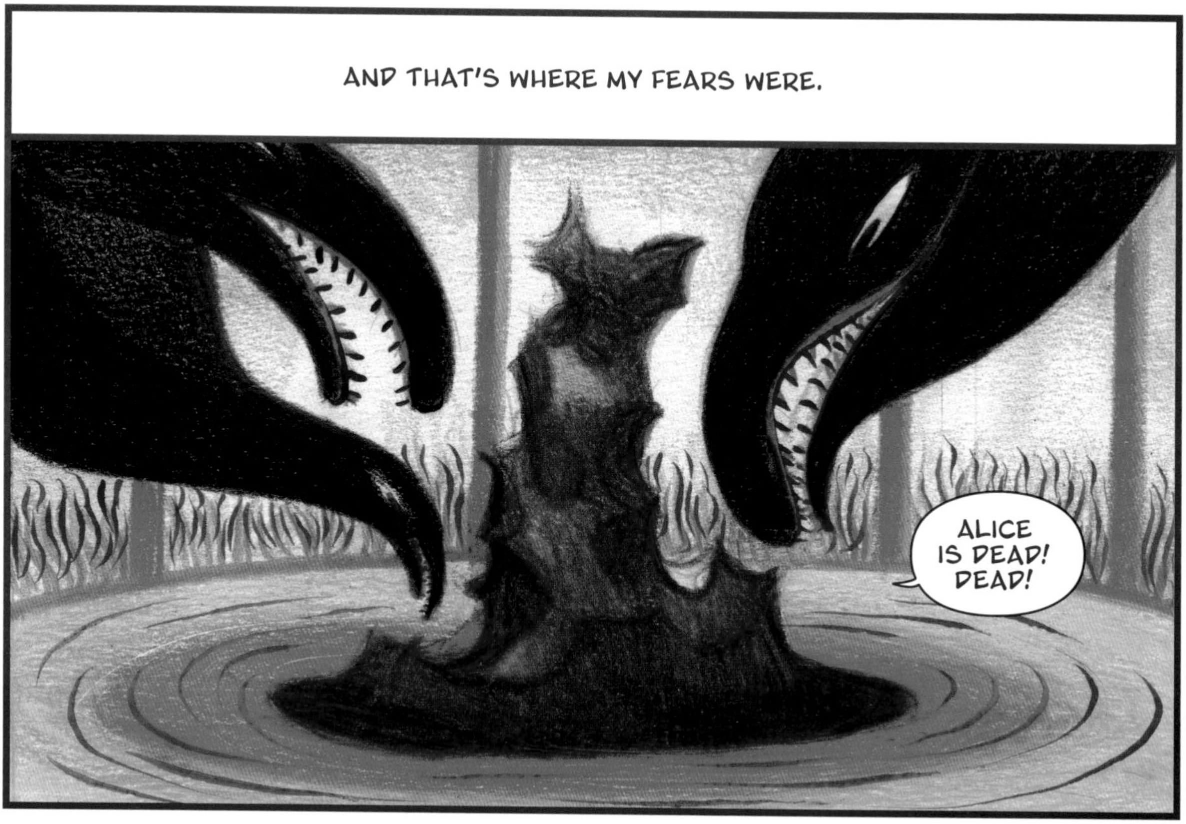
AND THAT'S WHERE MY FEARS WERE.
ALICE IS DEAD! DEAD!

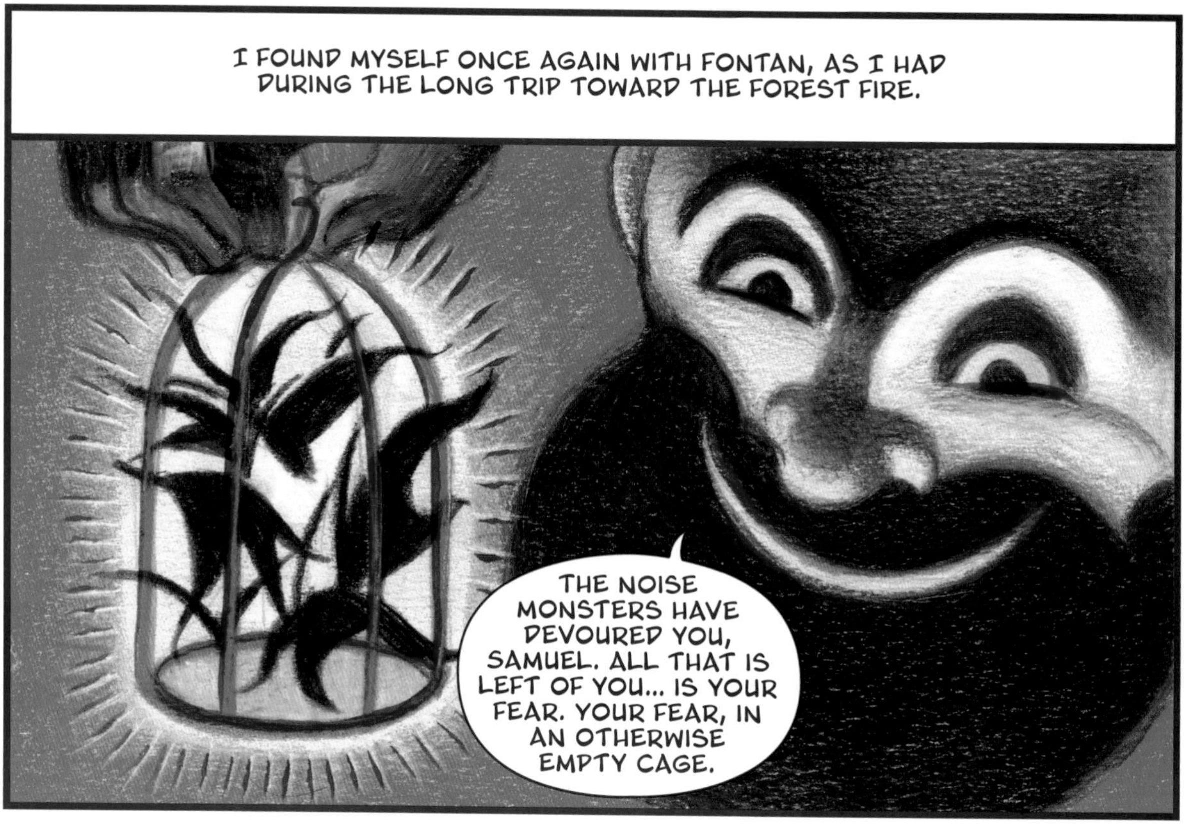
I FOUND MYSELF ONCE AGAIN WITH FONTAN, AS I HAD DURING THE LONG TRIP TOWARD THE FOREST FIRE.
THE NOISE MONSTERS HAVE DEVOURED YOU, SAMUEL. ALL THAT IS LEFT OF YOU... IS YOUR FEAR. YOUR FEAR, IN AN OTHERWISE EMPTY CAGE.

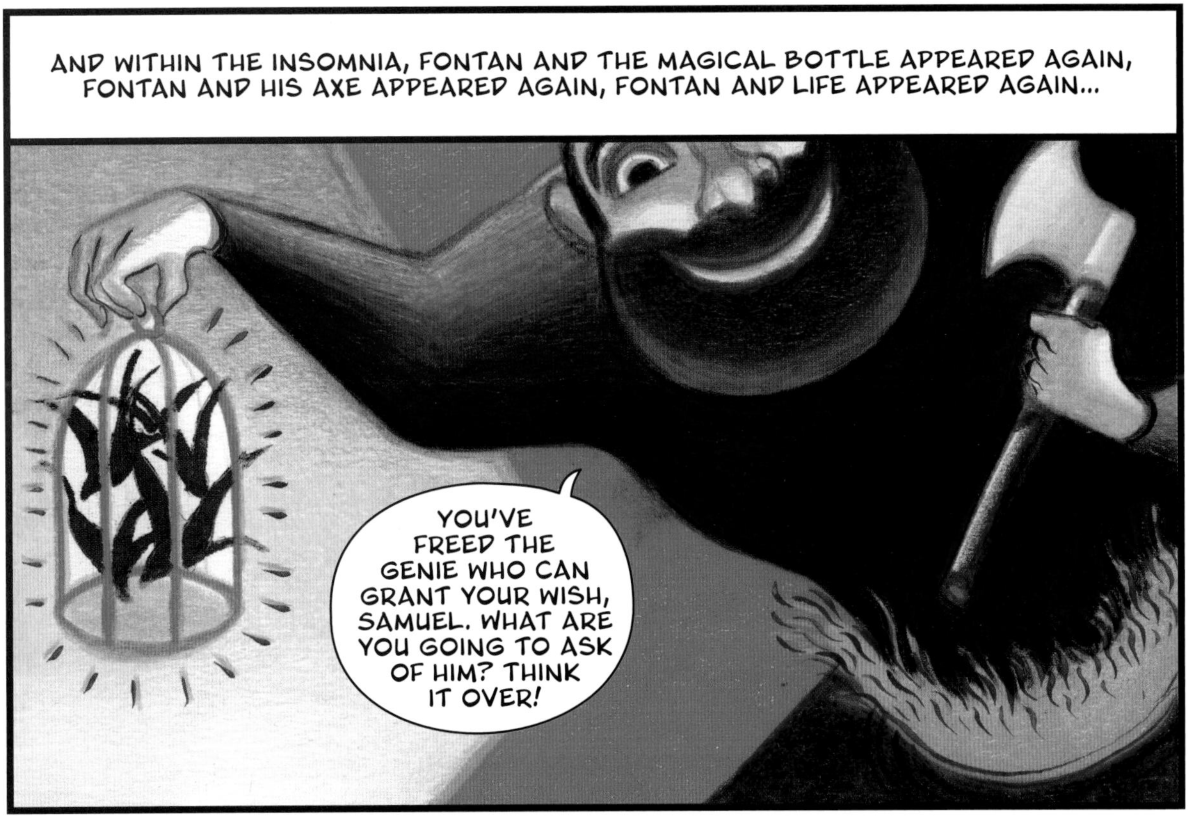
AND WITHIN THE INSOMNIA, FONTAN AND THE MAGICAL BOTTLE APPEARED AGAIN, FONTAN AND HIS AXE APPEARED AGAIN, FONTAN AND LIFE APPEARED AGAIN...
YOU'VE FREED THE GENIE WHO CAN GRANT YOUR WISH, SAMUEL. WHAT ARE YOU GOING TO ASK OF HIM? THINK IT OVER!

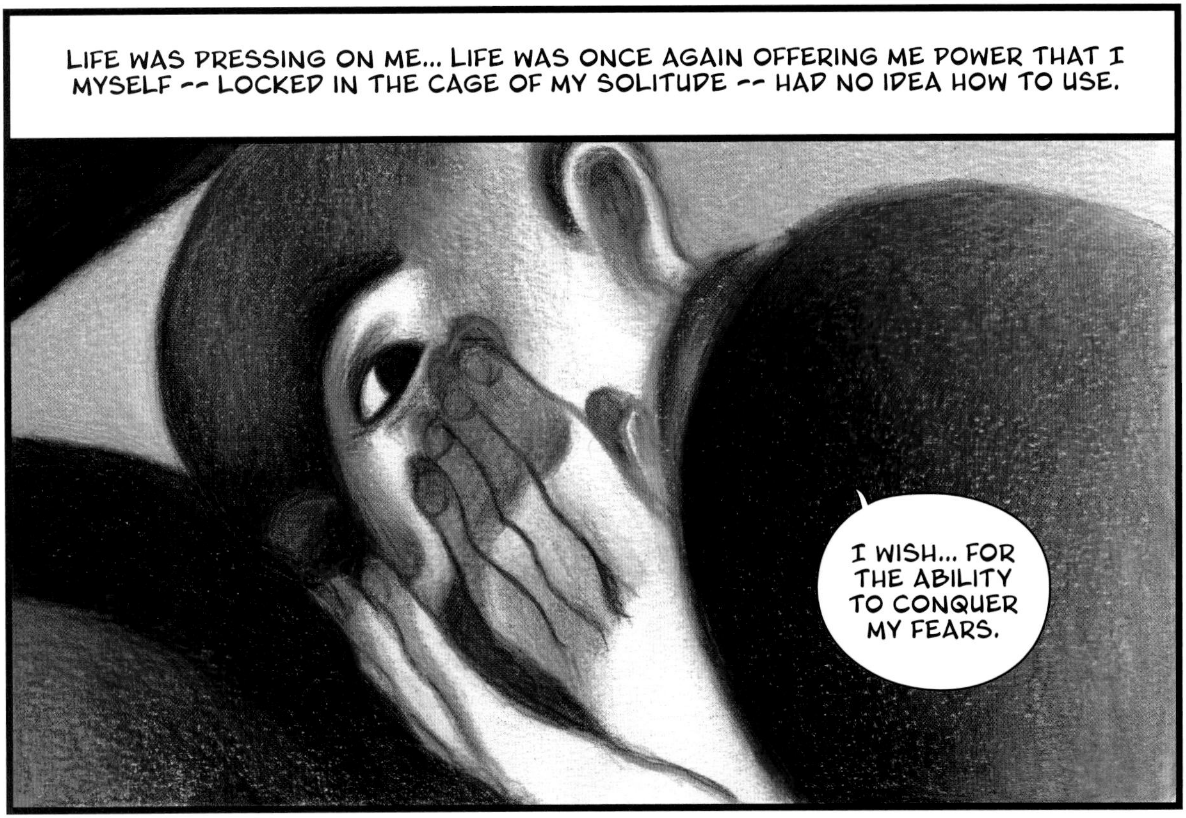
LIFE WAS PRESSING ON ME... LIFE WAS ONCE AGAIN OFFERING ME POWER THAT I MYSELF -- LOCKED IN THE CAGE OF MY SOLITUDE -- HAD NO IDEA HOW TO USE.
I WISH... FOR THE ABILITY TO CONQUER MY FEARS.

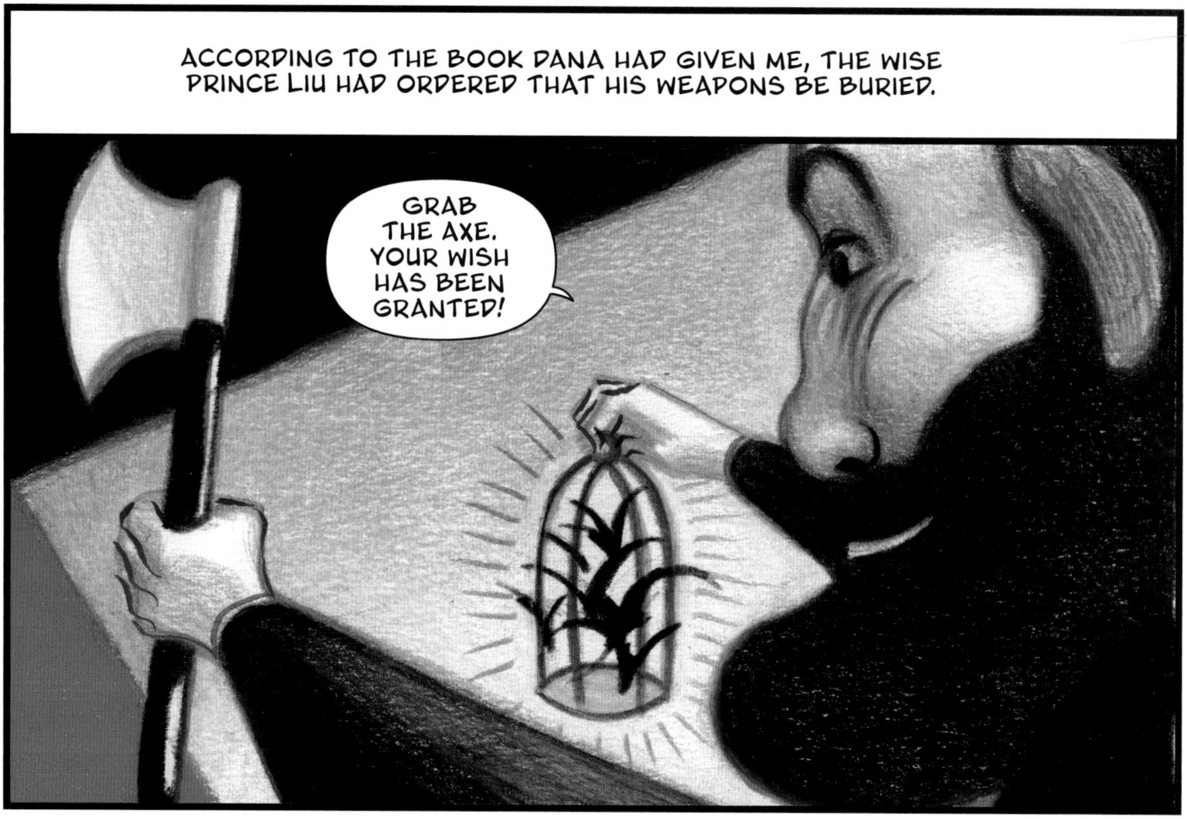
ACCORDING TO THE BOOK DANA HAD GIVEN ME, THE WISE PRINCE LIU HAD ORDERED THAT HIS WEAPONS BE BURIED.
GRAB THE AXE. YOUR WISH HAS BEEN GRANTED!

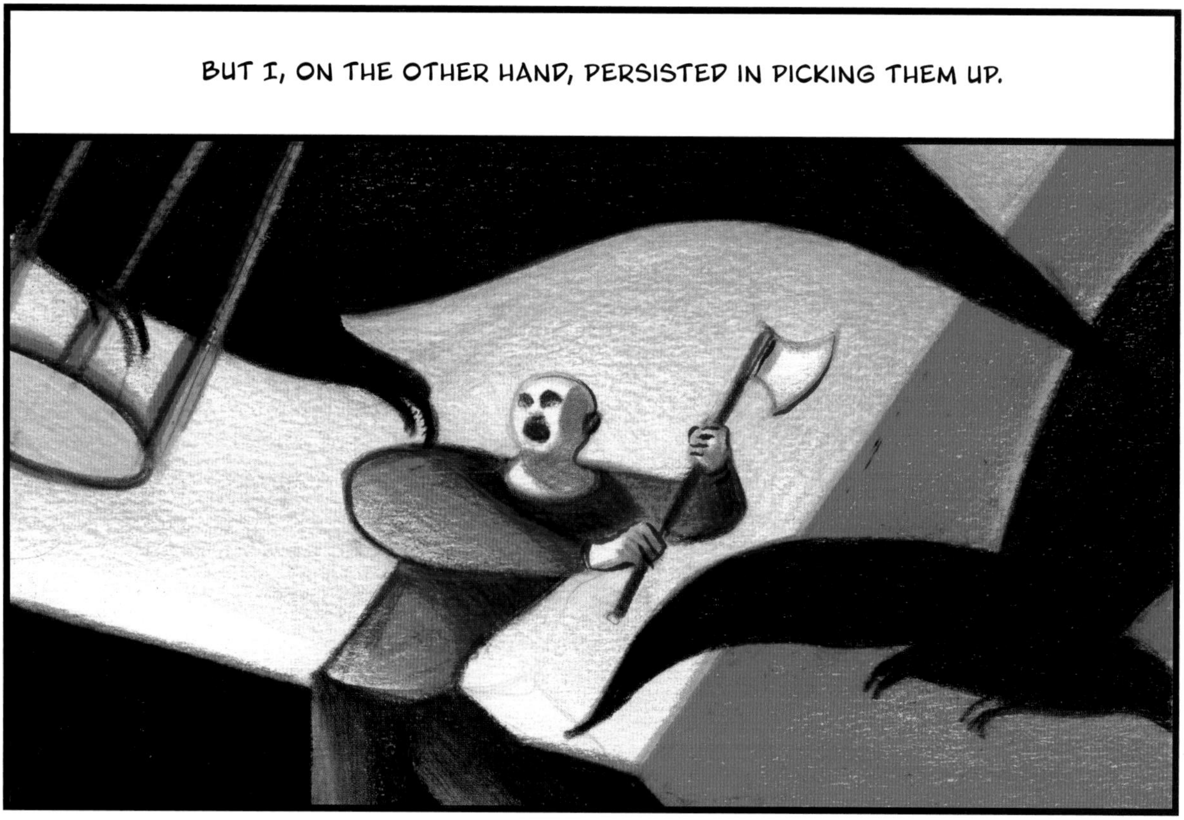
BUT I, ON THE OTHER HAND, PERSISTED IN PICKING THEM UP.

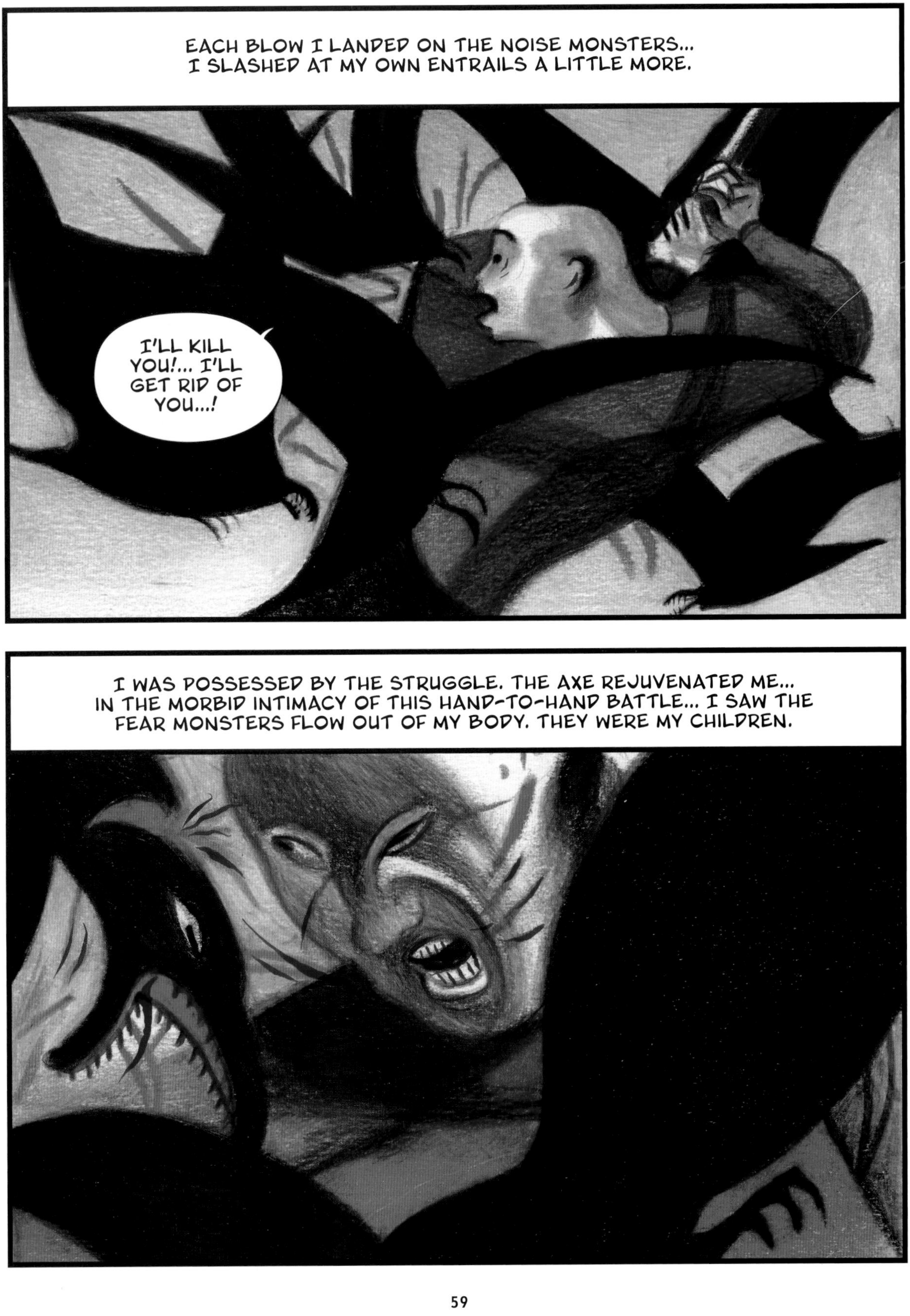
EACH BLOW I LANDED ON THE NOISE MONSTERS... I SLASHED AT MY OWN ENTRAILS A LITTLE MORE.
I'LL KILL YOU!... I'LL GET RID OF YOU...!
I WAS POSSESSED BY THE STRUGGLE. THE AXE REJUVENATED ME... IN THE MORBID INTIMACY OF THIS HAND-TO-HAND BATTLE... I SAW THE FEAR MONSTERS FLOW OUT OF MY BODY. THEY WERE MY CHILDREN.

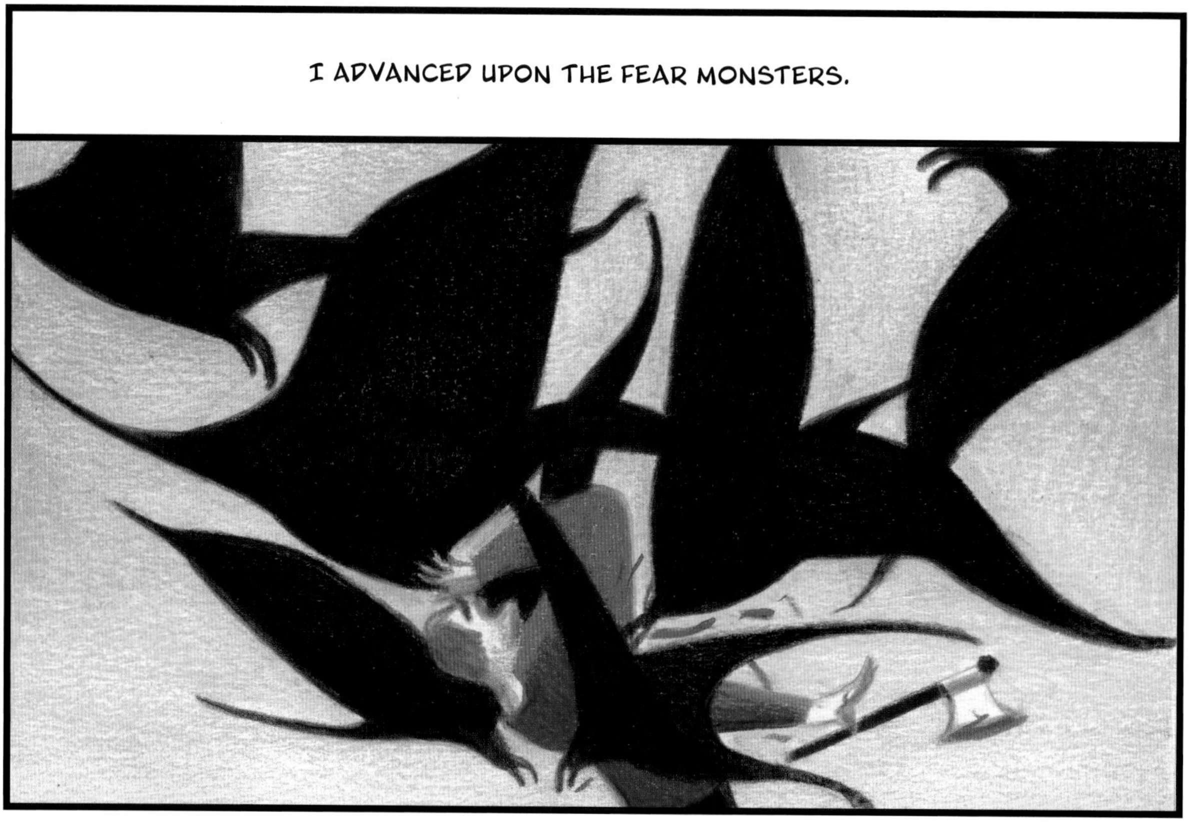
I ADVANCED UPON THE FEAR MONSTERS.

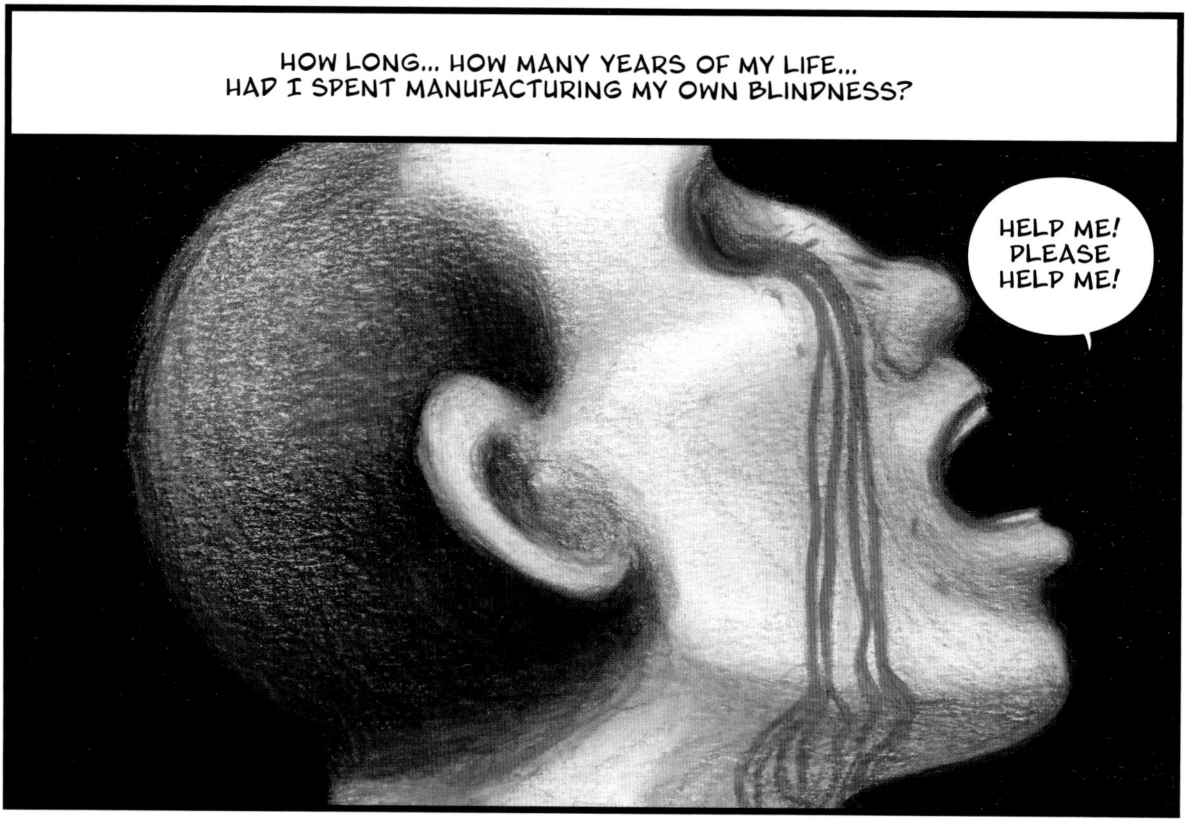
HOW LONG... HOW MANY YEARS OF MY LIFE... HAD I SPENT MANUFACTURING MY OWN BLINDNESS?
HELP ME! PLEASE HELP ME!

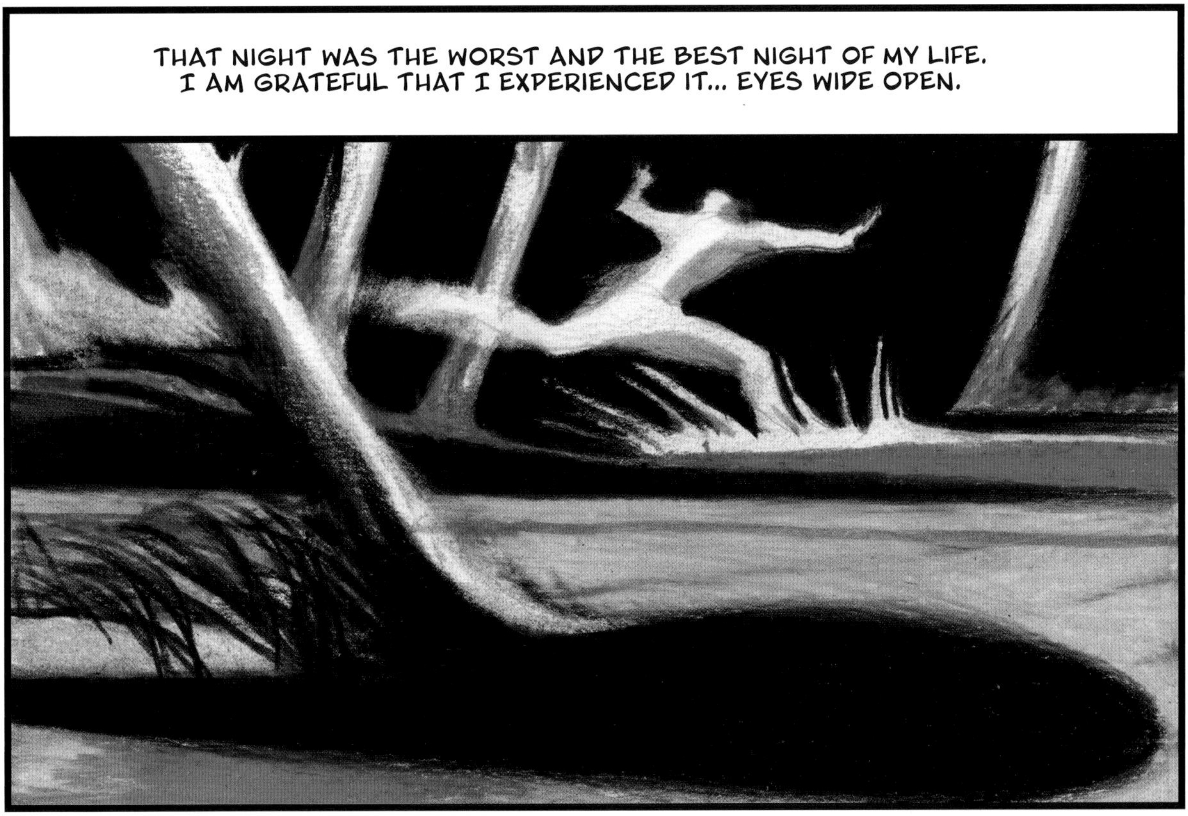
THAT NIGHT WAS THE WORST AND THE BEST NIGHT OF MY LIFE. I AM GRATEFUL THAT I EXPERIENCED IT... EYES WIDE OPEN.

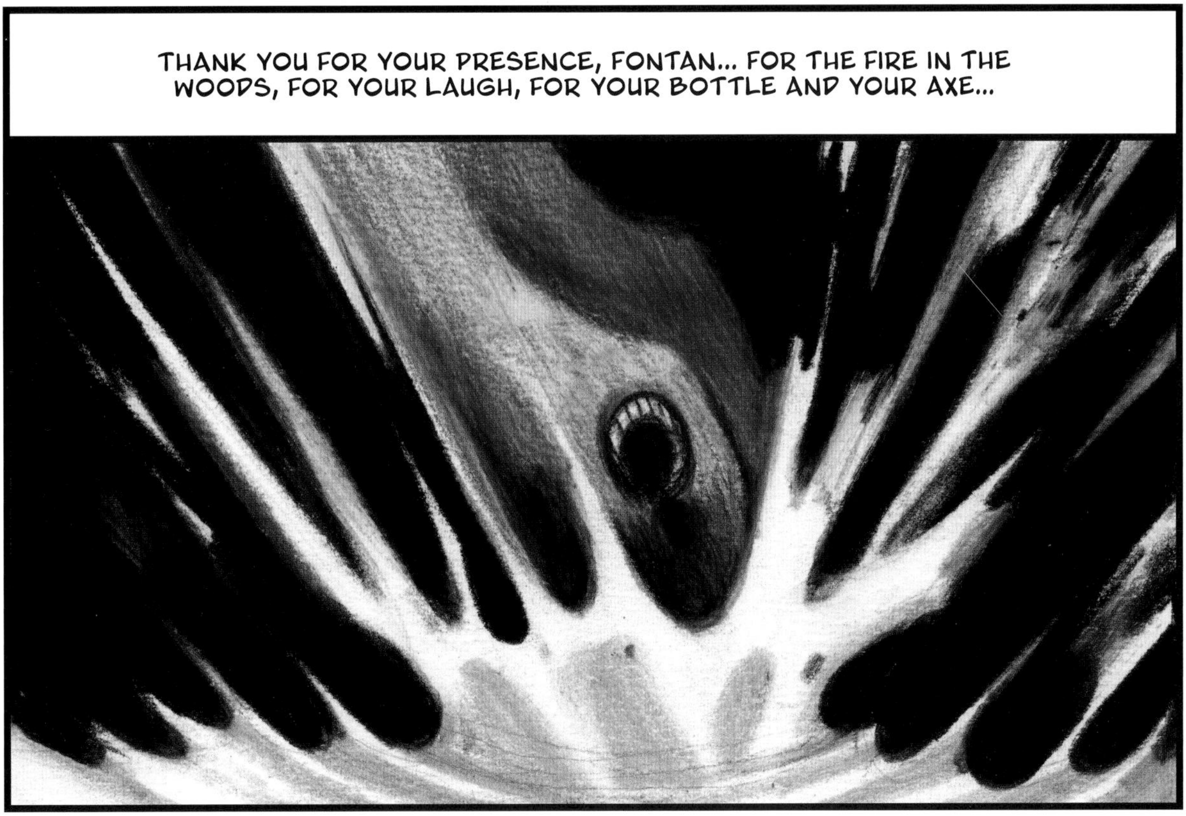
THANK YOU FOR YOUR PRESENCE, FONTAN... FOR THE FIRE IN THE WOODS, FOR YOUR LAUGH, FOR YOUR BOTTLE AND YOUR AXE...

THANK YOU FOR THE LIGHT, DOCTOR BERTHUIS.

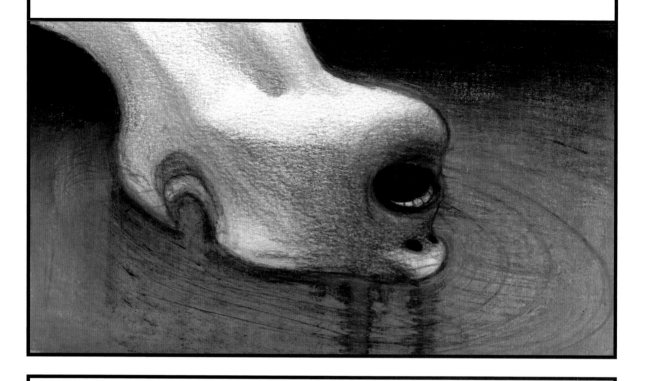

THANK YOU FOR THE VISIT TO THE RUINS OF THE PRIMITIVE CITY.
THANK YOU FOR THE VISIT TO MY OWN RUINS.

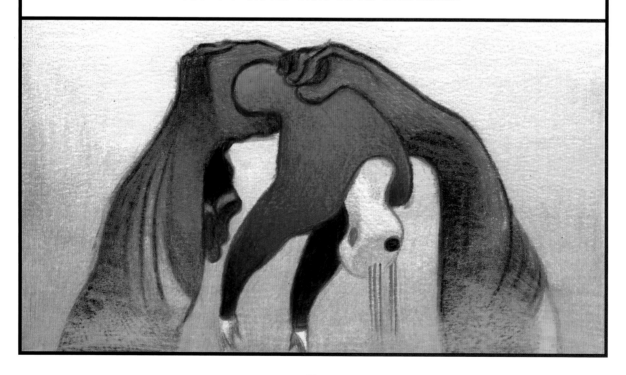

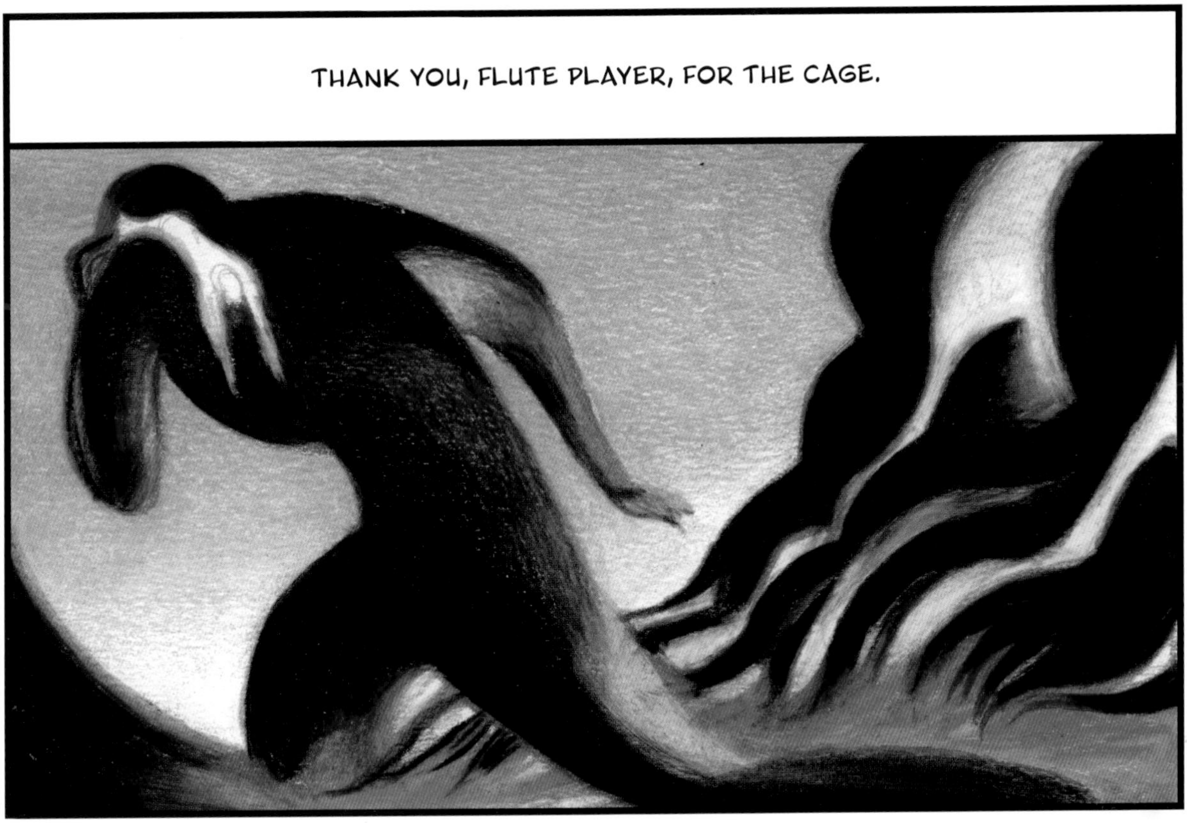
THANK YOU, FLUTE PLAYER, FOR THE CAGE.

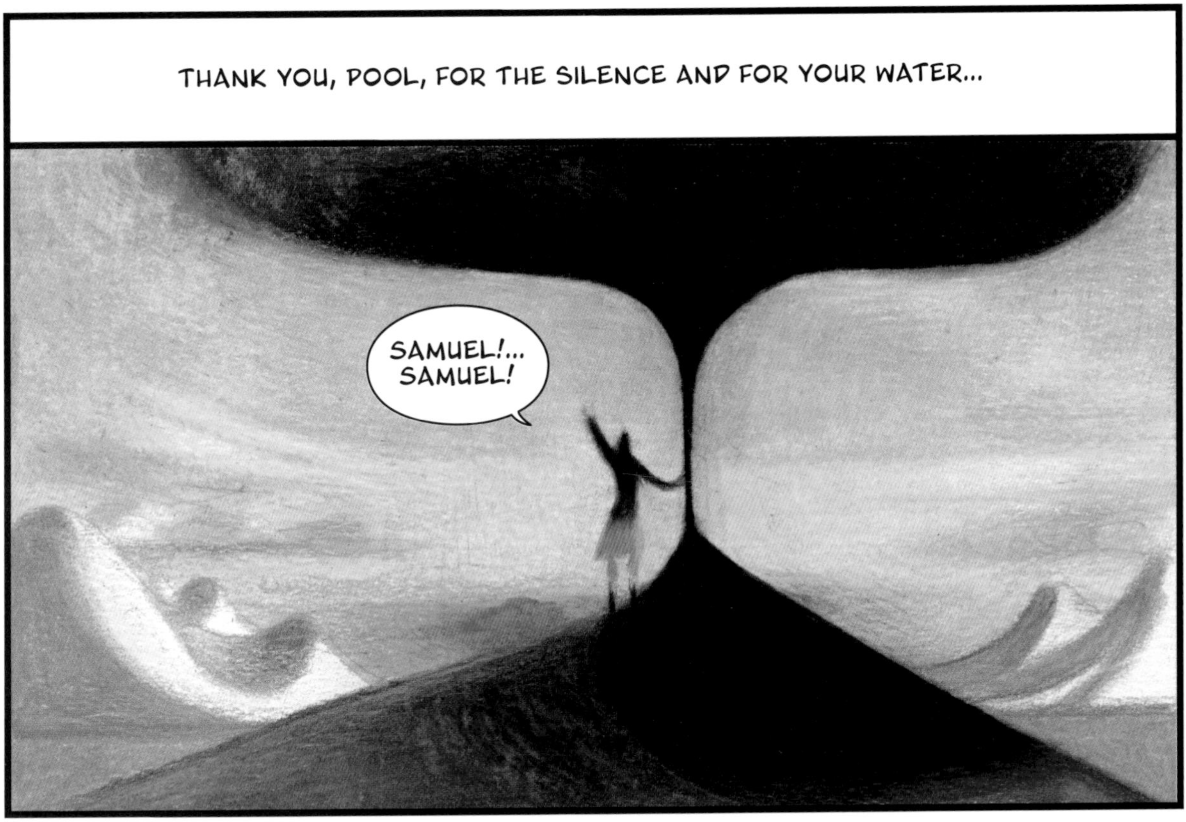
THANK YOU, POOL, FOR THE SILENCE AND FOR YOUR WATER...
SAMUEL!... SAMUEL!

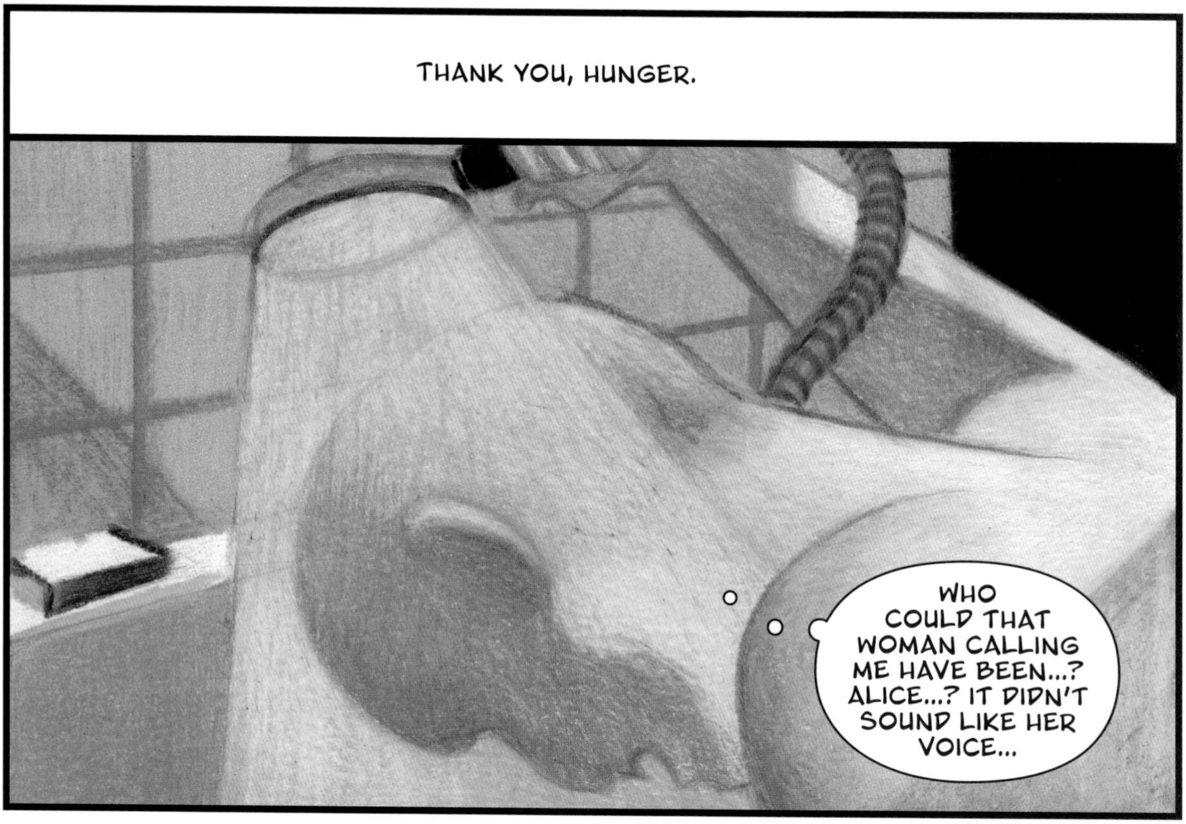
THANK YOU, HUNGER.
WHO COULD THAT WOMAN CALLING ME HAVE BEEN...? ALICE...? IT DIDN'T SOUND LIKE HER VOICE...

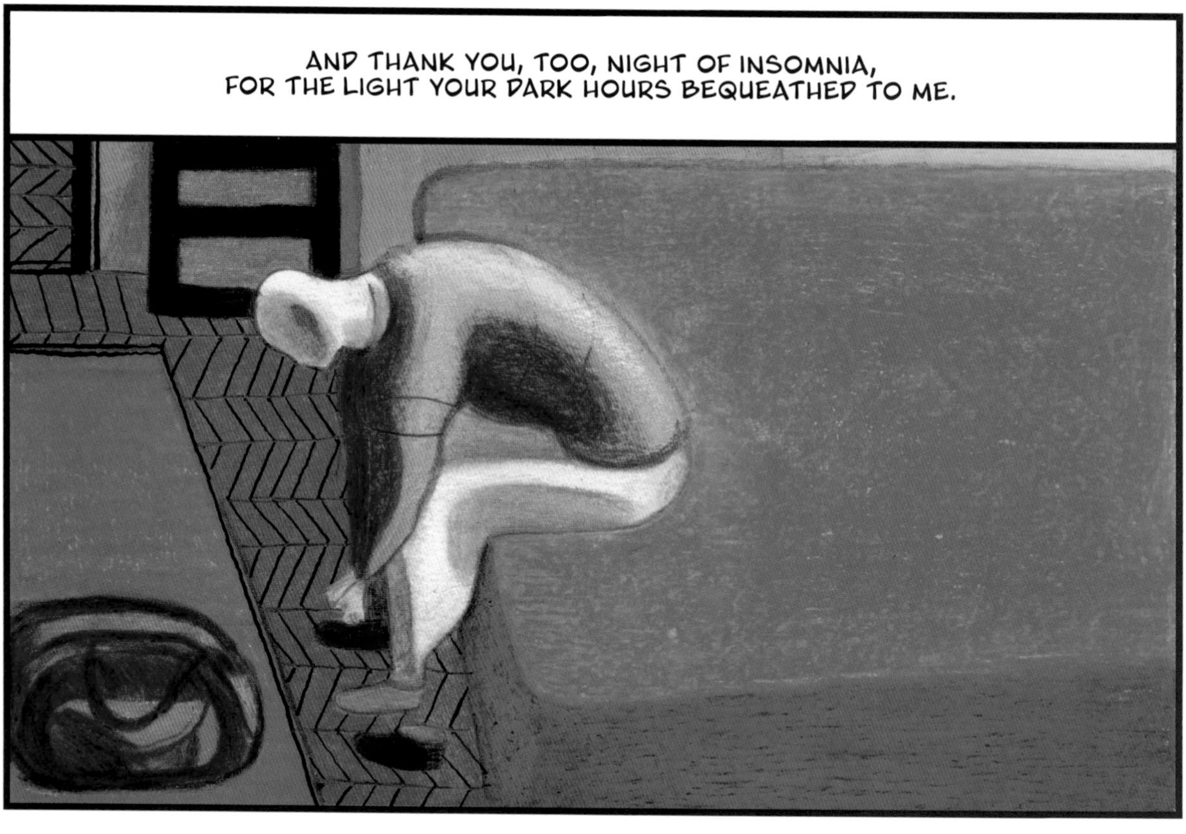
AND THANK YOU, TOO, NIGHT OF INSOMNIA, FOR THE LIGHT YOUR DARK HOURS BEQUEATHED TO ME.

4

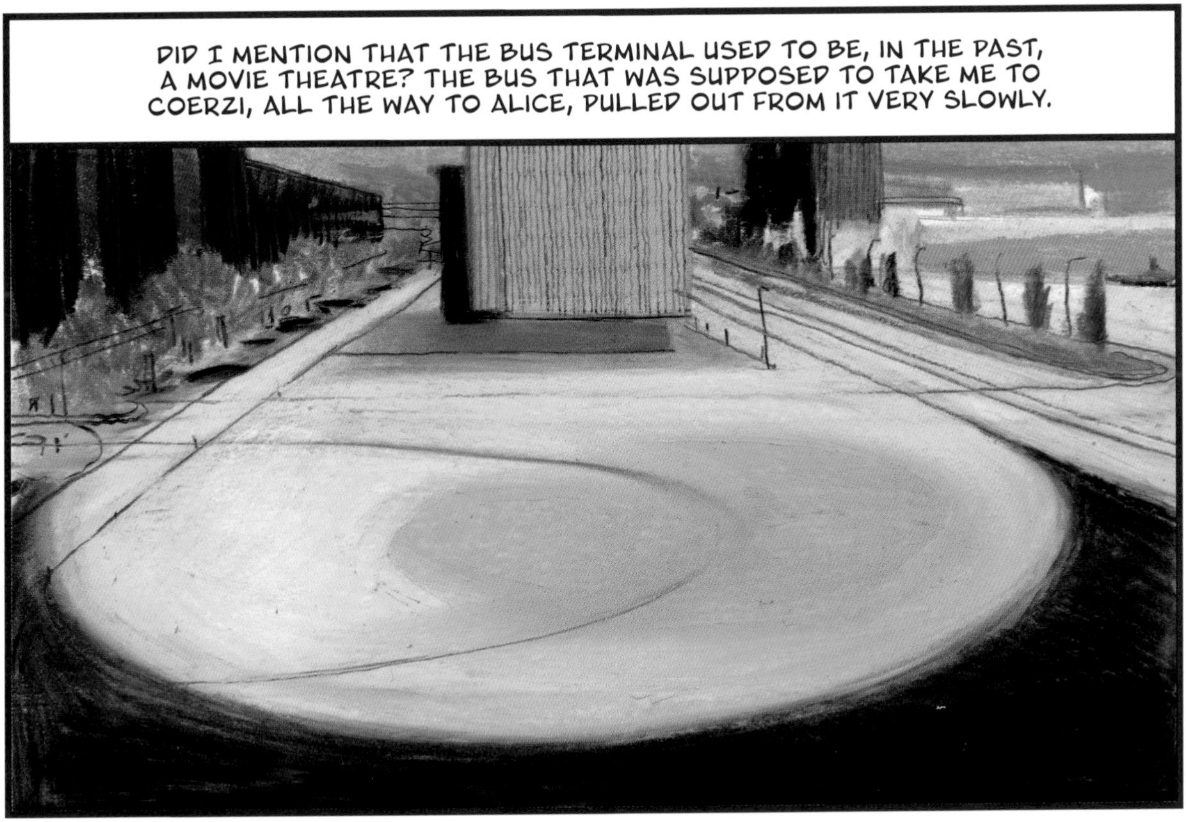
DID I MENTION THAT THE BUS TERMINAL USED TO BE, IN THE PAST, A MOVIE THEATRE? THE BUS THAT WAS SUPPOSED TO TAKE ME TO COERZI, ALL THE WAY TO ALICE, PULLED OUT FROM IT VERY SLOWLY.

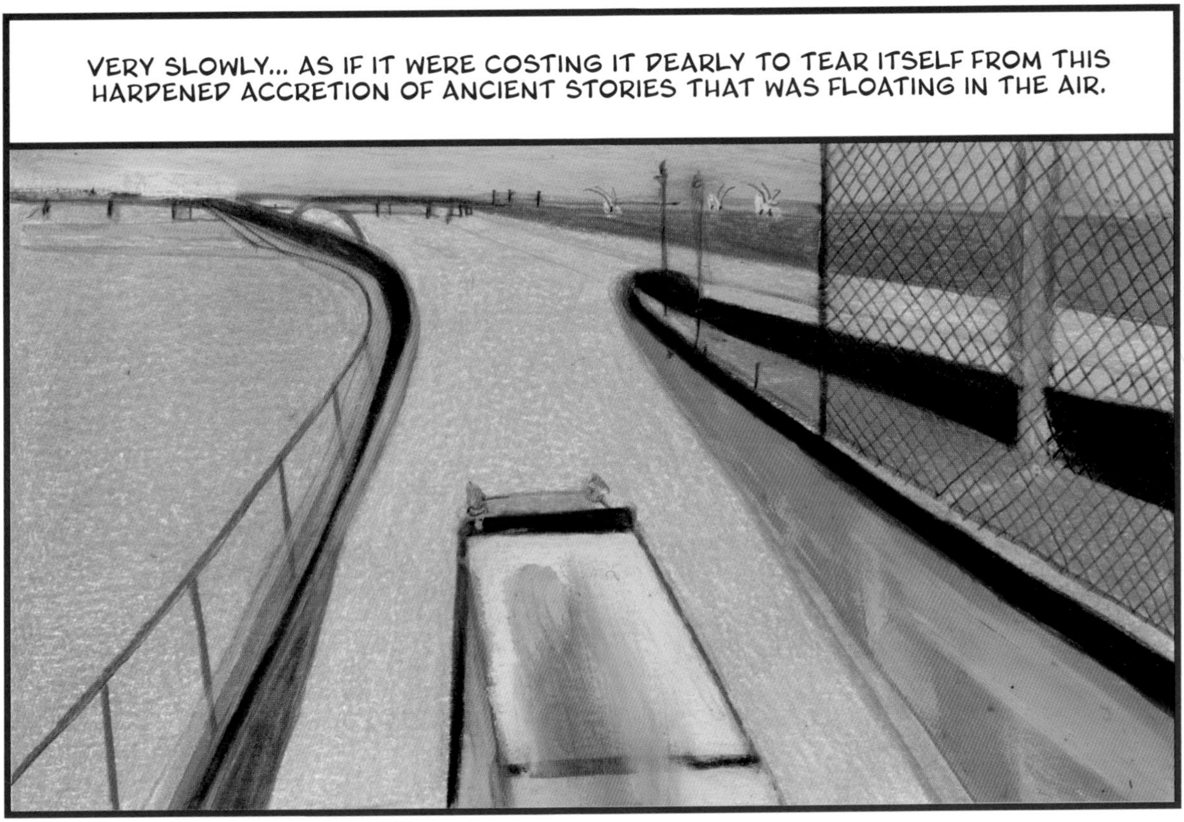
VERY SLOWLY... AS IF IT WERE COSTING IT DEARLY TO TEAR ITSELF FROM THIS HARDENED ACCRETION OF ANCIENT STORIES THAT WAS FLOATING IN THE AIR.

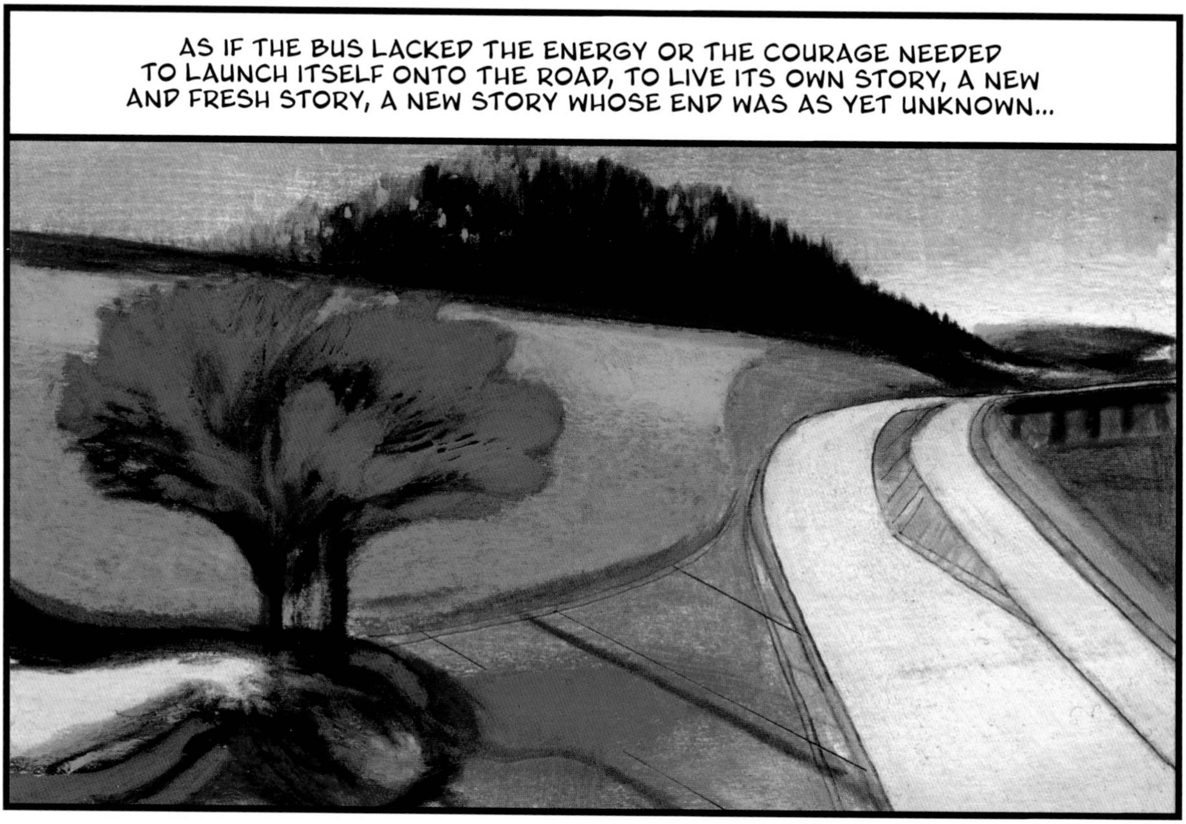
AS IF THE BUS LACKED THE ENERGY OR THE COURAGE NEEDED TO LAUNCH ITSELF ONTO THE ROAD, TO LIVE ITS OWN STORY, A NEW AND FRESH STORY, A NEW STORY WHOSE END WAS AS YET UNKNOWN...

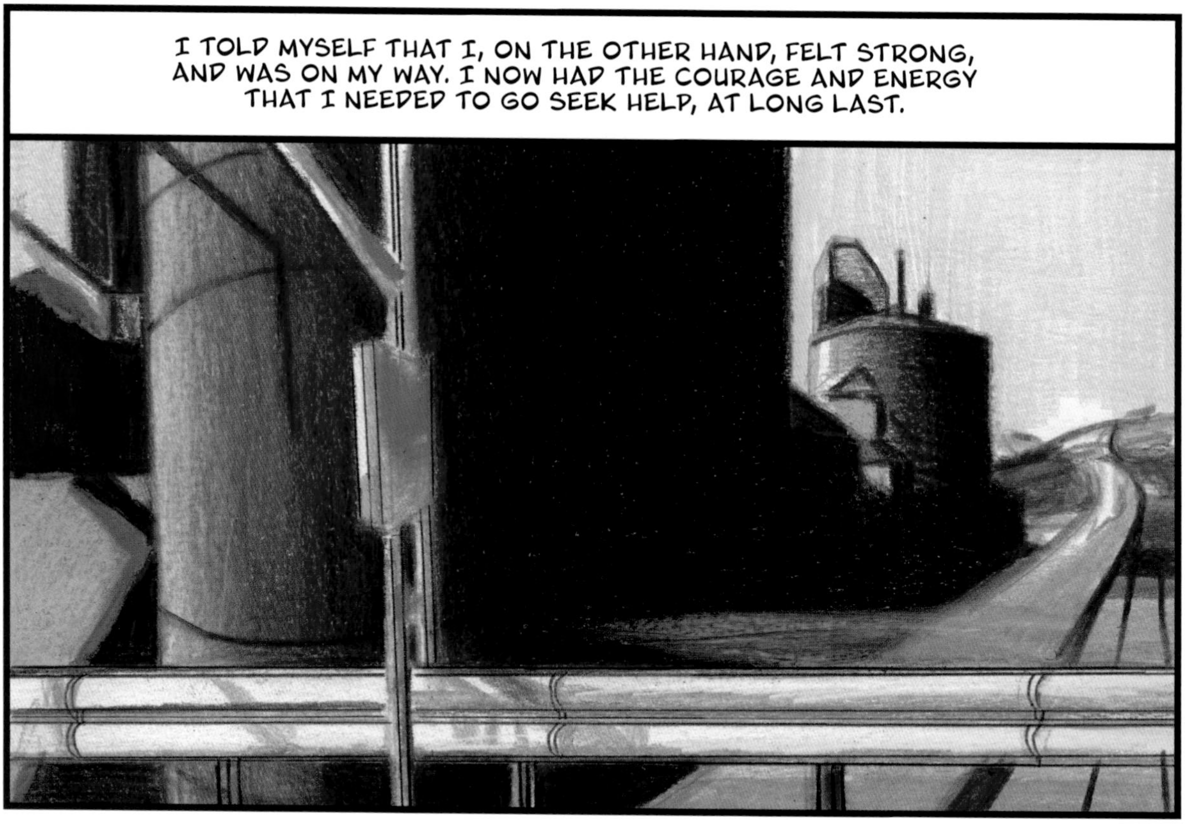
I TOLD MYSELF THAT I, ON THE OTHER HAND, FELT STRONG, AND WAS ON MY WAY. I NOW HAD THE COURAGE AND ENERGY THAT I NEEDED TO GO SEEK HELP, AT LONG LAST.

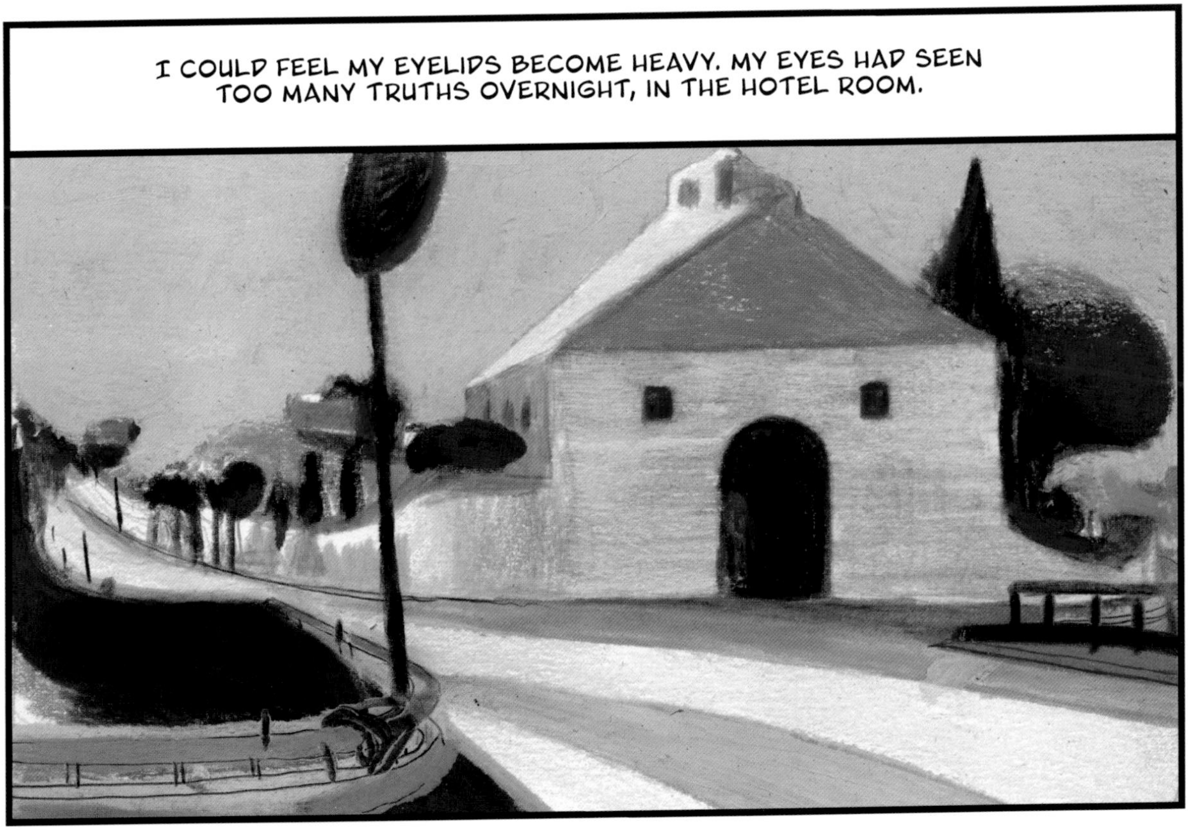
I COULD FEEL MY EYELIDS BECOME HEAVY. MY EYES HAD SEEN TOO MANY TRUTHS OVERNIGHT, IN THE HOTEL ROOM.

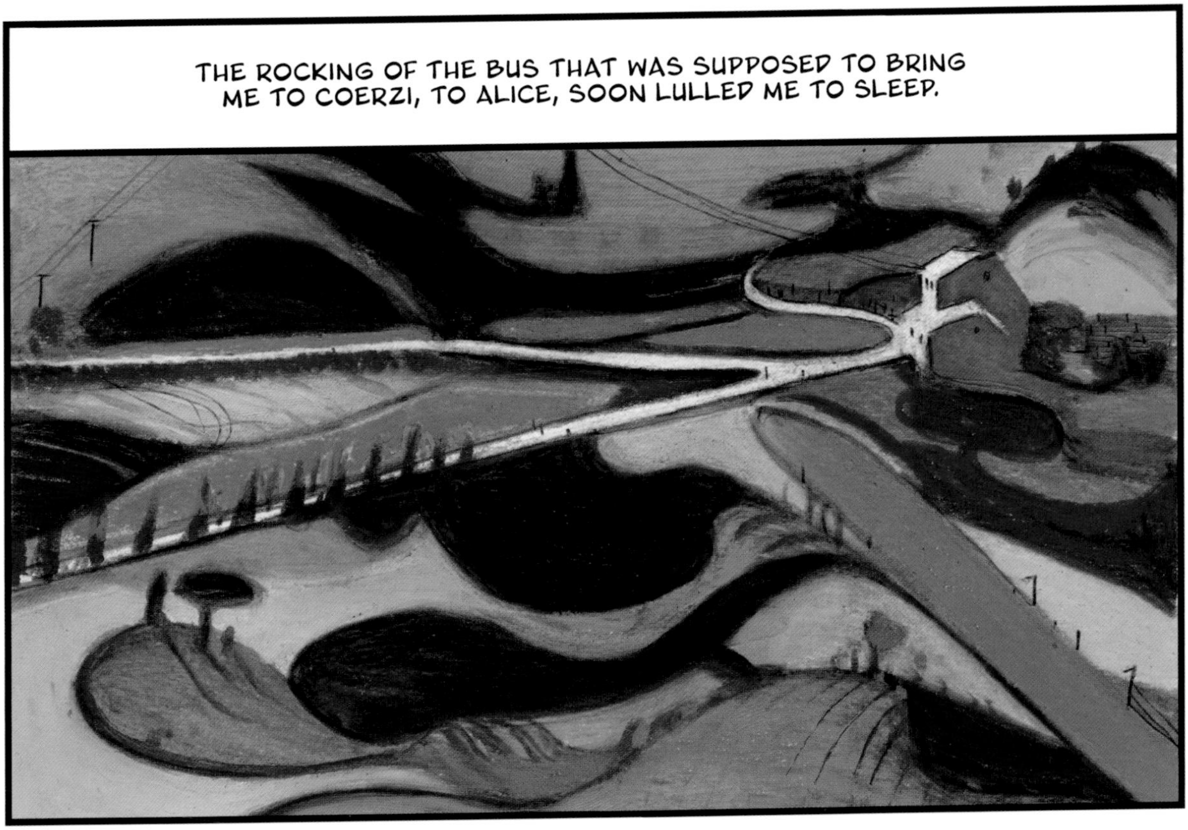
THE ROCKING OF THE BUS THAT WAS SUPPOSED TO BRING ME TO COERZI, TO ALICE, SOON LULLED ME TO SLEEP.

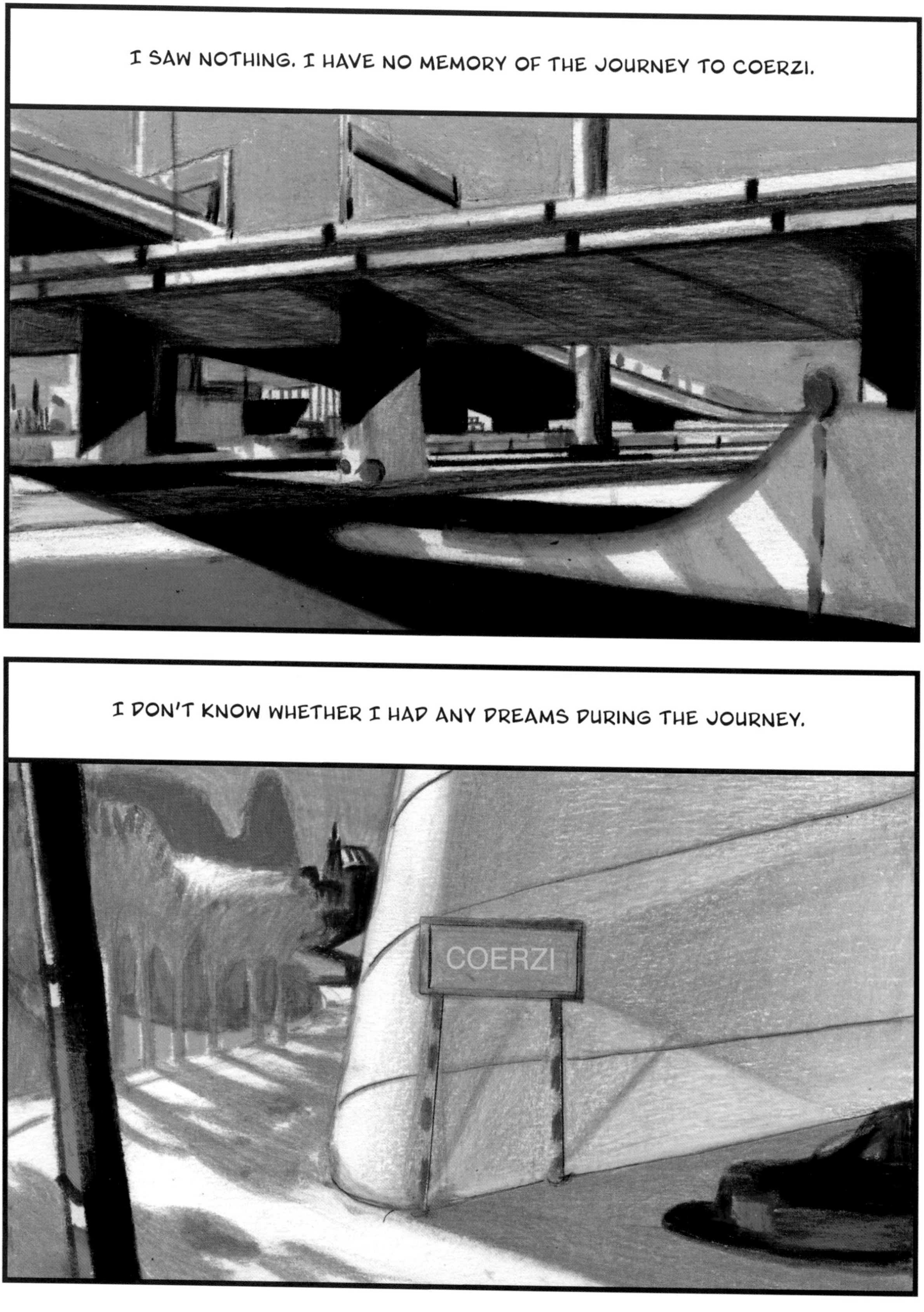
I SAW NOTHING. I HAVE NO MEMORY OF THE JOURNEY TO COERZI.
I DON'T KNOW WHETHER I HAD ANY DREAMS DURING THE JOURNEY.
COERZI

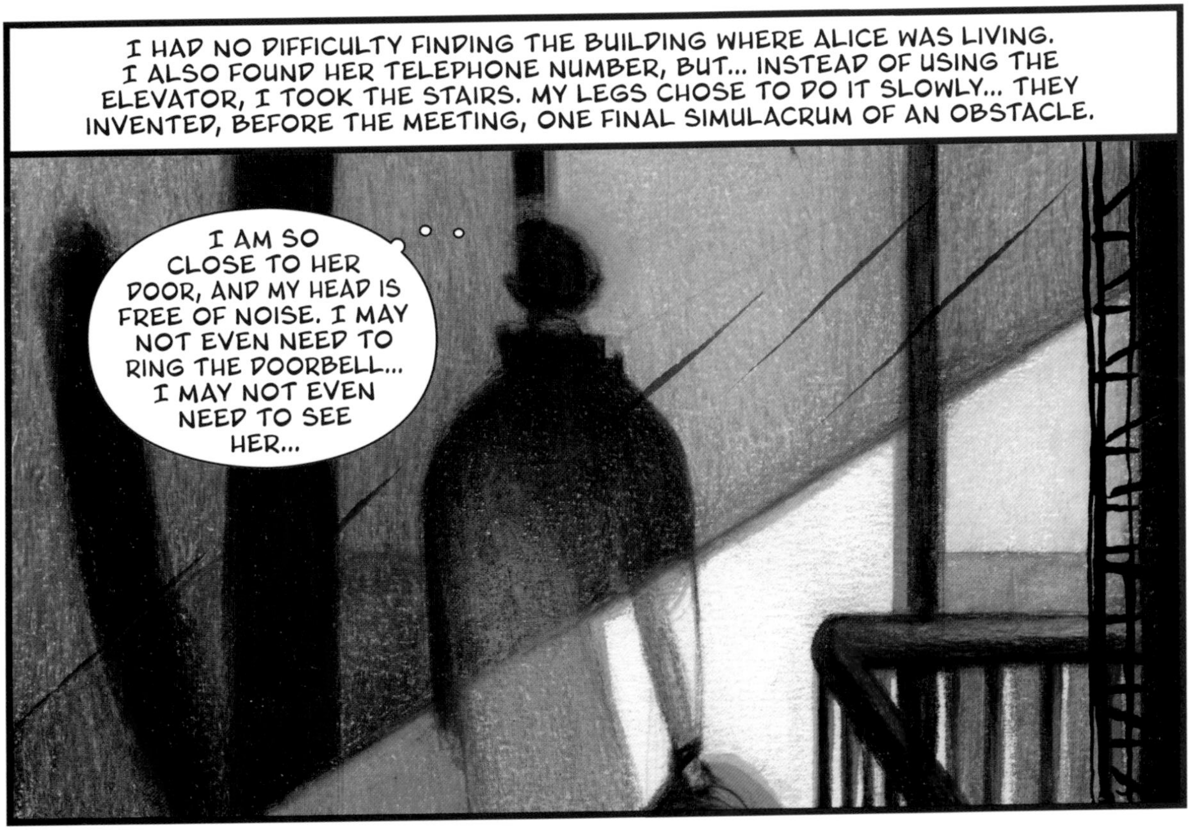
I HAD NO DIFFICULTY FINDING THE BUILDING WHERE ALICE WAS LIVING. I ALSO FOUND HER TELEPHONE NUMBER, BUT... INSTEAD OF USING THE ELEVATOR, I TOOK THE STAIRS. MY LEGS CHOSE TO DO IT SLOWLY... THEY INVENTED, BEFORE THE MEETING, ONE FINAL SIMULACRUM OF AN OBSTACLE.
I AM SO CLOSE TO HER DOOR, AND MY HEAD IS FREE OF NOISE. I MAY NOT EVEN NEED TO RING THE DOORBELL... I MAY NOT EVEN NEED TO SEE HER...

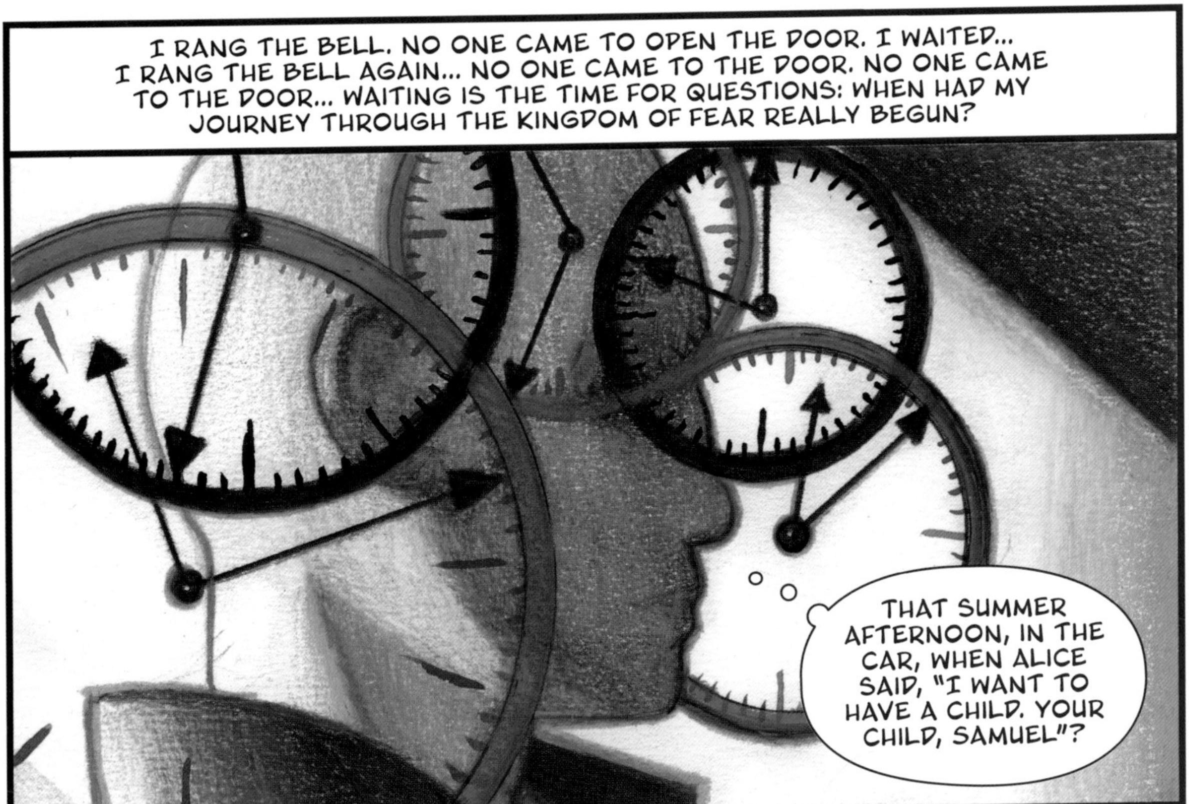
I RANG THE BELL. NO ONE CAME TO OPEN THE DOOR. I WAITED... I RANG THE BELL AGAIN... NO ONE CAME TO THE DOOR. NO ONE CAME TO THE DOOR... WAITING IS THE TIME FOR QUESTIONS: WHEN HAD MY JOURNEY THROUGH THE KINGDOM OF FEAR REALLY BEGUN?
THAT SUMMER AFTERNOON, IN THE CAR, WHEN ALICE SAID, "I WANT TO HAVE A CHILD. YOUR CHILD, SAMUEL"?

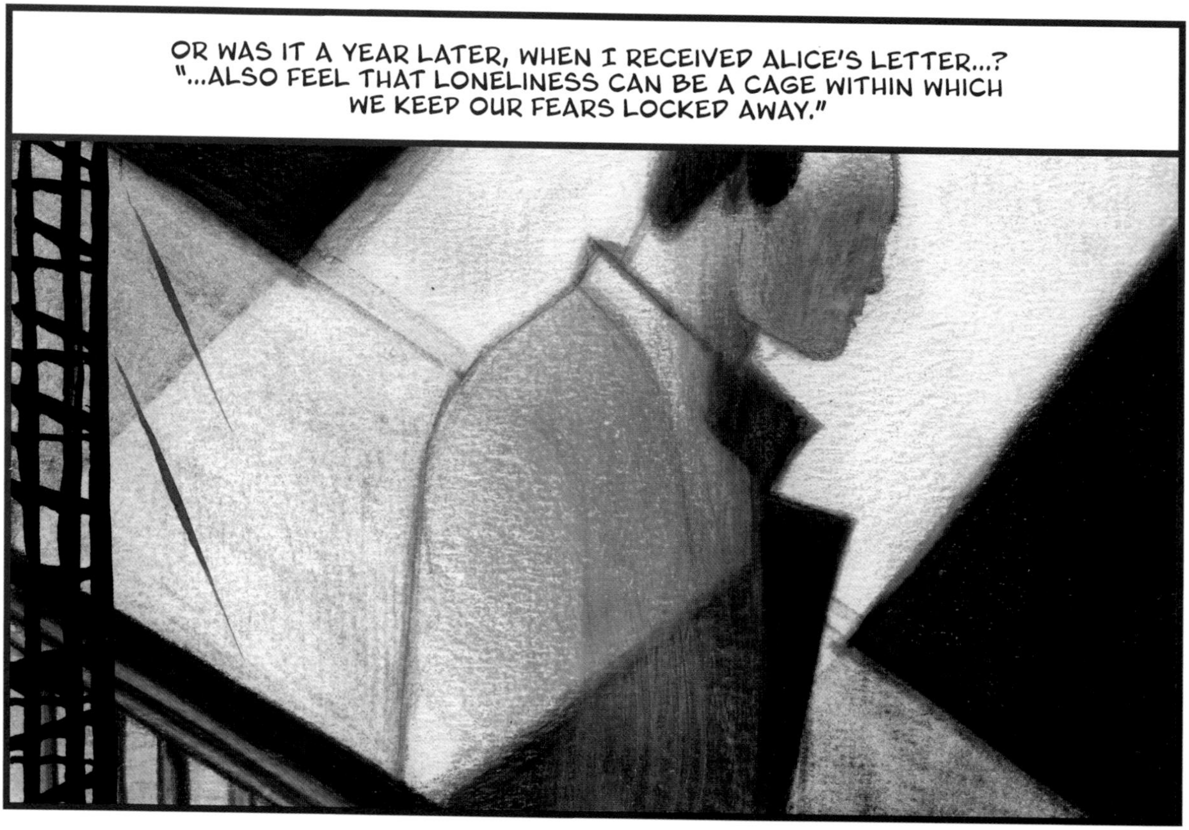
OR WAS IT A YEAR LATER, WHEN I RECEIVED ALICE'S LETTER...? "...ALSO FEEL THAT LONELINESS CAN BE A CAGE WITHIN WHICH WE KEEP OUR FEARS LOCKED AWAY."

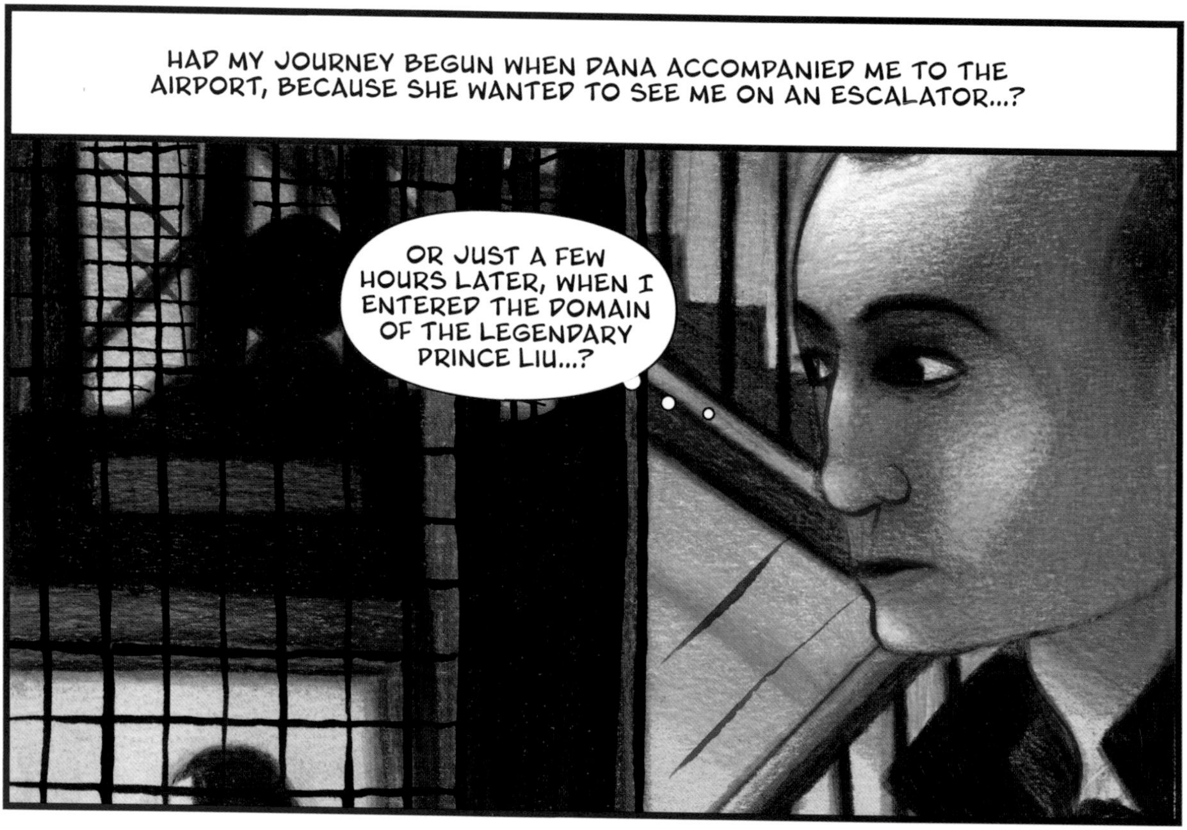
HAD MY JOURNEY BEGUN WHEN DANA ACCOMPANIED ME TO THE AIRPORT, BECAUSE SHE WANTED TO SEE ME ON AN ESCALATOR...?
OR JUST A FEW HOURS LATER, WHEN I ENTERED THE DOMAIN OF THE LEGENDARY PRINCE LIU...?

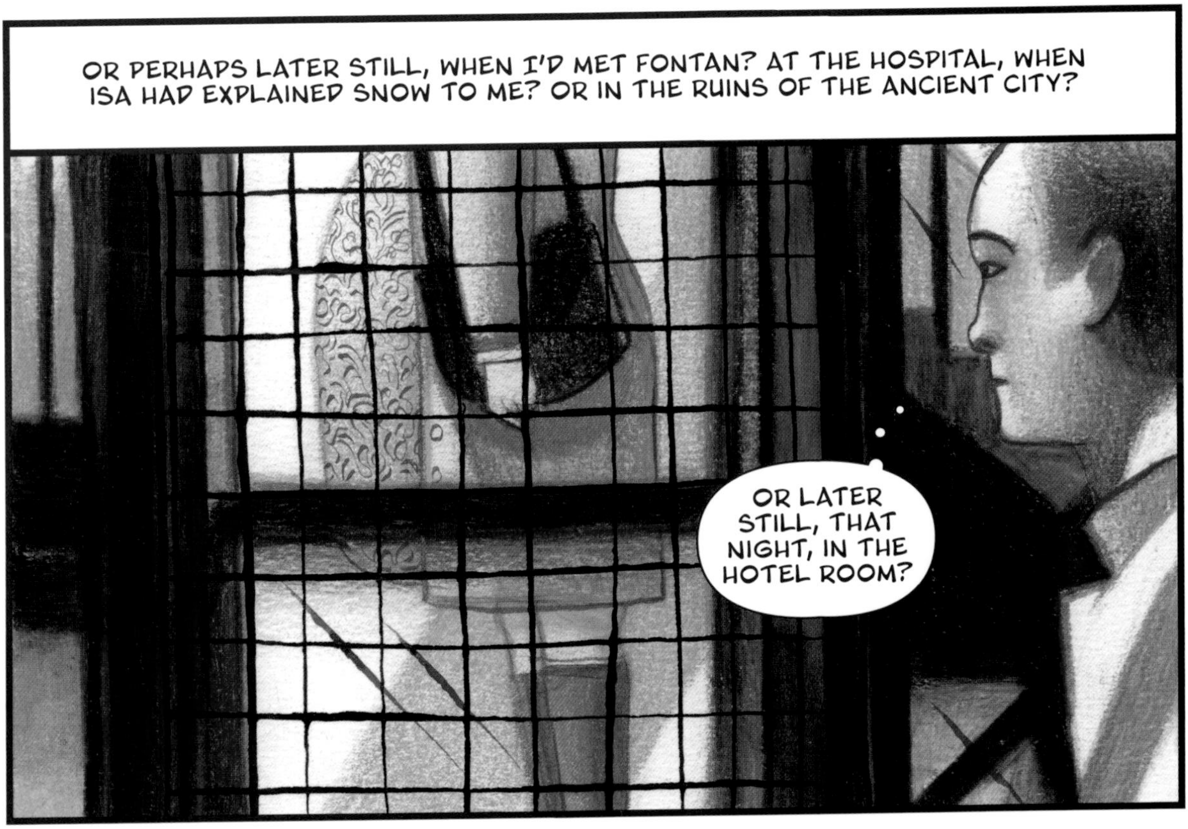
OR PERHAPS LATER STILL, WHEN I'D MET FONTAN? AT THE HOSPITAL, WHEN ISA HAD EXPLAINED SNOW TO ME? OR IN THE RUINS OF THE ANCIENT CITY?
OR LATER STILL, THAT NIGHT, IN THE HOTEL ROOM?

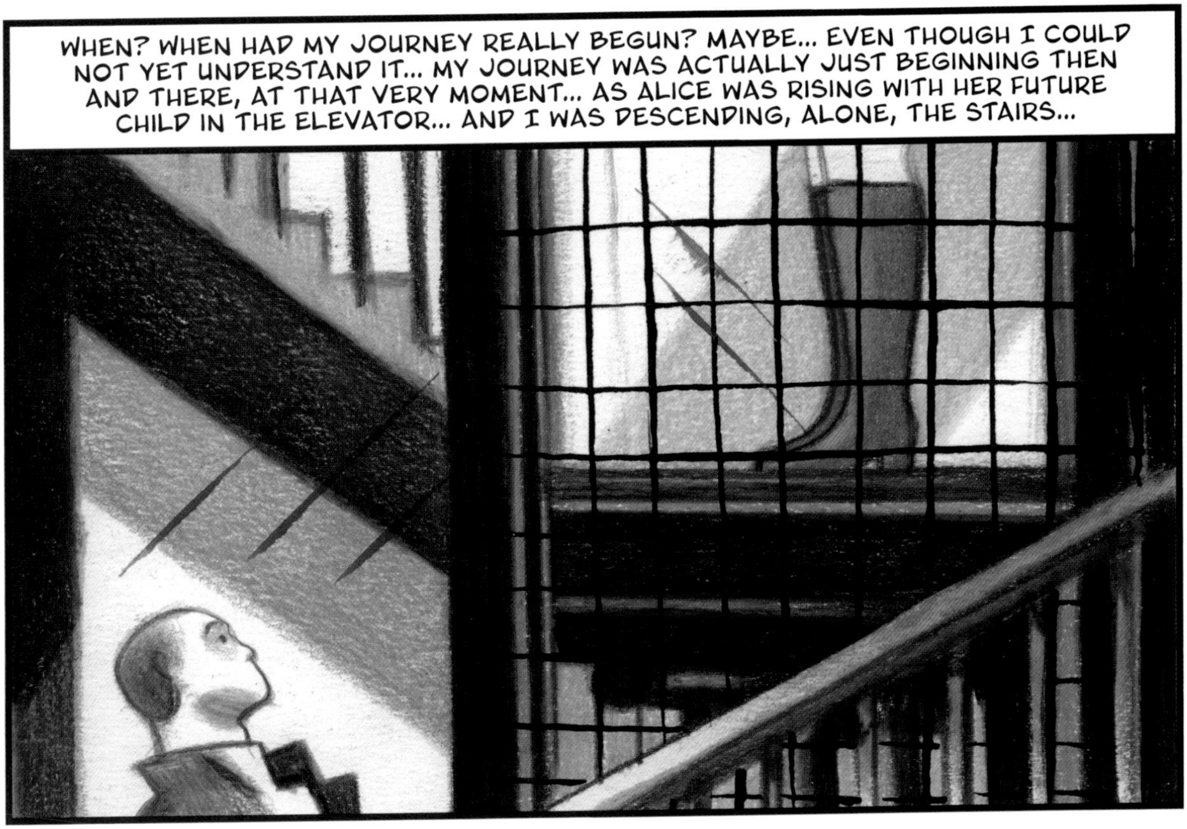
WHEN? WHEN HAD MY JOURNEY REALLY BEGUN? MAYBE... EVEN THOUGH I COULD NOT YET UNDERSTAND IT... MY JOURNEY WAS ACTUALLY JUST BEGINNING THEN AND THERE, AT THAT VERY MOMENT... AS ALICE WAS RISING WITH HER FUTURE CHILD IN THE ELEVATOR... AND I WAS DESCENDING, ALONE, THE STAIRS...

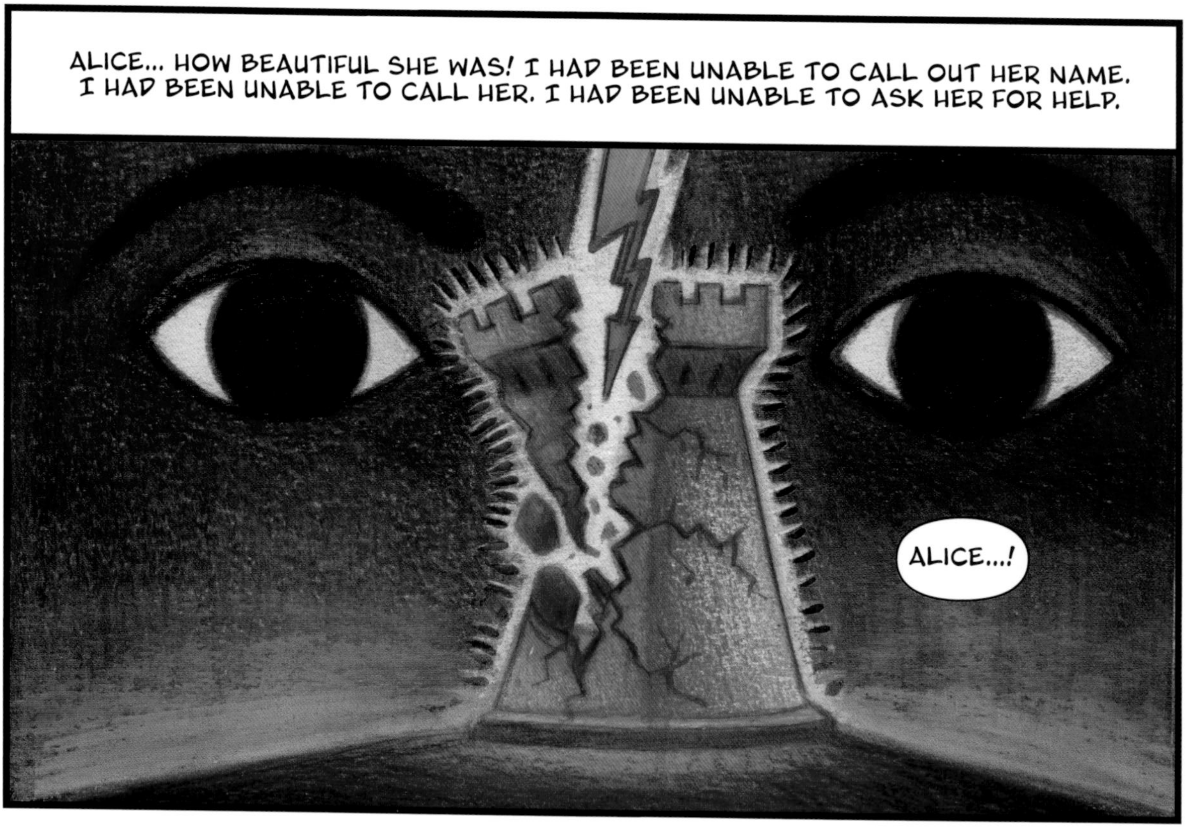
ALICE... HOW BEAUTIFUL SHE WAS! I HAD BEEN UNABLE TO CALL OUT HER NAME. I HAD BEEN UNABLE TO CALL HER. I HAD BEEN UNABLE TO ASK HER FOR HELP.
ALICE...!

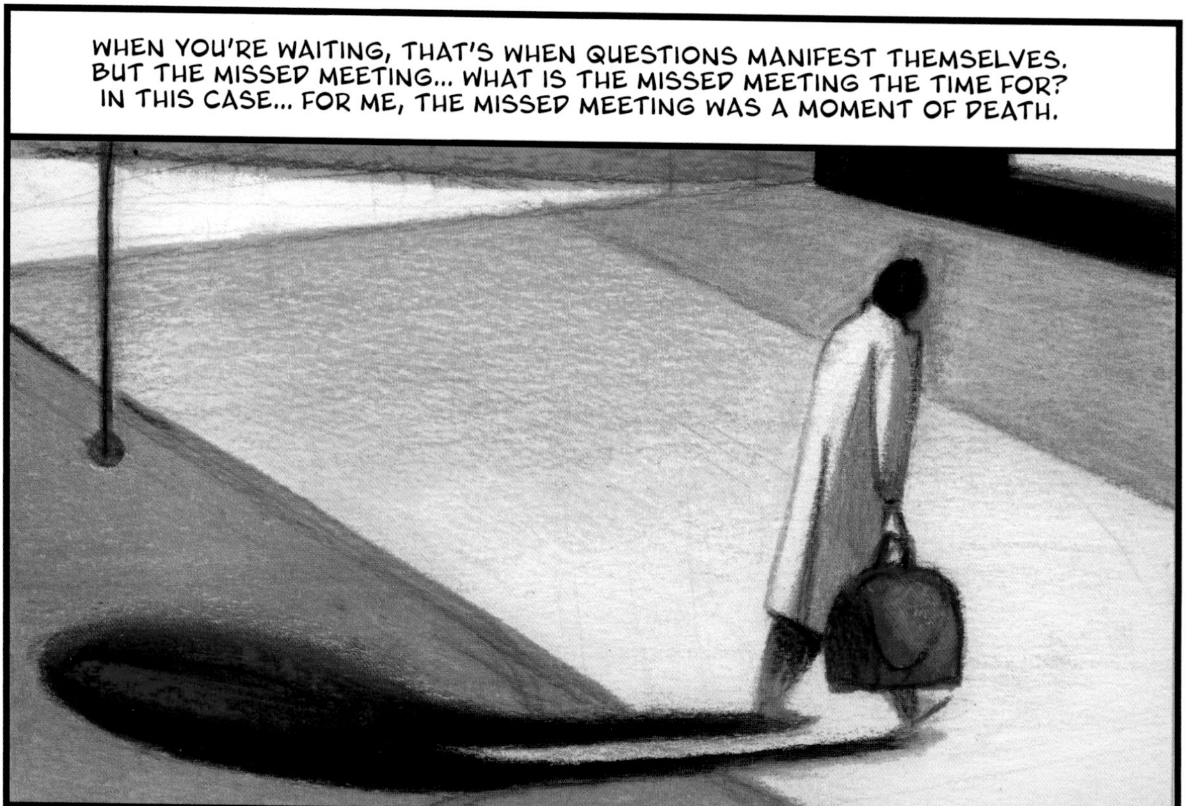
WHEN YOU'RE WAITING, THAT'S WHEN QUESTIONS MANIFEST THEMSELVES. BUT THE MISSED MEETING... WHAT IS THE MISSED MEETING THE TIME FOR? IN THIS CASE... FOR ME, THE MISSED MEETING WAS A MOMENT OF DEATH.

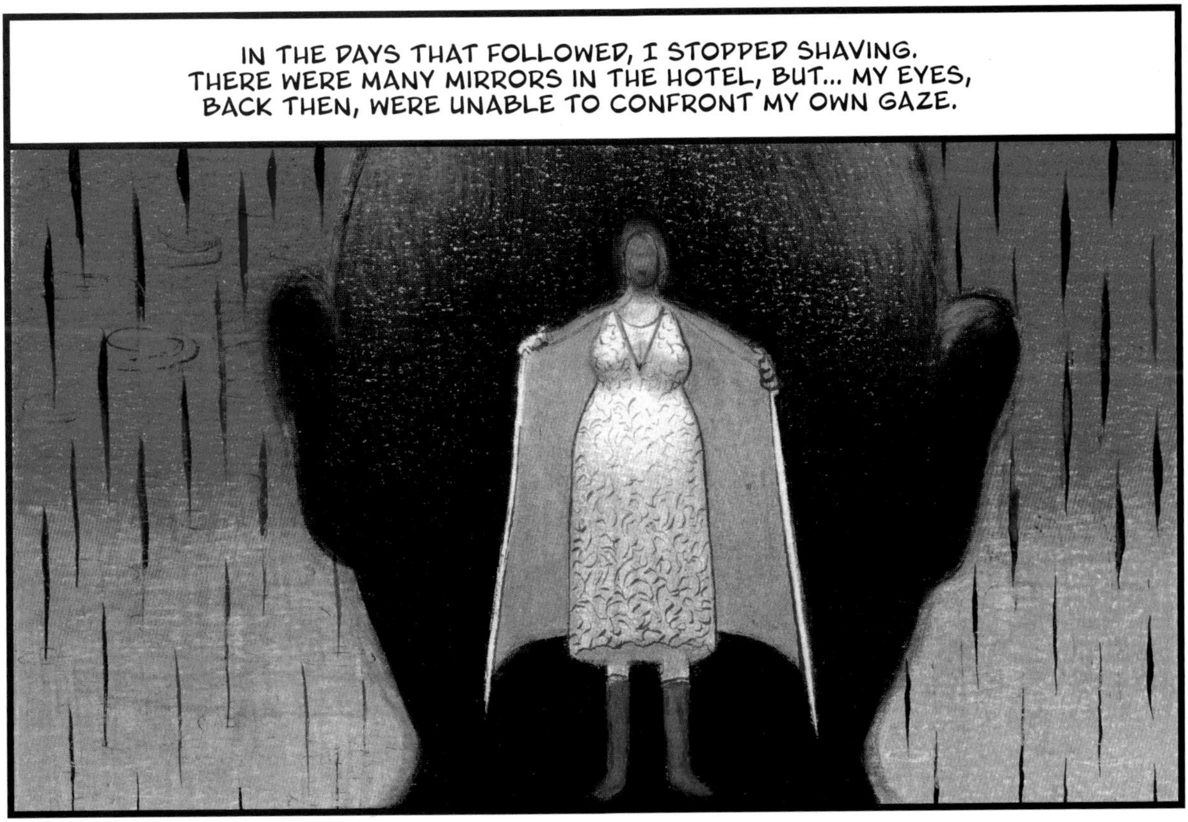
IN THE DAYS THAT FOLLOWED, I STOPPED SHAVING. THERE WERE MANY MIRRORS IN THE HOTEL, BUT... MY EYES, BACK THEN, WERE UNABLE TO CONFRONT MY OWN GAZE.

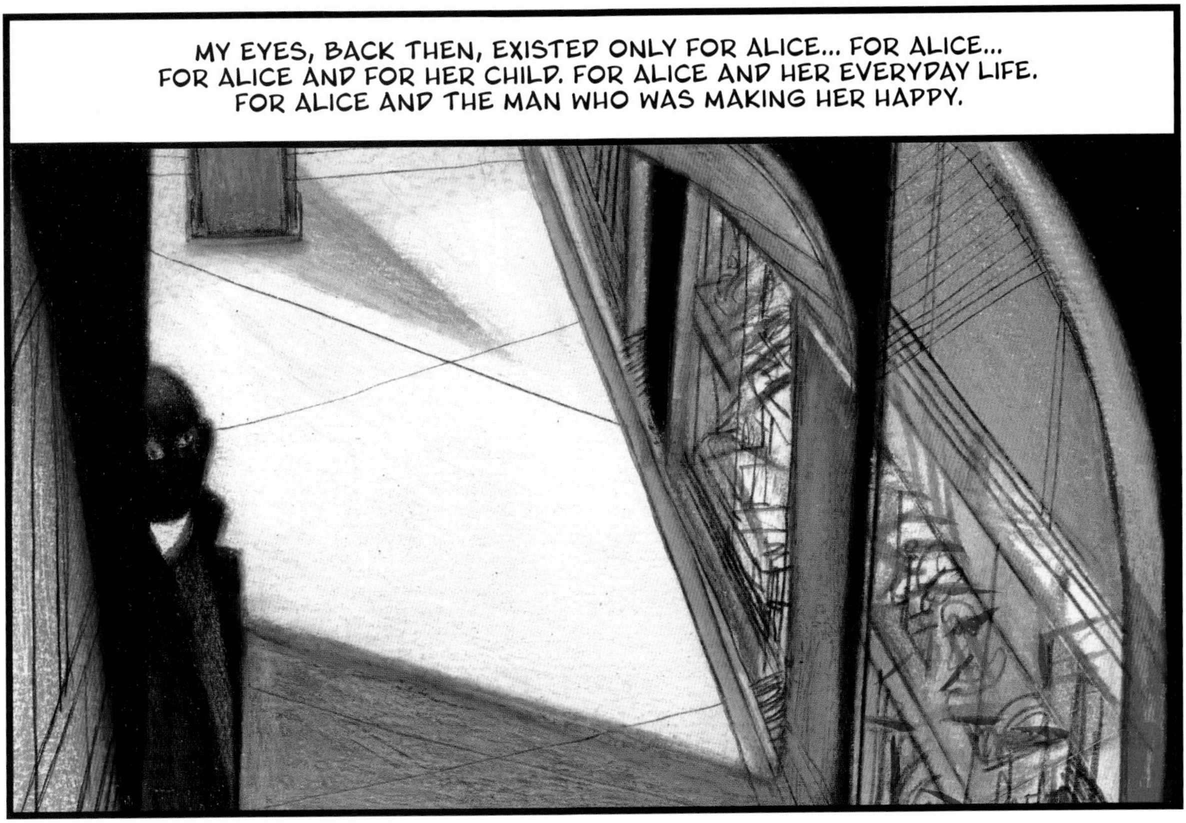
MY EYES, BACK THEN, EXISTED ONLY FOR ALICE... FOR ALICE... FOR ALICE AND FOR HER CHILD. FOR ALICE AND HER EVERYDAY LIFE. FOR ALICE AND THE MAN WHO WAS MAKING HER HAPPY.

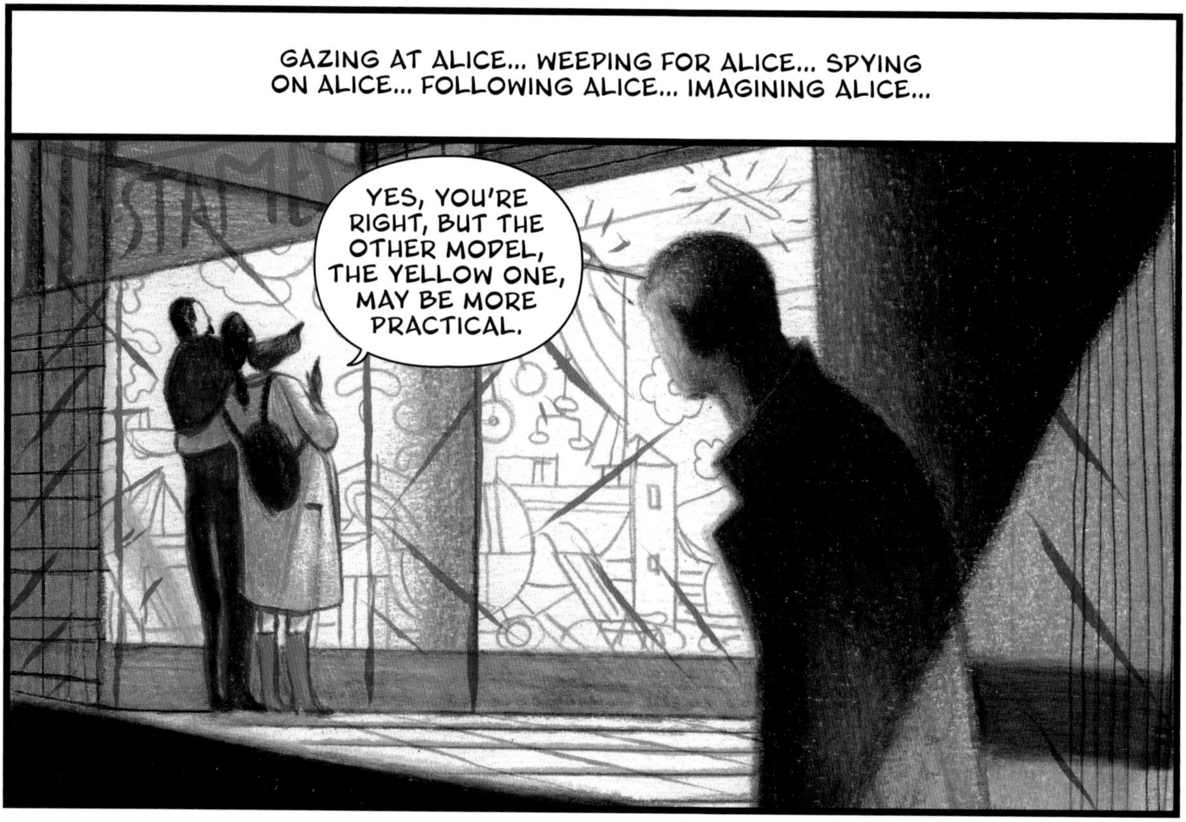
GAZING AT ALICE... WEEPING FOR ALICE... SPYING ON ALICE... FOLLOWING ALICE... IMAGINING ALICE...
YES, YOU'RE RIGHT, BUT THE OTHER MODEL, THE YELLOW ONE, MAY BE MORE PRACTICAL.

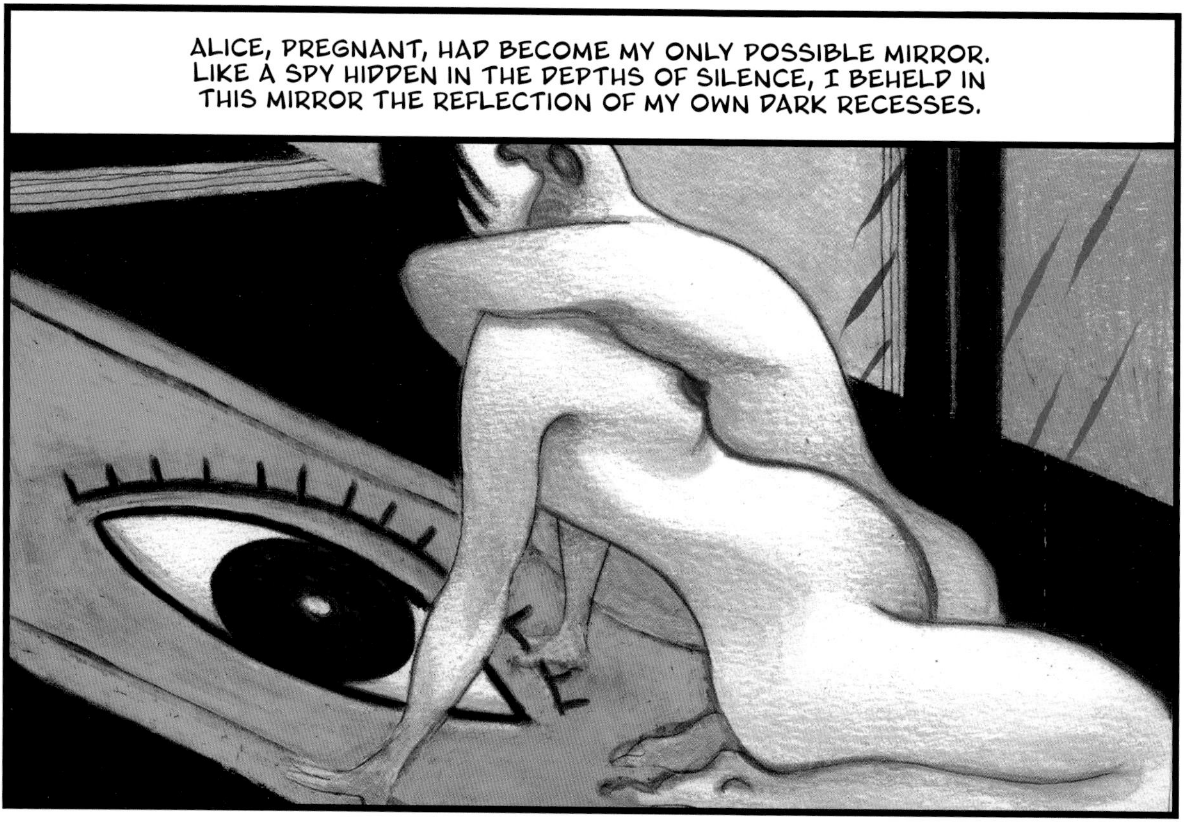
ALICE, PREGNANT, HAD BECOME MY ONLY POSSIBLE MIRROR. LIKE A SPY HIDDEN IN THE DEPTHS OF SILENCE, I BEHELD IN THIS MIRROR THE REFLECTION OF MY OWN DARK RECESSES.

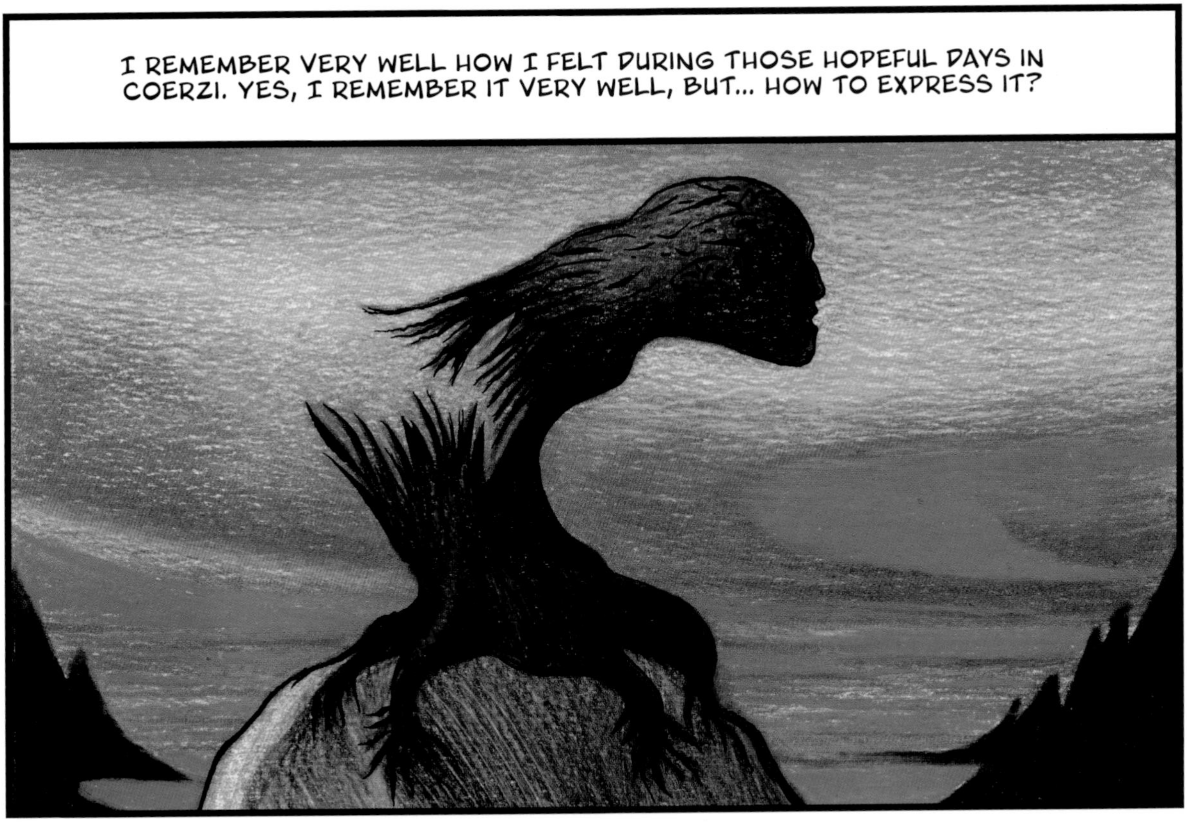
I REMEMBER VERY WELL HOW I FELT DURING THOSE HOPEFUL DAYS IN COERZI. YES, I REMEMBER IT VERY WELL, BUT... HOW TO EXPRESS IT?

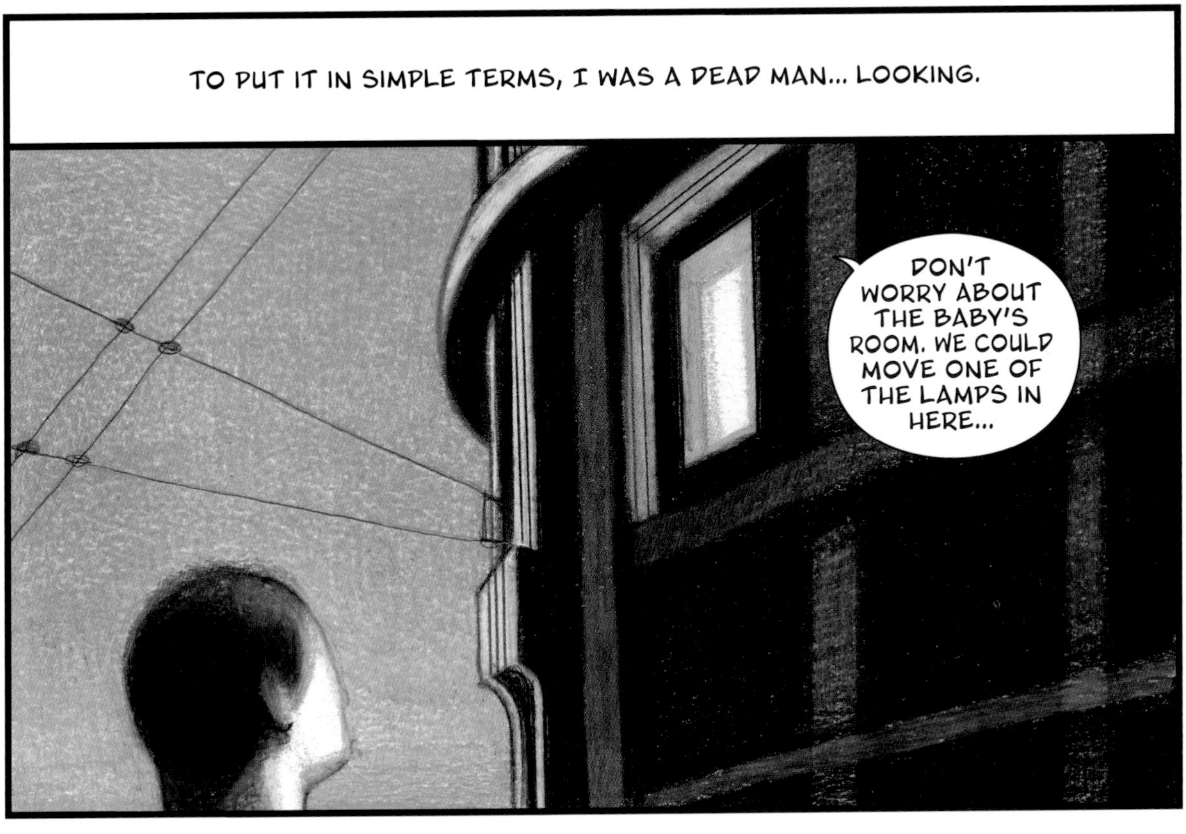
TO PUT IT IN SIMPLE TERMS, I WAS A DEAD MAN... LOOKING.
DON'T WORRY ABOUT THE BABY'S ROOM. WE COULD MOVE ONE OF THE LAMPS IN HERE...

A DEAD MAN WHOSE CHEST WAS FULL OF PAIN, OF JEALOUSY, BUT ALSO BRIMMING WITH A SINCERE JOY FOR ALICE'S HAPPINESS... A DEAD MAN WHO STILL HAD THE ABILITY TO LACERATE HIS HEART WITH PHANTASMS...

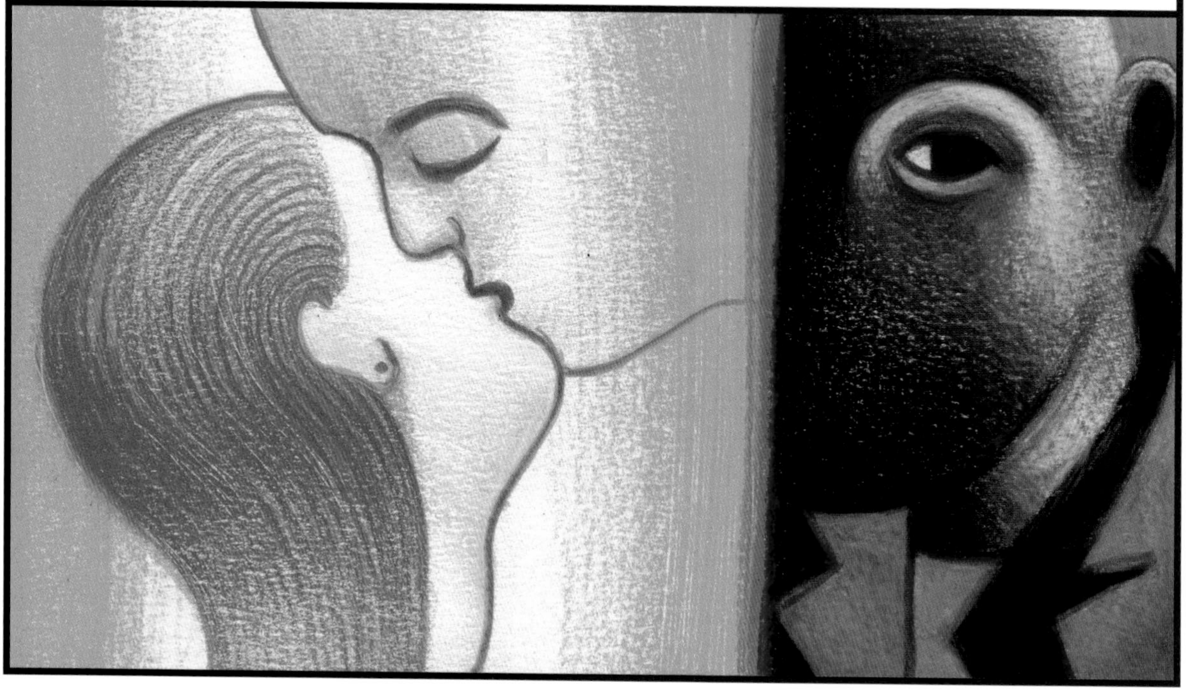

I WAS A DEAD MAN WITH FEELINGS. I WAS THE WORST KIND OF DEAD MAN.

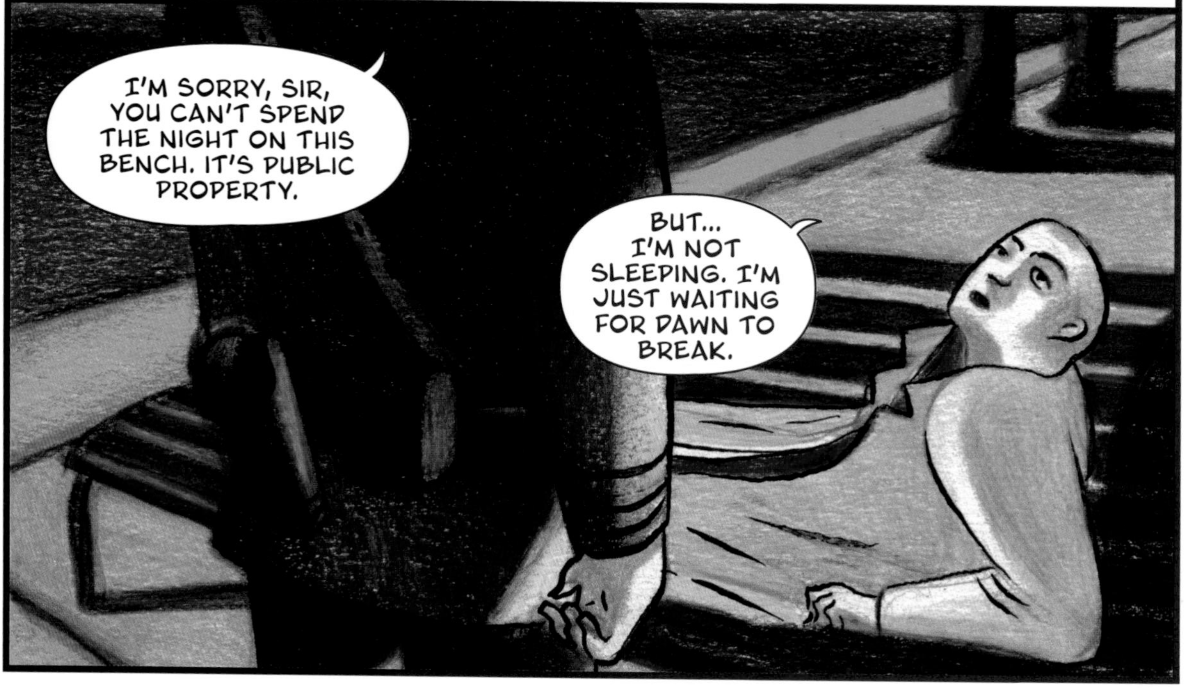
I'M SORRY, SIR, YOU CAN'T SPEND THE NIGHT ON THIS BENCH. IT'S PUBLIC PROPERTY.
BUT... I'M NOT SLEEPING. I'M JUST WAITING FOR DAWN TO BREAK.

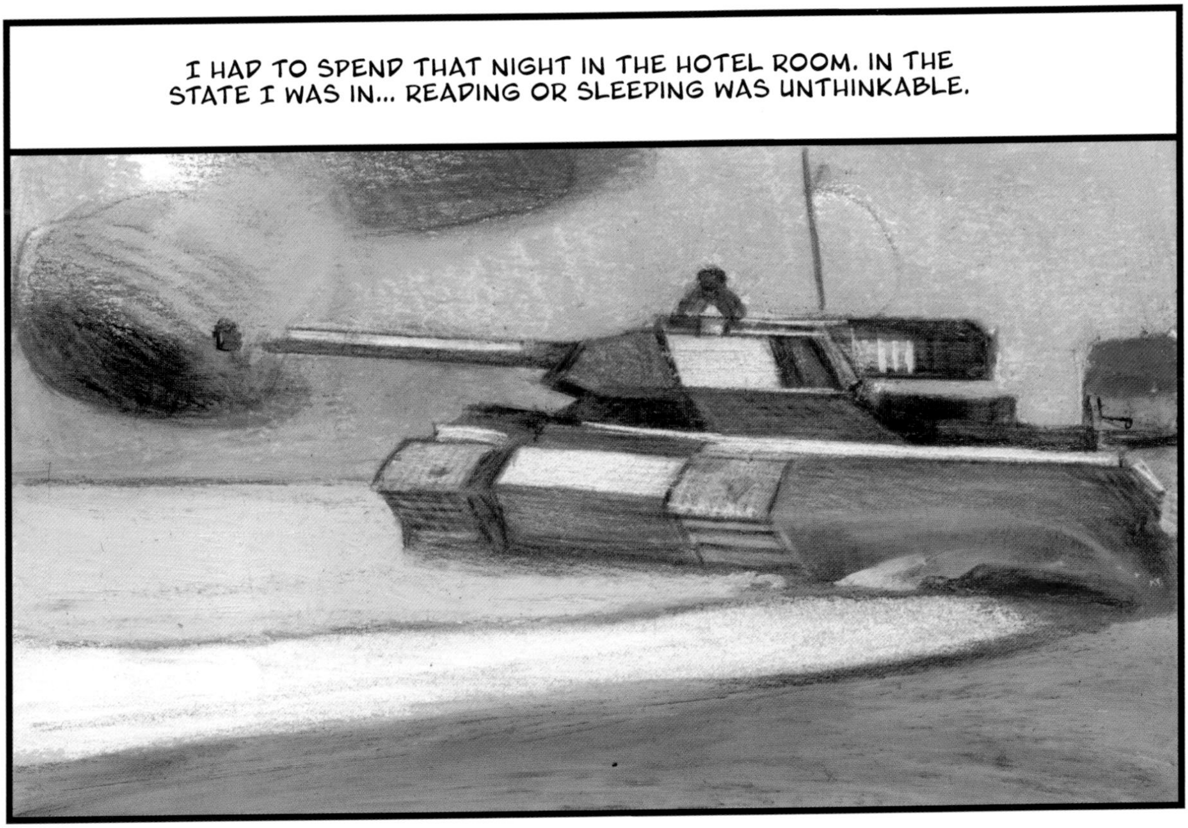
I HAD TO SPEND THAT NIGHT IN THE HOTEL ROOM. IN THE STATE I WAS IN... READING OR SLEEPING WAS UNTHINKABLE.

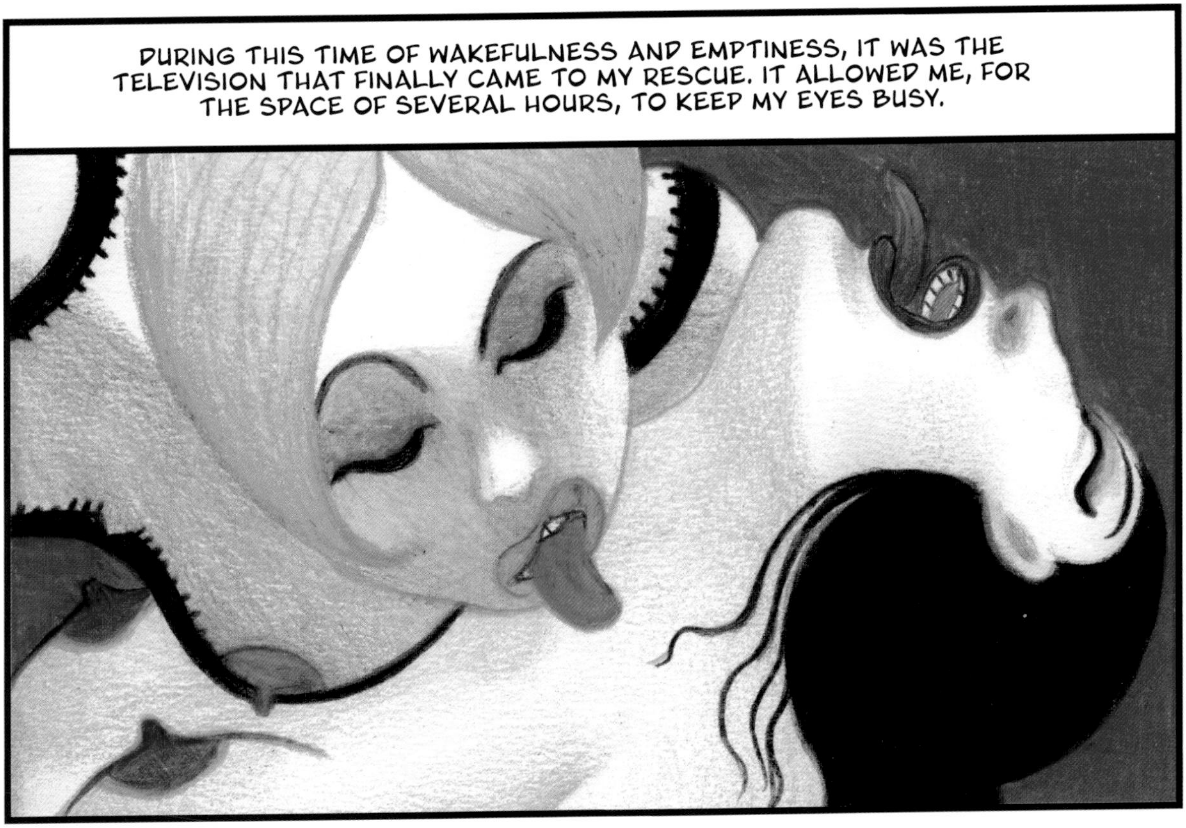
DURING THIS TIME OF WAKEFULNESS AND EMPTINESS, IT WAS THE TELEVISION THAT FINALLY CAME TO MY RESCUE. IT ALLOWED ME, FOR THE SPACE OF SEVERAL HOURS, TO KEEP MY EYES BUSY.

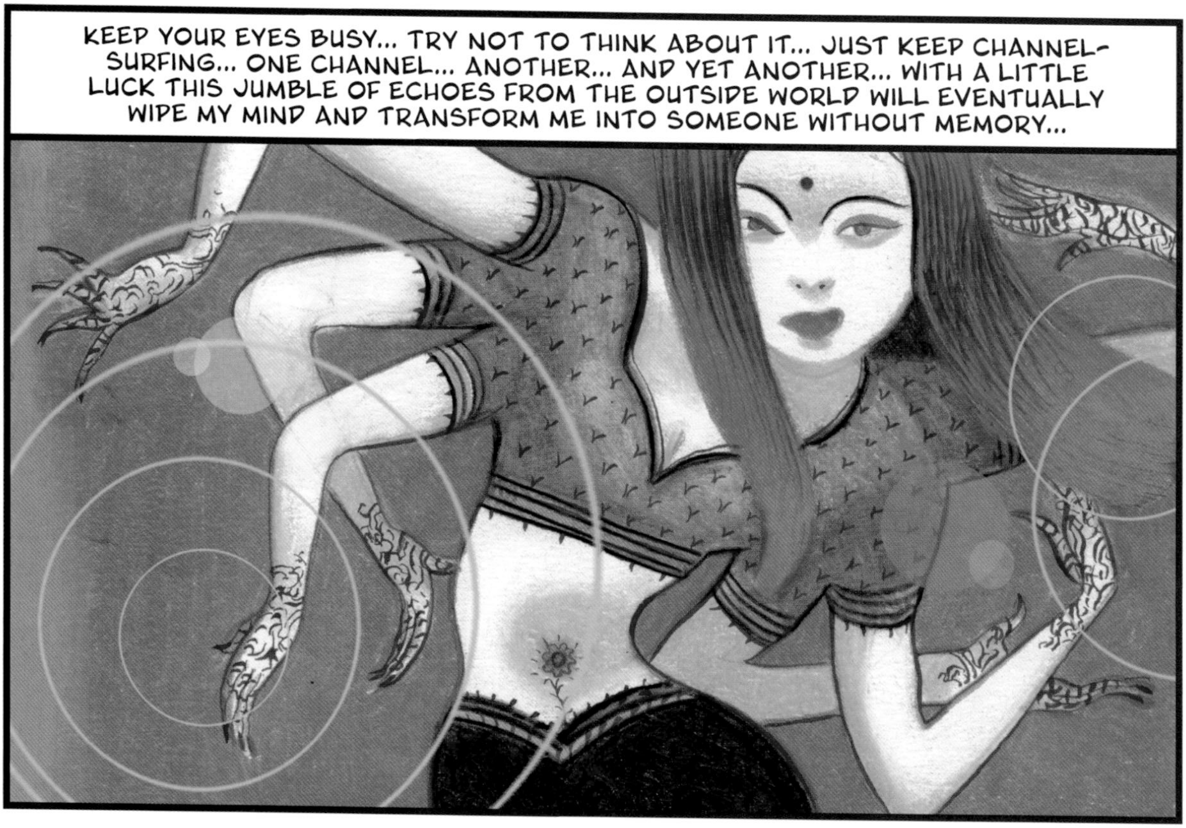
KEEP YOUR EYES BUSY... TRY NOT TO THINK ABOUT IT... JUST KEEP CHANNEL-SURFING... ONE CHANNEL... ANOTHER... AND YET ANOTHER... WITH A LITTLE LUCK THIS JUMBLE OF ECHOES FROM THE OUTSIDE WORLD WILL EVENTUALLY WIPE MY MIND AND TRANSFORM ME INTO SOMEONE WITHOUT MEMORY...

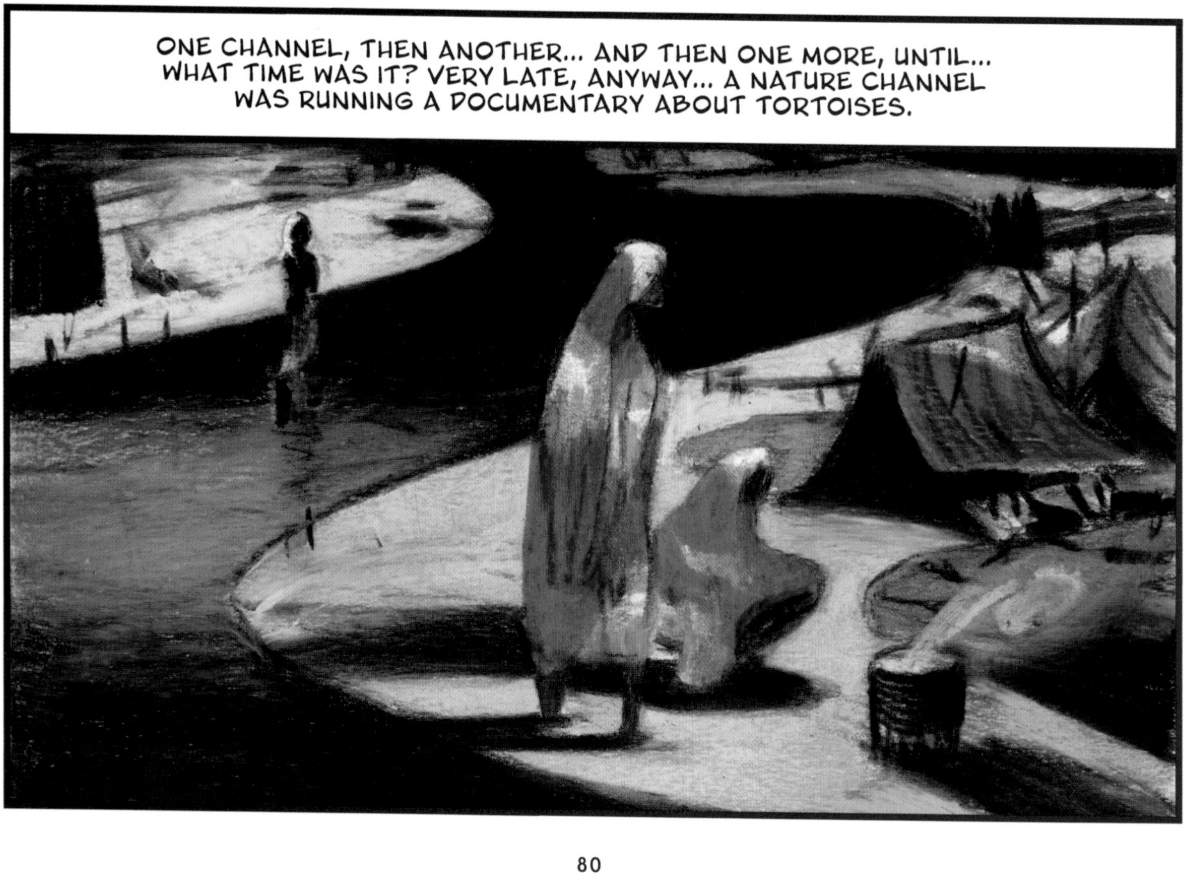
ONE CHANNEL, THEN ANOTHER... AND THEN ONE MORE, UNTIL... WHAT TIME WAS IT? VERY LATE, ANYWAY... A NATURE CHANNEL WAS RUNNING A DOCUMENTARY ABOUT TORTOISES.

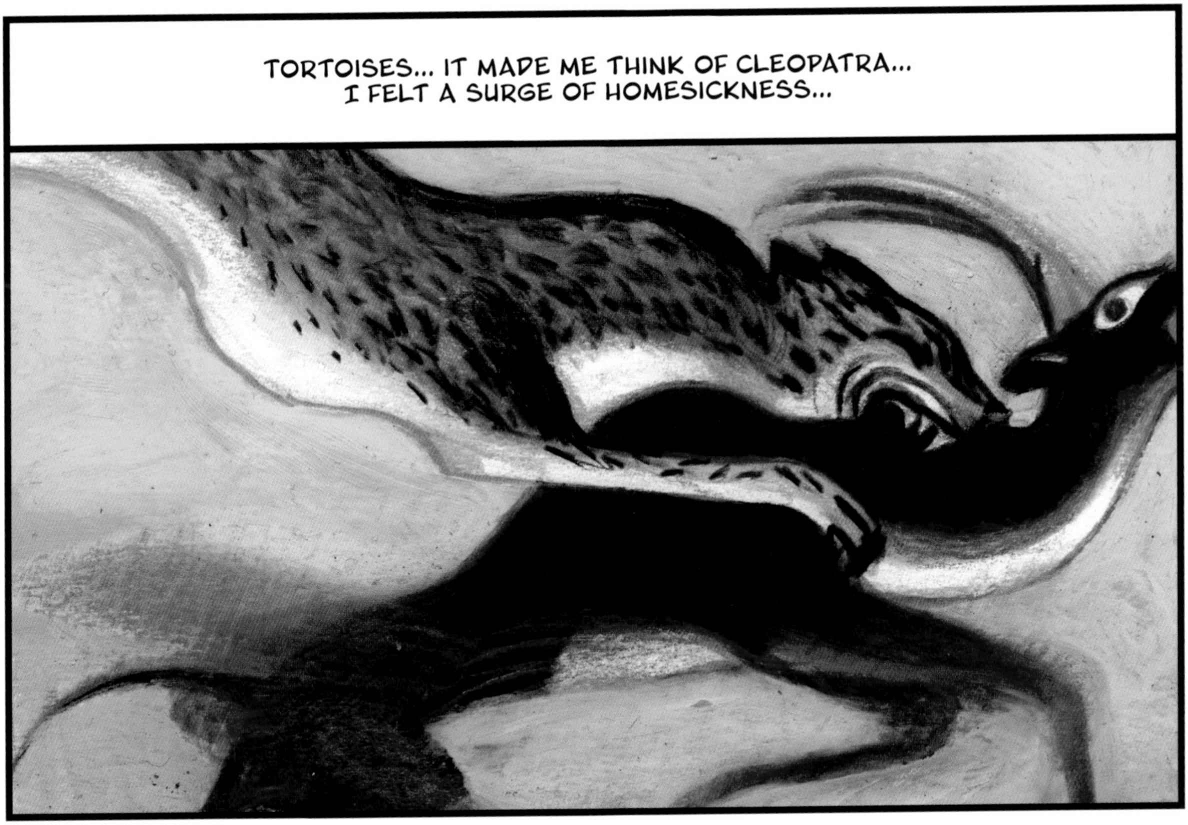
TORTOISES... IT MADE ME THINK OF CLEOPATRA... I FELT A SURGE OF HOMESICKNESS...

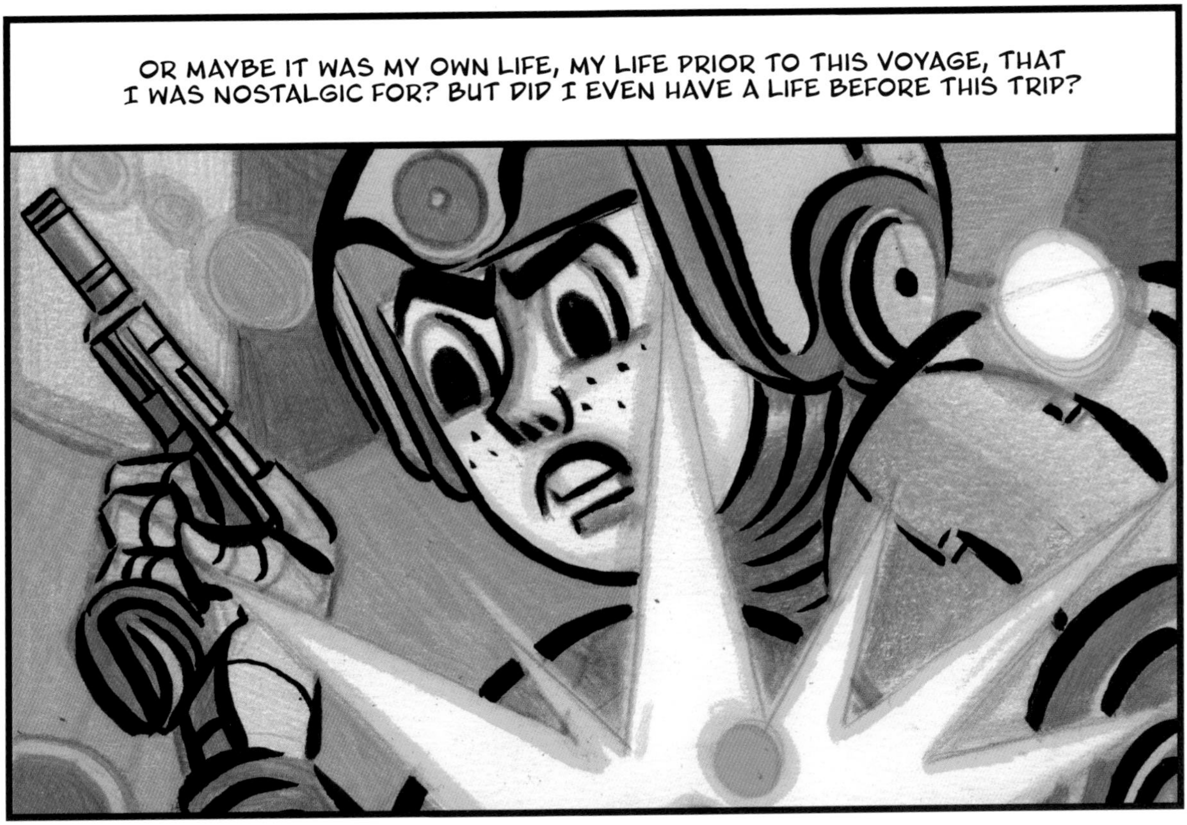
OR MAYBE IT WAS MY OWN LIFE, MY LIFE PRIOR TO THIS VOYAGE, THAT I WAS NOSTALGIC FOR? BUT DID I EVEN HAVE A LIFE BEFORE THIS TRIP?

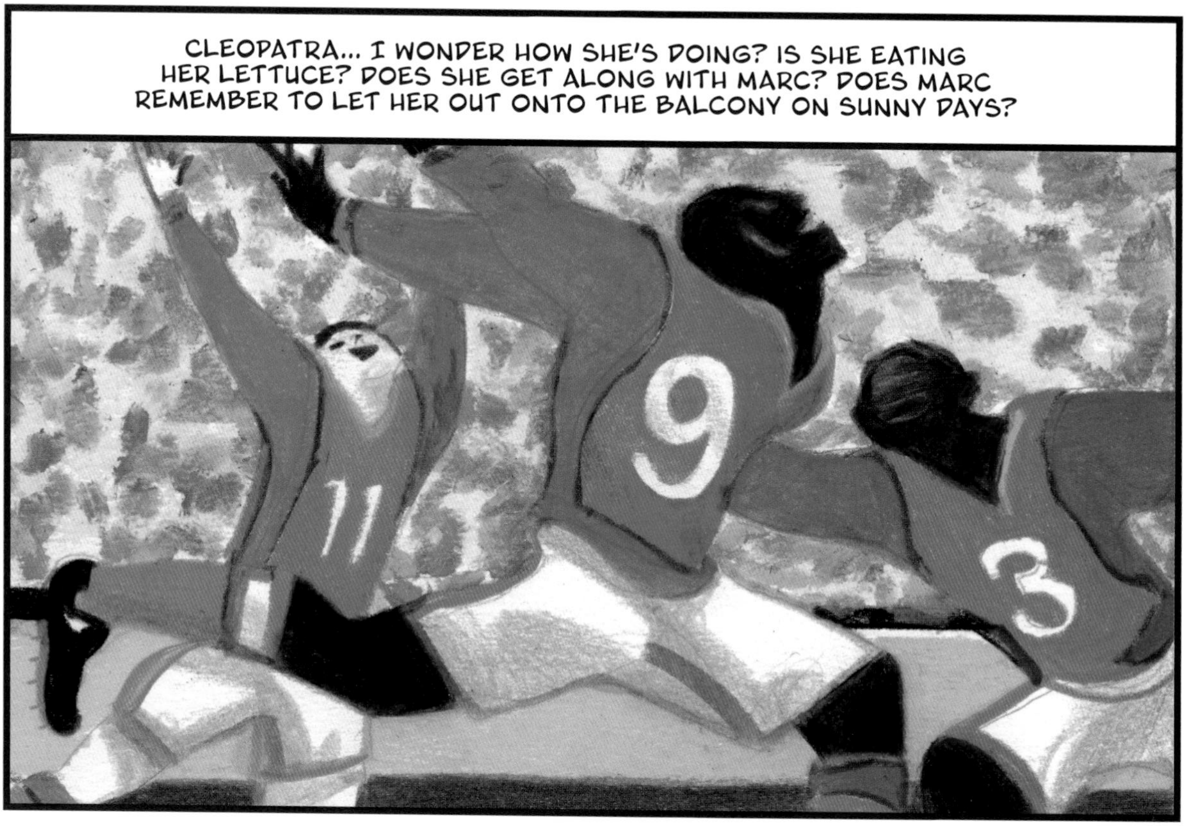
CLEOPATRA... I WONDER HOW SHE'S DOING? IS SHE EATING HER LETTUCE? DOES SHE GET ALONG WITH MARC? DOES MARC REMEMBER TO LET HER OUT ONTO THE BALCONY ON SUNNY DAYS?

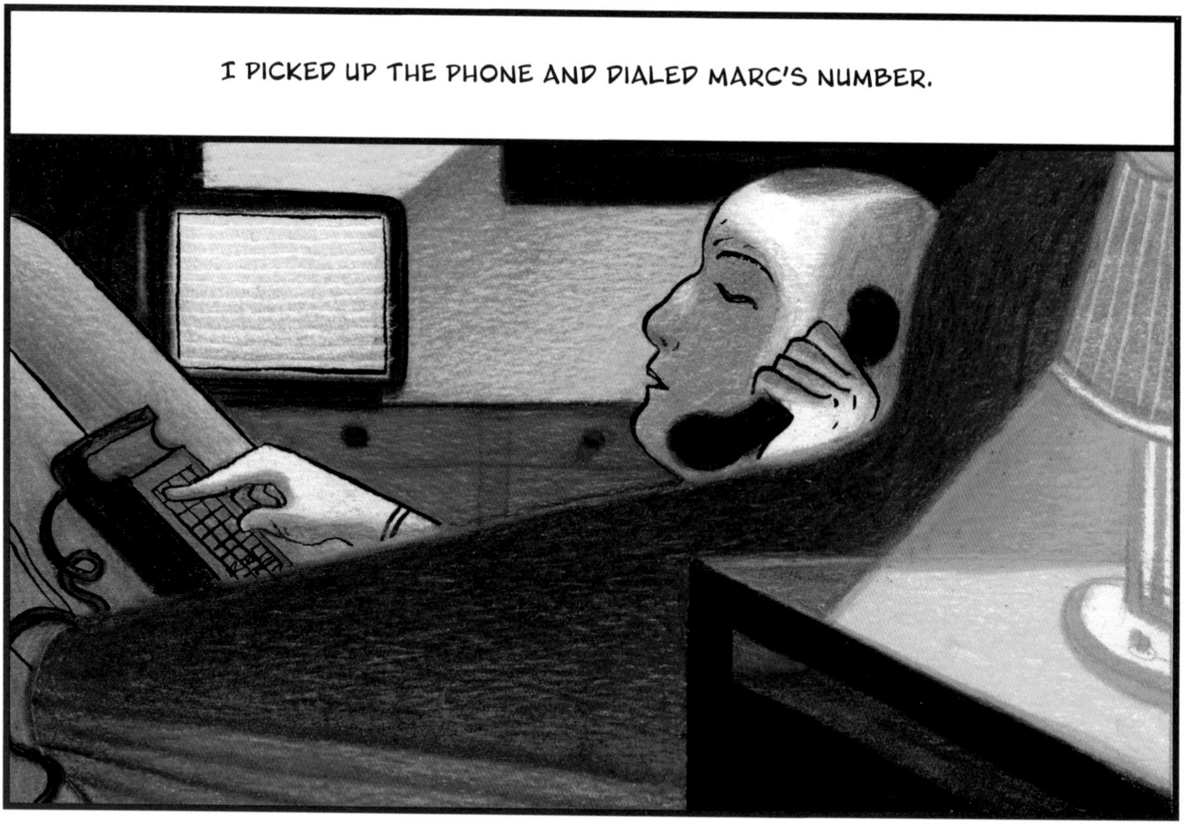
I PICKED UP THE PHONE AND DIALED MARC'S NUMBER.

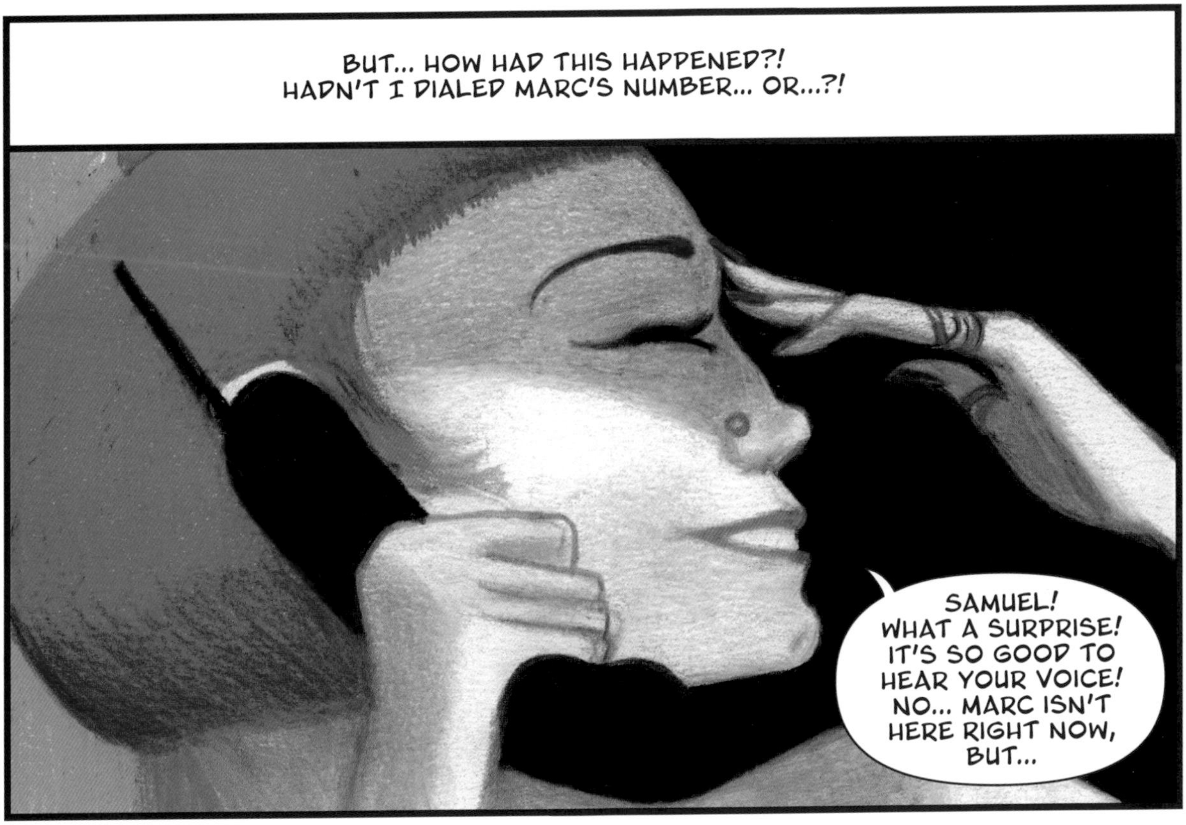
BUT... HOW HAD THIS HAPPENED?! HADN'T I DIALED MARC'S NUMBER... OR...?!
SAMUEL! WHAT A SURPRISE! IT'S SO GOOD TO HEAR YOUR VOICE! NO... MARC ISN'T HERE RIGHT NOW, BUT...

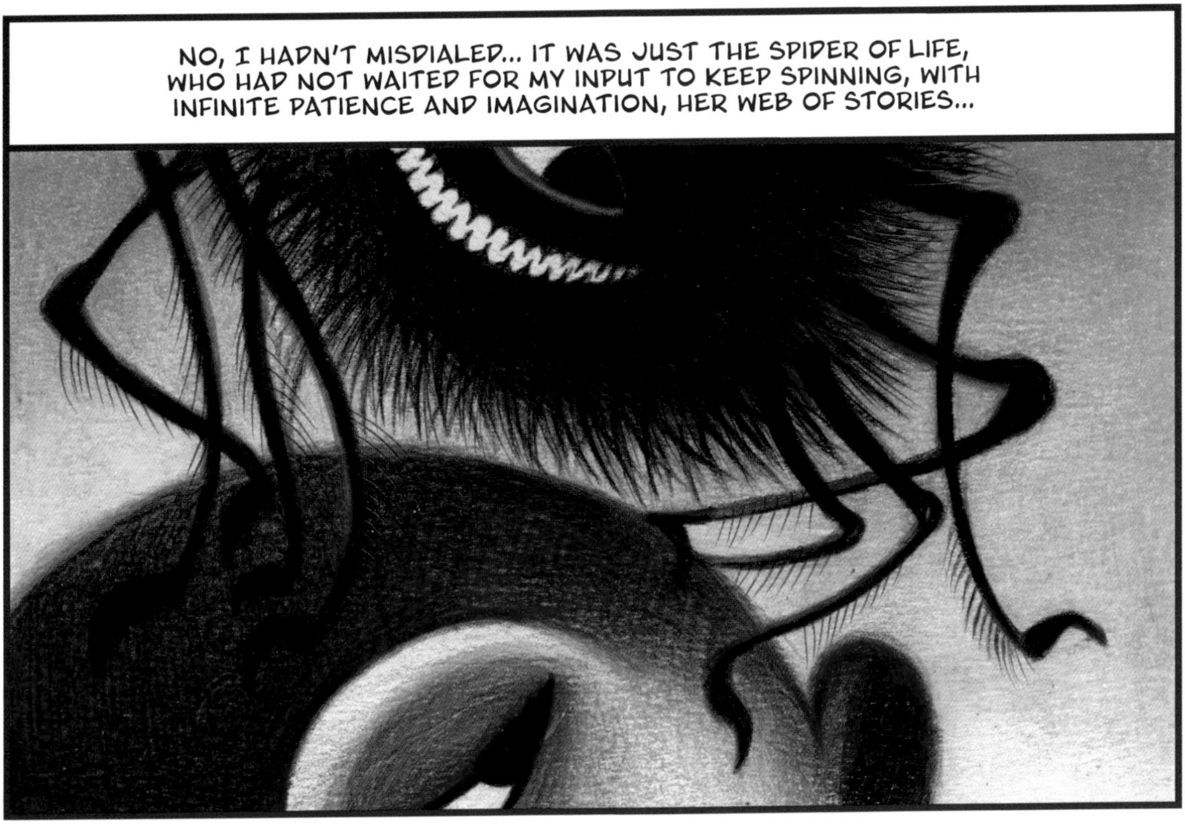
NO, I HADN'T MISDIALED... IT WAS JUST THE SPIDER OF LIFE, WHO HAD NOT WAITED FOR MY INPUT TO KEEP SPINNING, WITH INFINITE PATIENCE AND IMAGINATION, HER WEB OF STORIES...

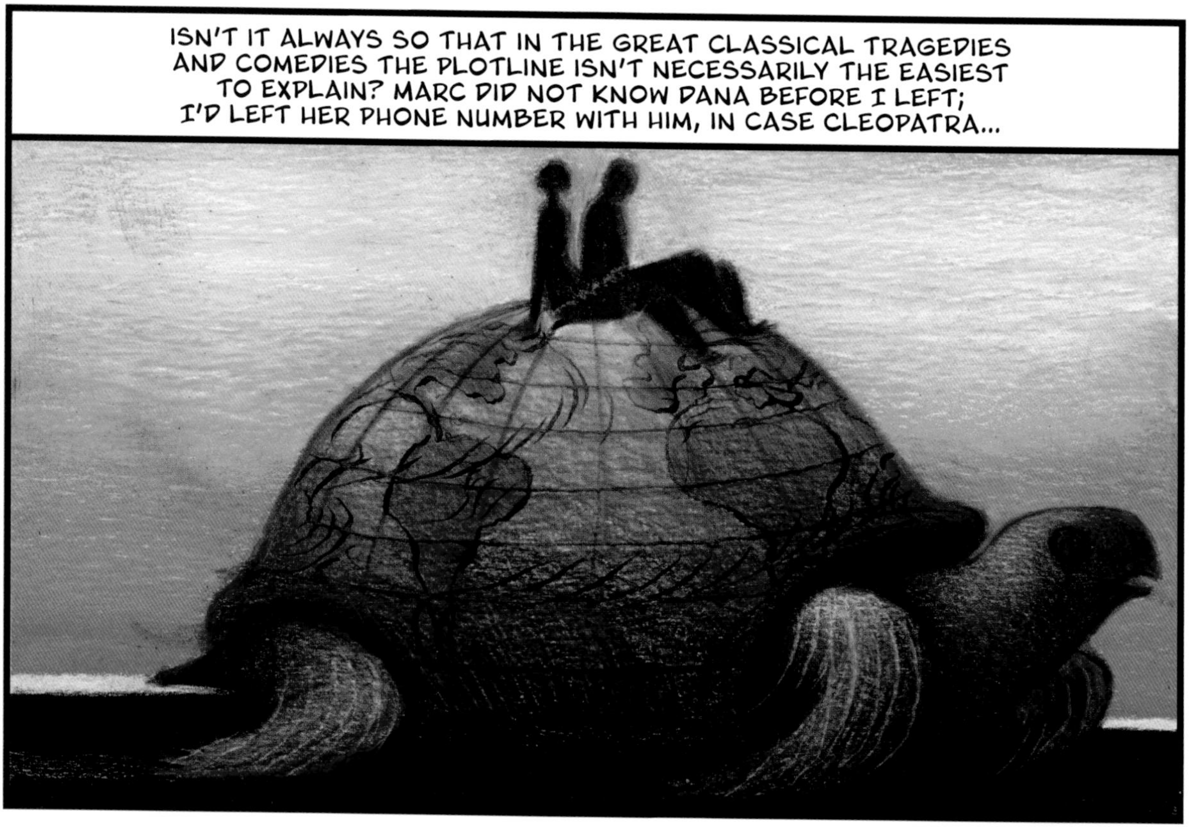
ISN'T IT ALWAYS SO THAT IN THE GREAT CLASSICAL TRAGEDIES AND COMEDIES THE PLOTLINE ISN'T NECESSARILY THE EASIEST TO EXPLAIN? MARC DID NOT KNOW DANA BEFORE I LEFT; I'D LEFT HER PHONE NUMBER WITH HIM, IN CASE CLEOPATRA...

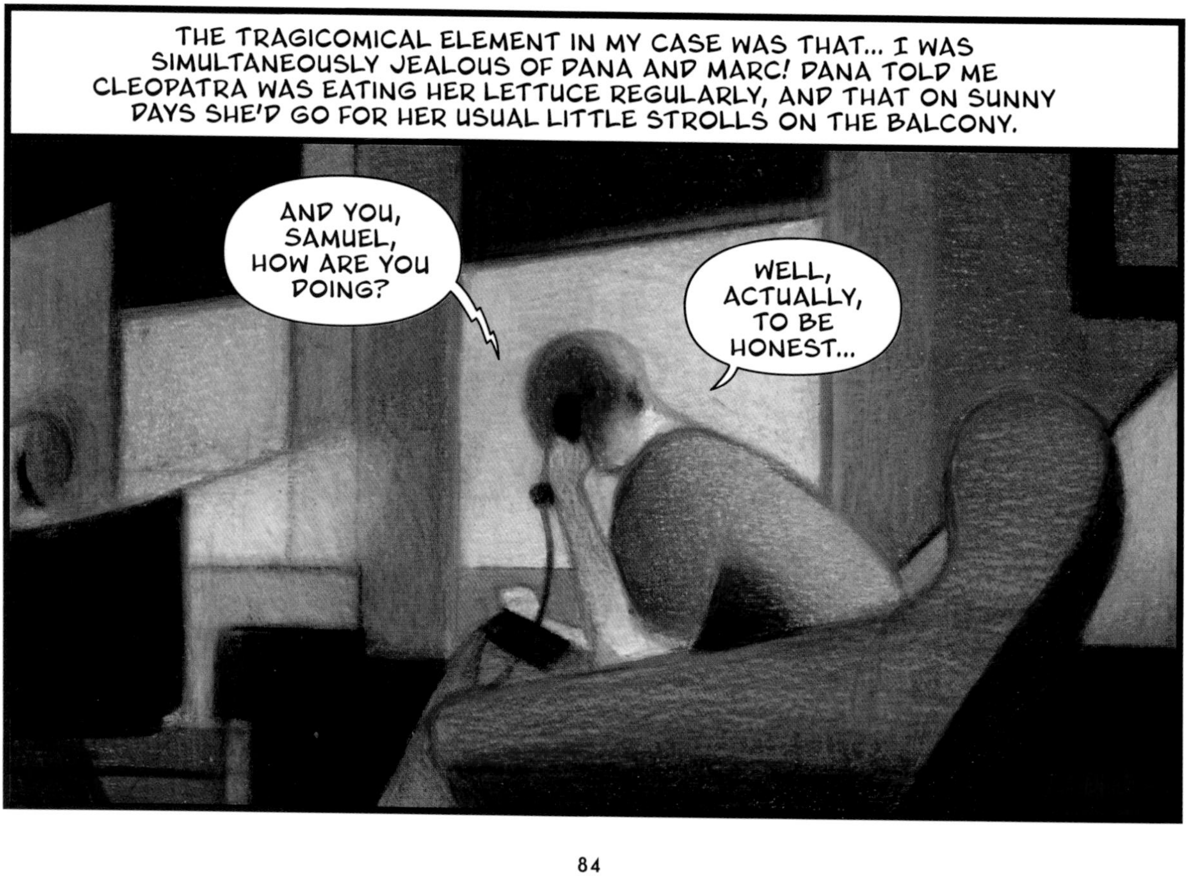
THE TRAGICOMICAL ELEMENT IN MY CASE WAS THAT... I WAS SIMULTANEOUSLY JEALOUS OF DANA AND MARC! DANA TOLD ME CLEOPATRA WAS EATING HER LETTUCE REGULARLY, AND THAT ON SUNNY DAYS SHE'D GO FOR HER USUAL LITTLE STROLLS ON THE BALCONY.
AND YOU, SAMUEL, HOW ARE YOU DOING?
WELL, ACTUALLY, TO BE HONEST...

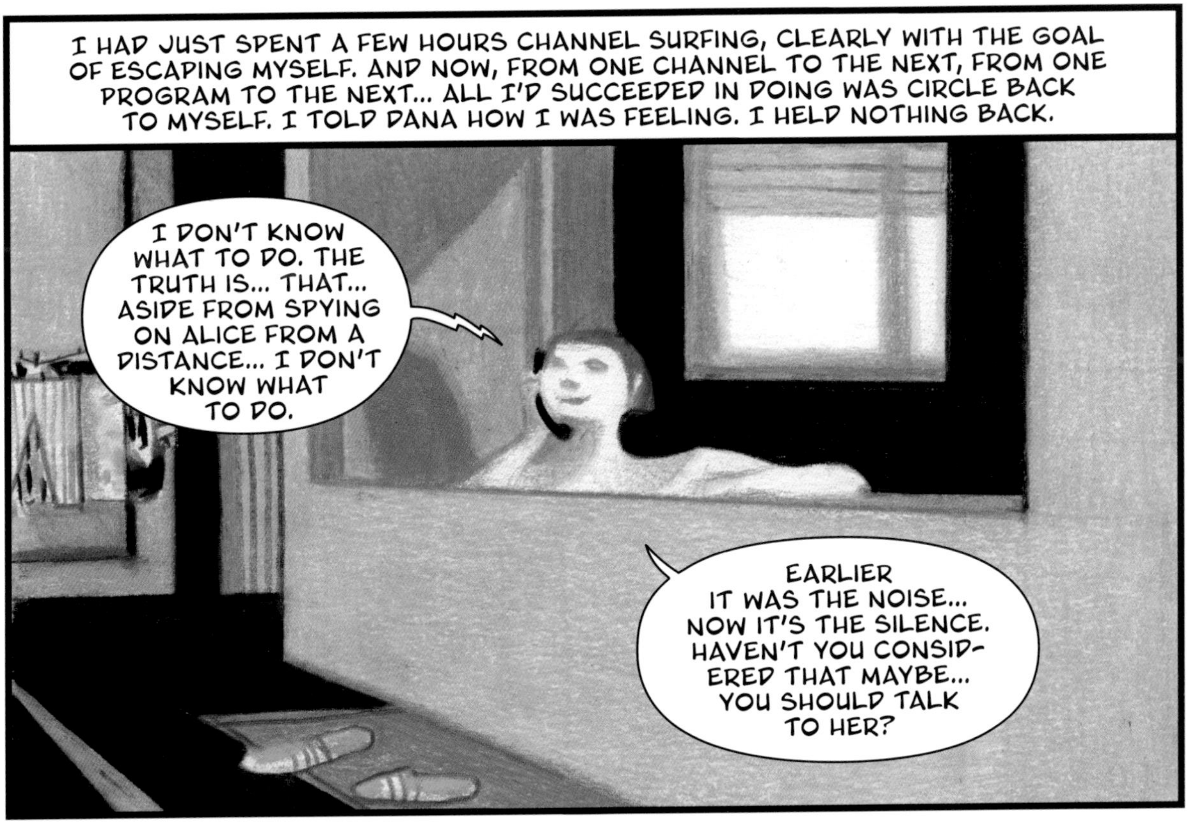
I HAD JUST SPENT A FEW HOURS CHANNEL SURFING, CLEARLY WITH THE GOAL OF ESCAPING MYSELF. AND NOW, FROM ONE CHANNEL TO THE NEXT, FROM ONE PROGRAM TO THE NEXT... ALL I'D SUCCEEDED IN DOING WAS CIRCLE BACK TO MYSELF. I TOLD DANA HOW I WAS FEELING. I HELD NOTHING BACK.
I DON'T KNOW WHAT TO DO. THE TRUTH IS... THAT... ASIDE FROM SPYING ON ALICE FROM A DISTANCE... I DON'T KNOW WHAT TO DO.
EARLIER IT WAS THE NOISE... NOW IT'S THE SILENCE. HAVEN'T YOU CONSIDERED THAT MAYBE... YOU SHOULD TALK TO HER?

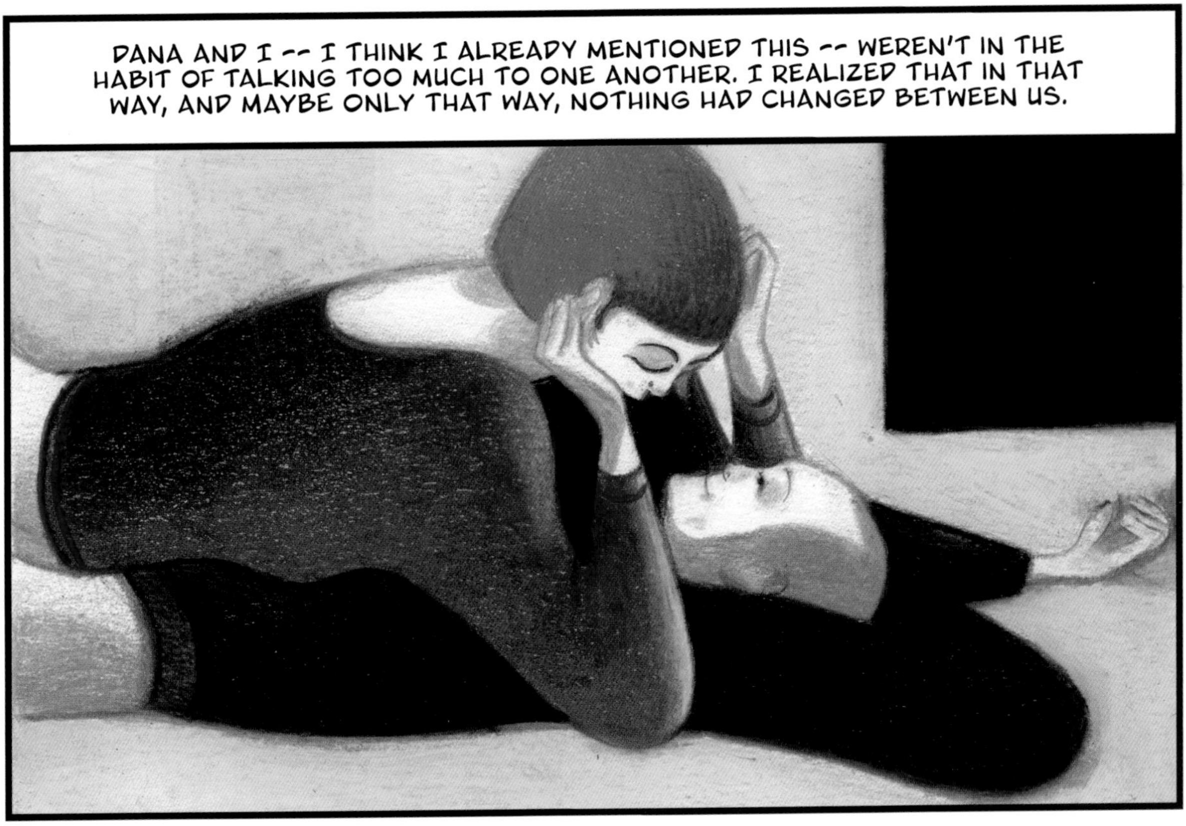
DANA AND I -- I THINK I ALREADY MENTIONED THIS -- WEREN'T IN THE HABIT OF TALKING TOO MUCH TO ONE ANOTHER. I REALIZED THAT IN THAT WAY, AND MAYBE ONLY THAT WAY, NOTHING HAD CHANGED BETWEEN US.

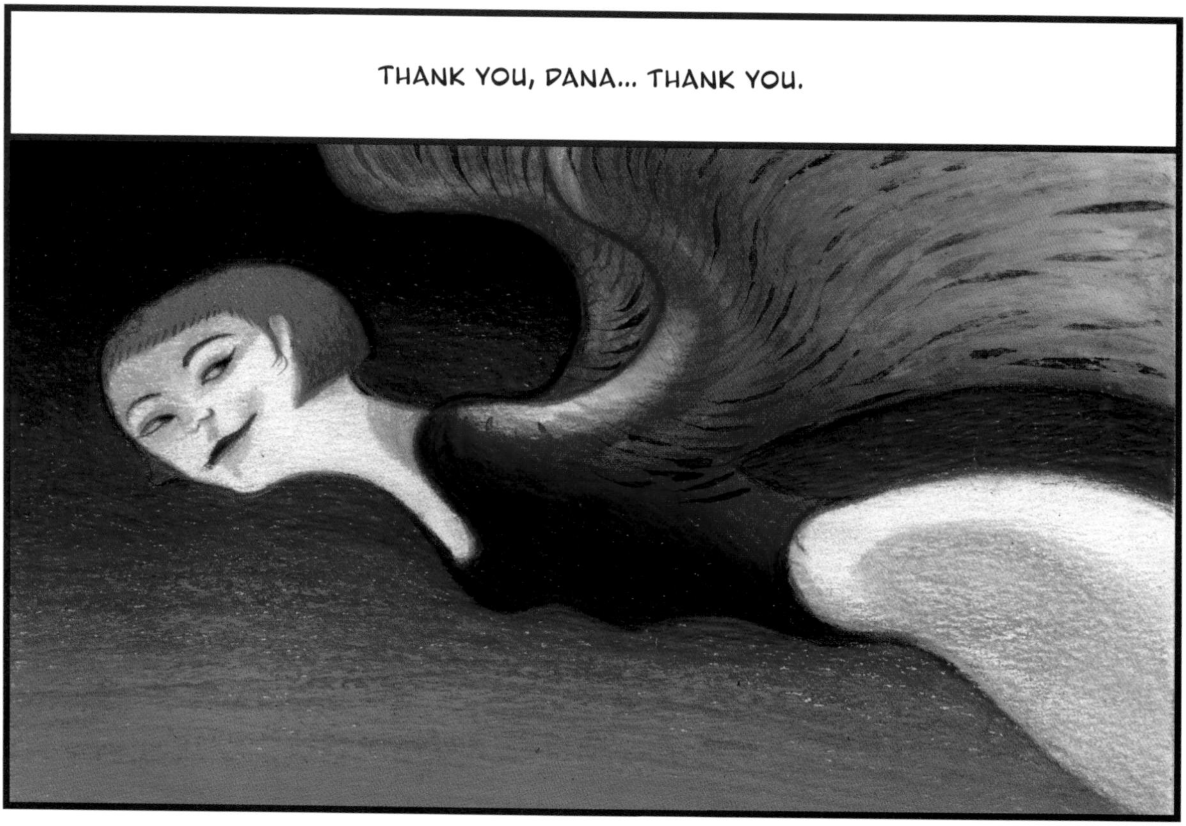
THANK YOU, DANA... THANK YOU.

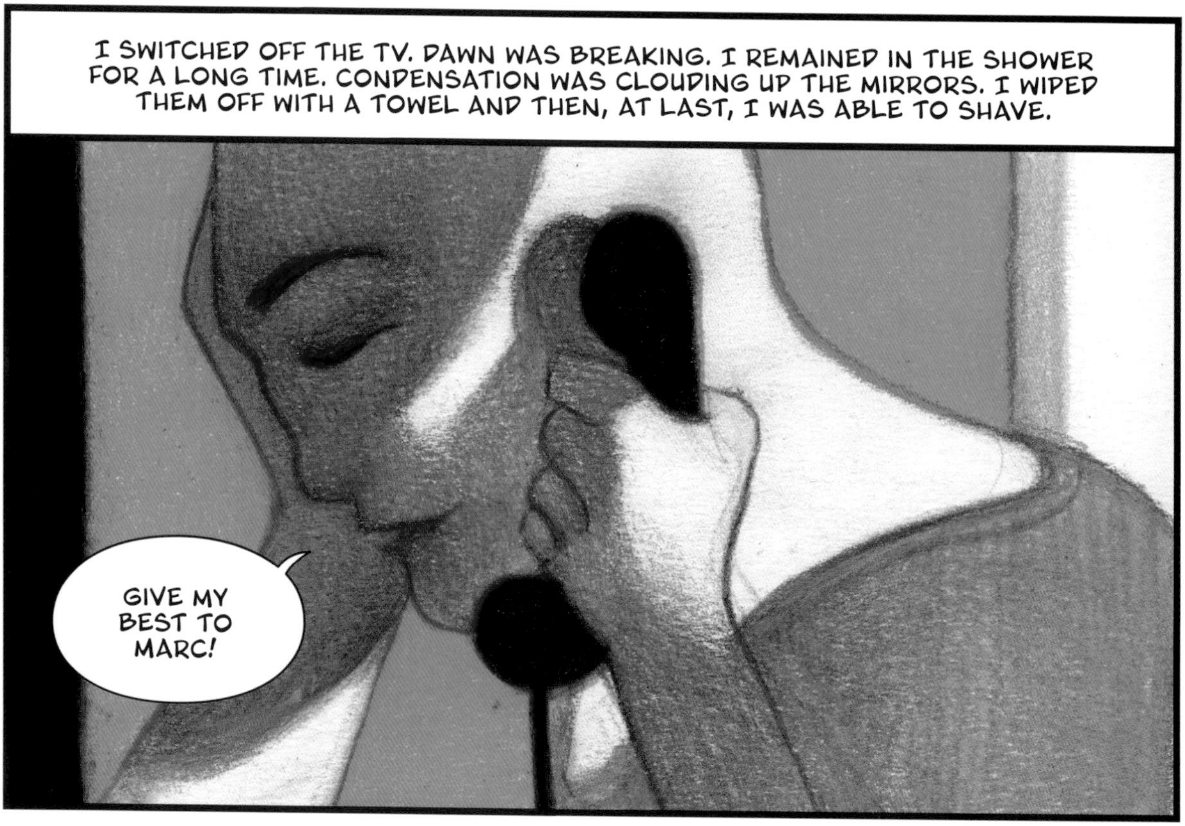
I SWITCHED OFF THE TV. DAWN WAS BREAKING. I REMAINED IN THE SHOWER FOR A LONG TIME. CONDENSATION WAS CLOUDING UP THE MIRRORS. I WIPED THEM OFF WITH A TOWEL AND THEN, AT LAST, I WAS ABLE TO SHAVE.
GIVE MY BEST TO MARC!

5

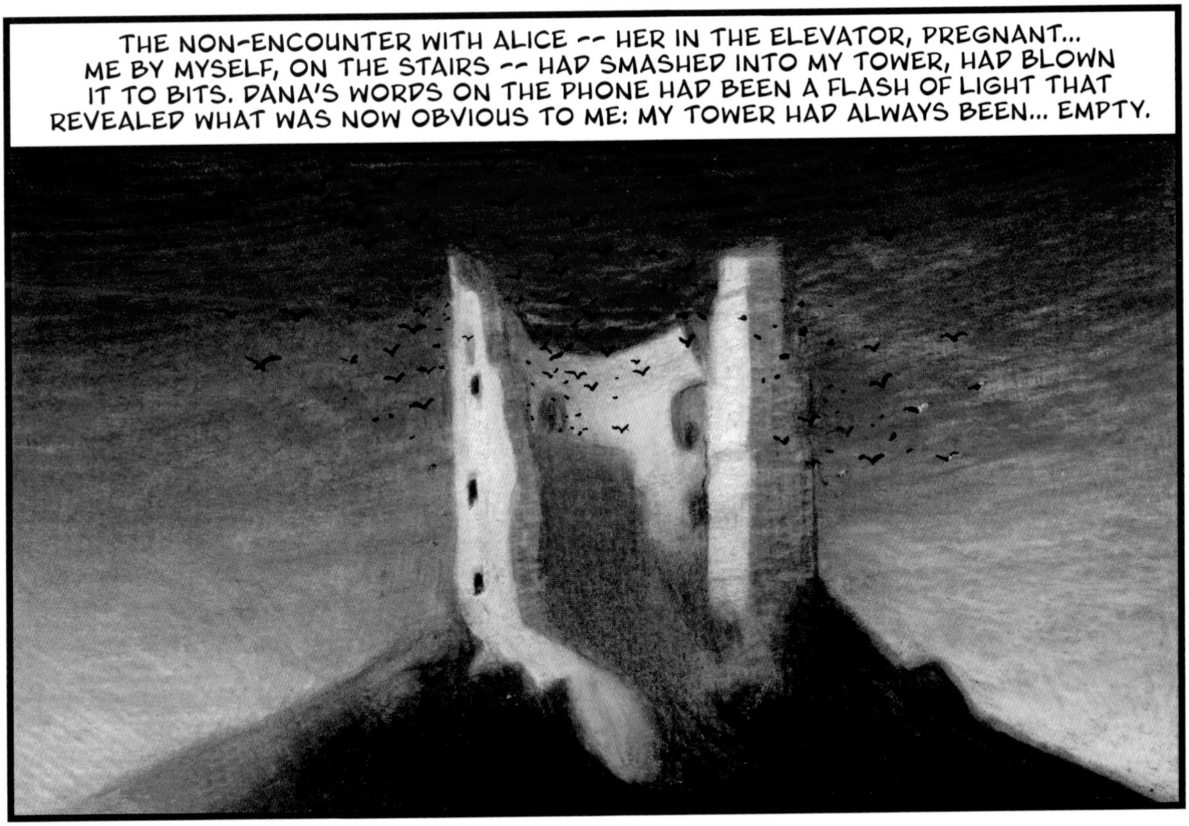
THE NON-ENCOUNTER WITH ALICE -- HER IN THE ELEVATOR, PREGNANT... ME BY MYSELF, ON THE STAIRS -- HAD SMASHED INTO MY TOWER, HAD BLOWN IT TO BITS. DANA'S WORDS ON THE PHONE HAD BEEN A FLASH OF LIGHT THAT REVEALED WHAT WAS NOW OBVIOUS TO ME: MY TOWER HAD ALWAYS BEEN... EMPTY.

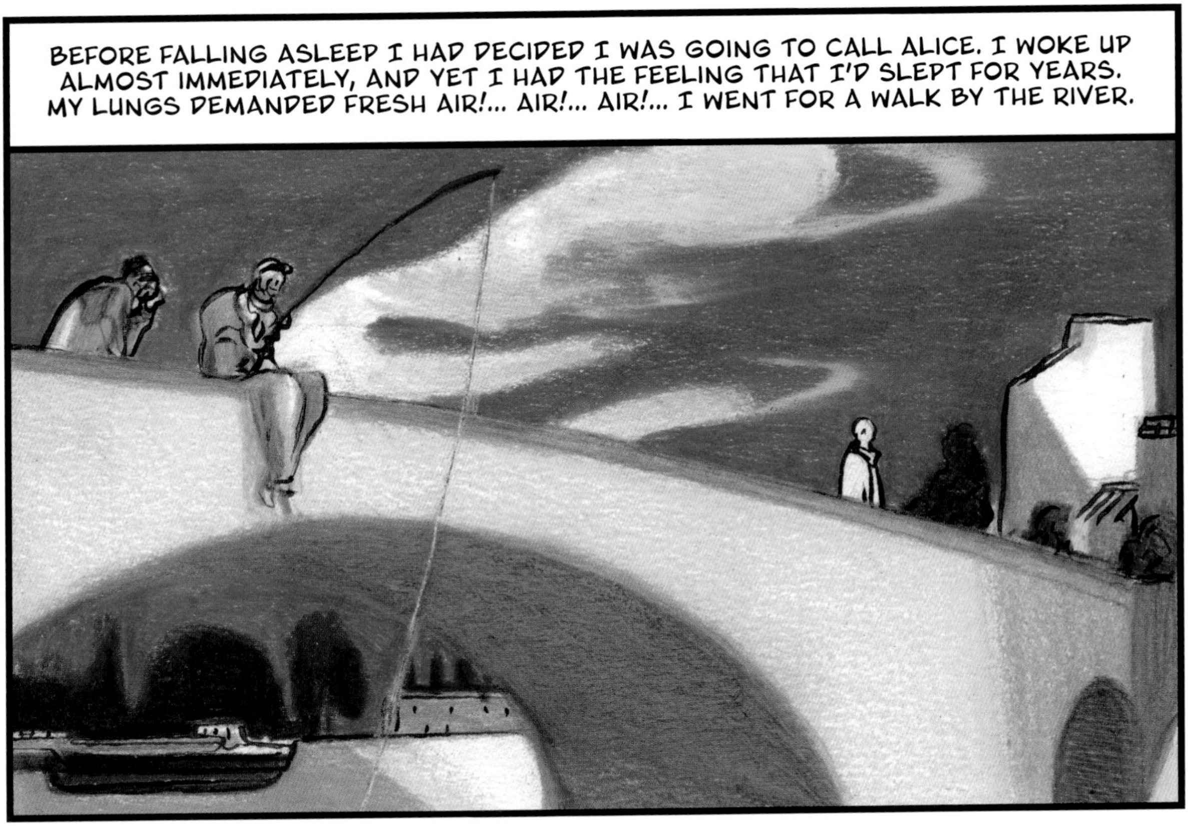
BEFORE FALLING ASLEEP I HAD DECIDED I WAS GOING TO CALL ALICE. I WOKE UP ALMOST IMMEDIATELY, AND YET I HAD THE FEELING THAT I'D SLEPT FOR YEARS. MY LUNGS DEMANDED FRESH AIR!... AIR!... AIR!... I WENT FOR A WALK BY THE RIVER.

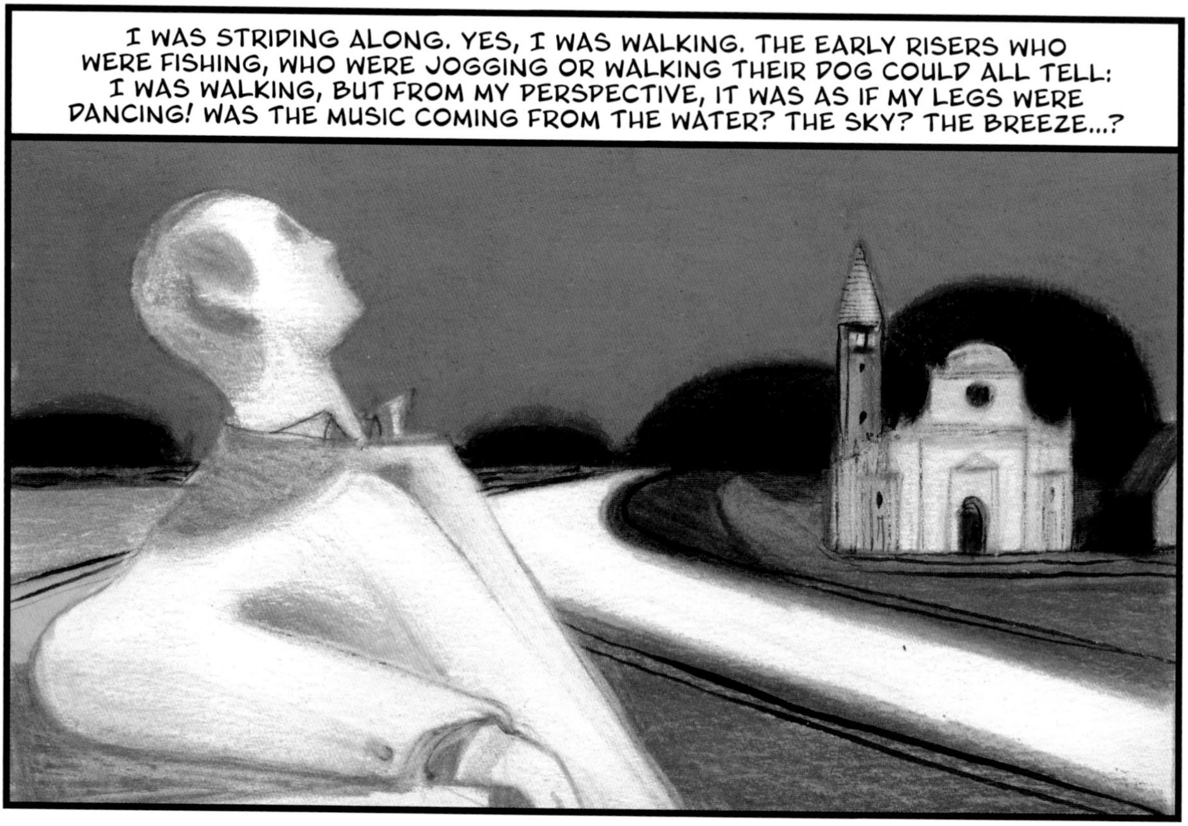
I WAS STRIDING ALONG. YES, I WAS WALKING. THE EARLY RISERS WHO WERE FISHING, WHO WERE JOGGING OR WALKING THEIR DOG COULD ALL TELL: I WAS WALKING, BUT FROM MY PERSPECTIVE, IT WAS AS IF MY LEGS WERE DANCING! WAS THE MUSIC COMING FROM THE WATER? THE SKY? THE BREEZE...?

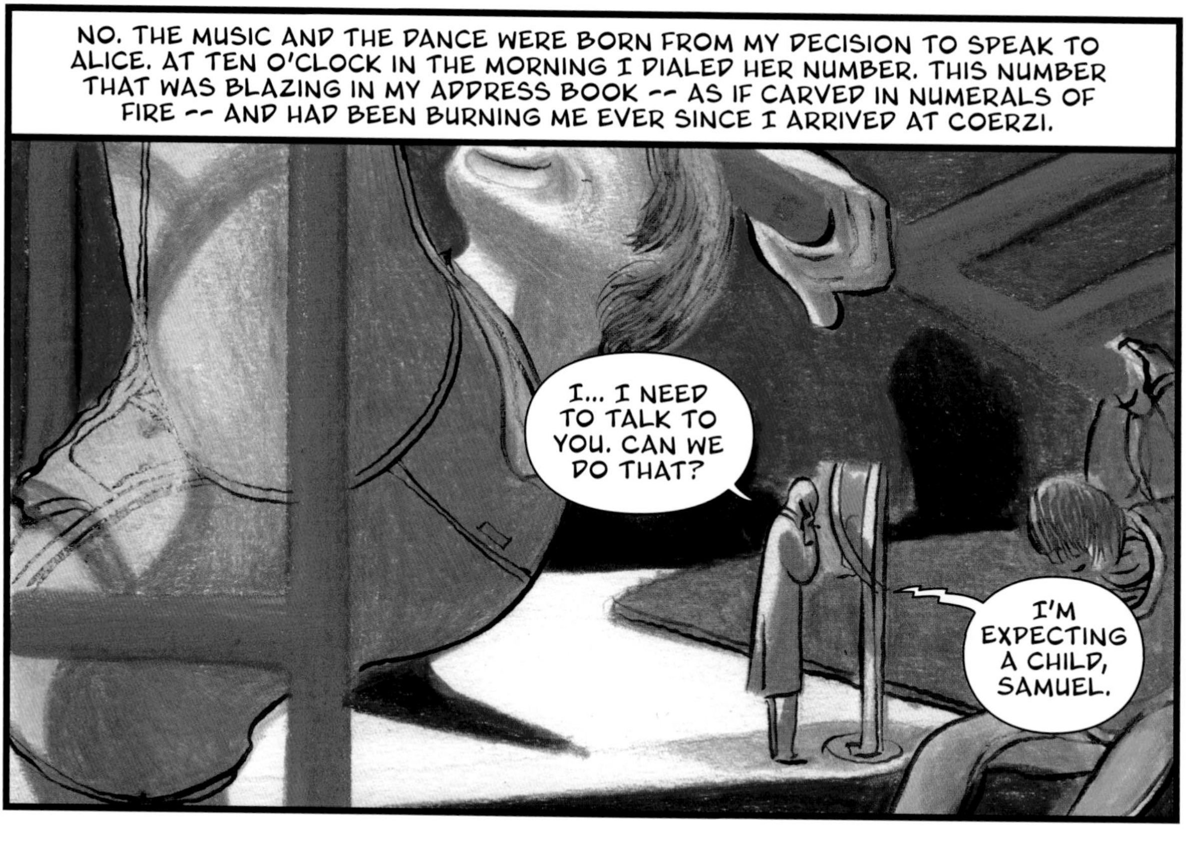
NO. THE MUSIC AND THE DANCE WERE BORN FROM MY DECISION TO SPEAK TO ALICE. AT TEN O'CLOCK IN THE MORNING I DIALED HER NUMBER. THIS NUMBER THAT WAS BLAZING IN MY ADDRESS BOOK -- AS IF CARVED IN NUMERALS OF FIRE -- AND HAD BEEN BURNING ME EVER SINCE I ARRIVED AT COERZI.
I... I NEED TO TALK TO YOU. CAN WE DO THAT?
I'M EXPECTING A CHILD, SAMUEL.

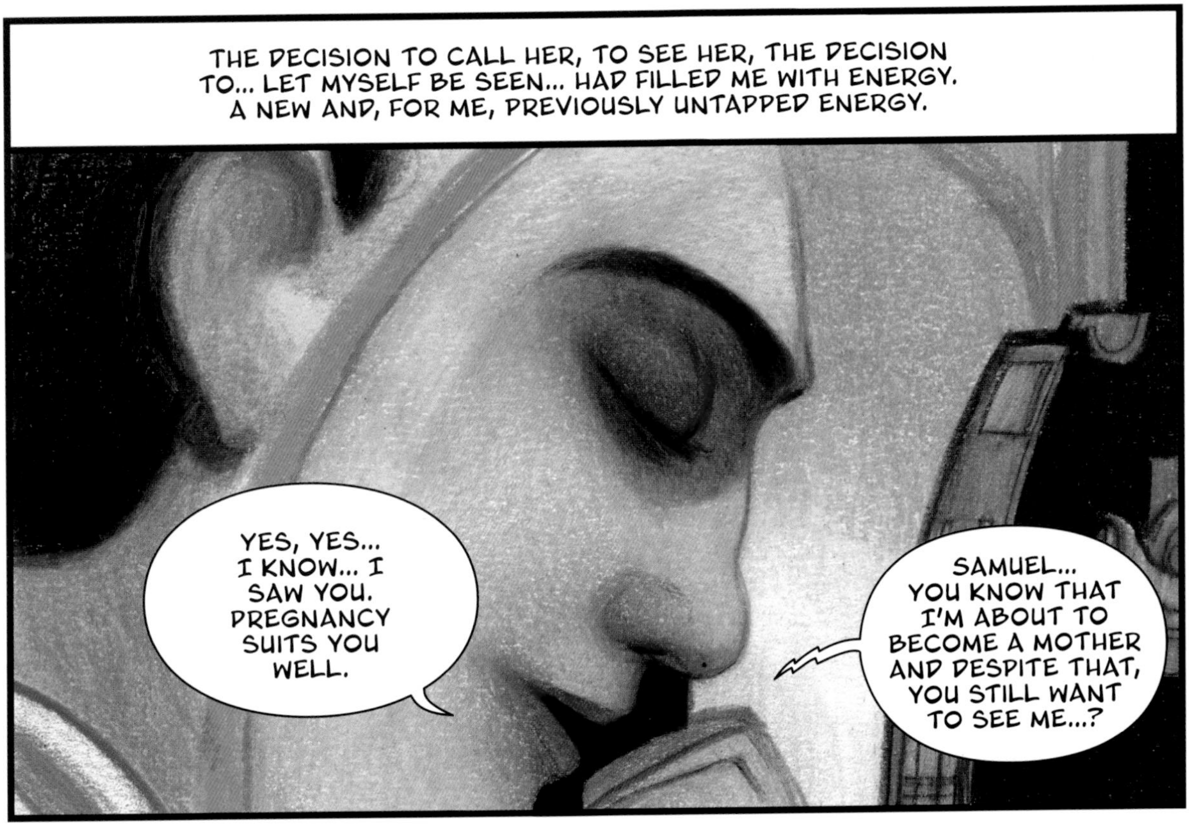
THE DECISION TO CALL HER, TO SEE HER, THE DECISION TO... LET MYSELF BE SEEN... HAD FILLED ME WITH ENERGY. A NEW AND, FOR ME, PREVIOUSLY UNTAPPED ENERGY.
SAMUEL... YOU KNOW THAT I'M ABOUT TO BECOME A MOTHER AND DESPITE THAT, YOU STILL WANT TO SEE ME...?
YES, YES... I KNOW... I SAW YOU. PREGNANCY SUITS YOU WELL.

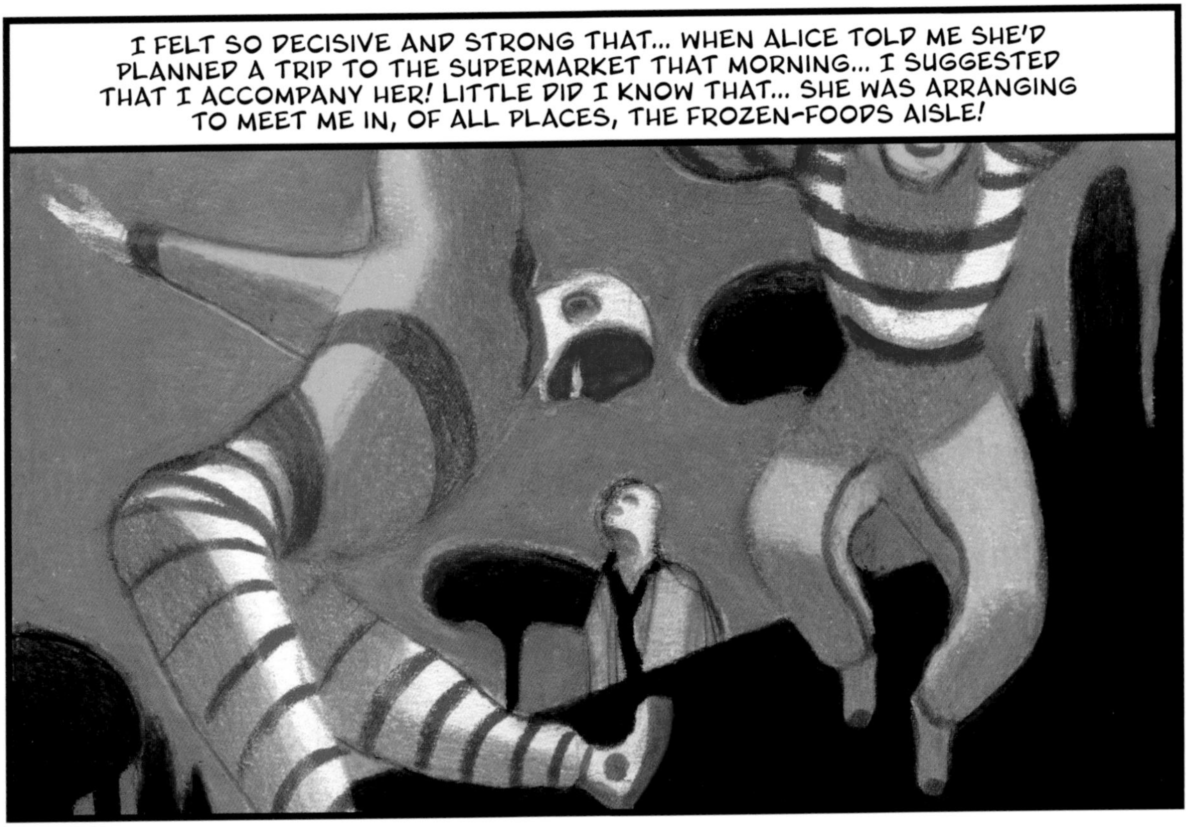
I FELT SO DECISIVE AND STRONG THAT... WHEN ALICE TOLD ME SHE'D PLANNED A TRIP TO THE SUPERMARKET THAT MORNING... I SUGGESTED THAT I ACCOMPANY HER! LITTLE DID I KNOW THAT... SHE WAS ARRANGING TO MEET ME IN, OF ALL PLACES, THE FROZEN-FOODS AISLE!

BUT I HAVE TO ADMIT THAT I FELT A HUGE RELIEF WHEN WE DECIDED TO MEET ONE HOUR LATER AT THE CAFETERIA IN THE SHOPPING MALL INSTEAD. ONE HOUR. ENOUGH TIME TO BUY HER FLOWERS SEVERAL TIMES OVER.

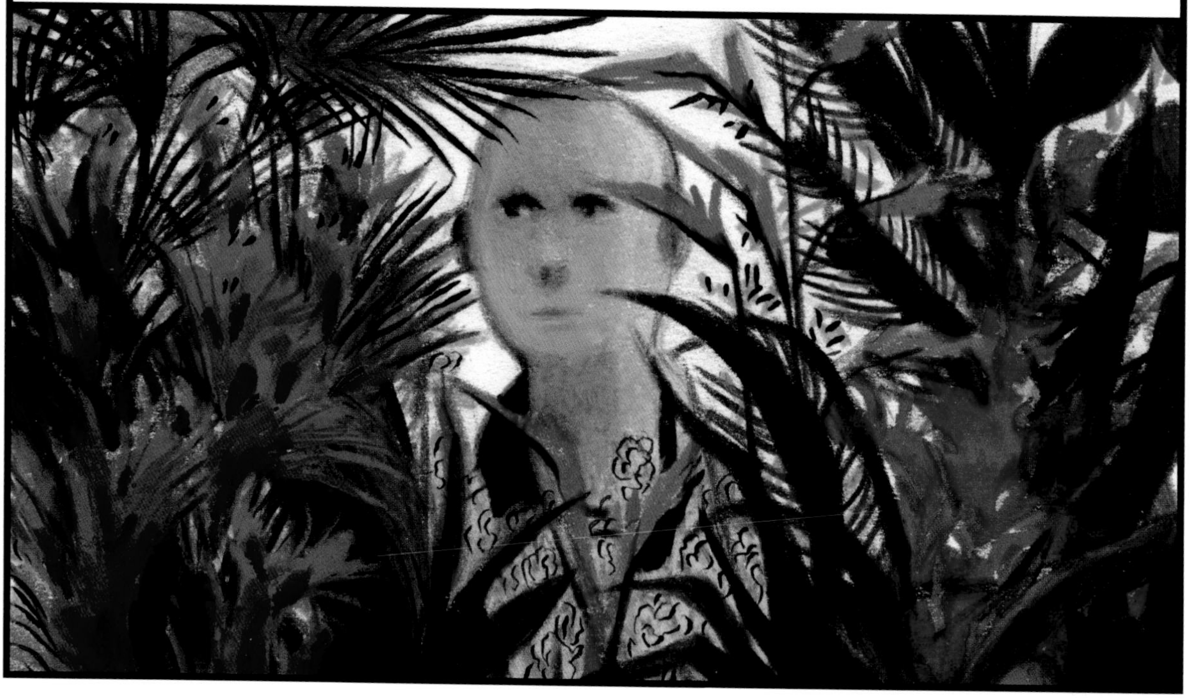

THREE BOUQUETS ENDED UP IN THE TRASH CAN. THE FLORIST WAS STARTING TO GIVE ME FUNNY LOOKS... DID I ULTIMATELY BUY THE RIGHT FLOWERS...?

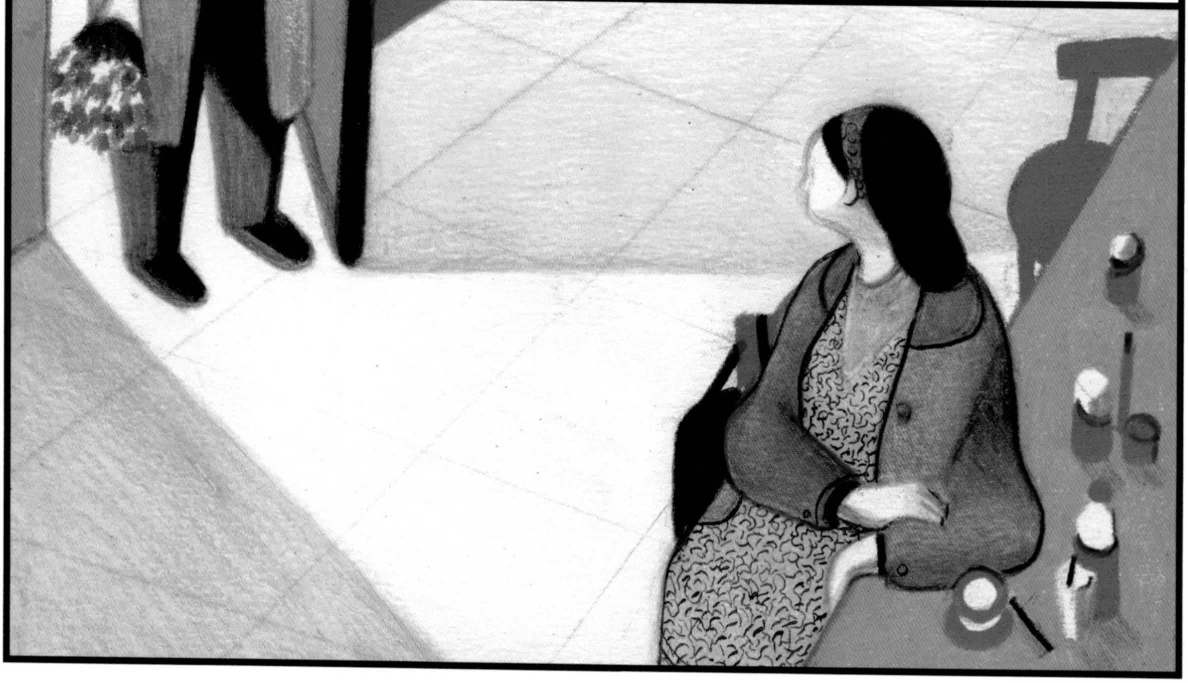

BECAUSE OF THE FLOWERS -- WELL, BECAUSE OF MY HESITATION -- I ARRIVED AT THE RENDEZVOUS SLIGHTLY LATE. HERE SHE WAS, FINALLY, THE REAL ALICE, IN FLESH AND BLOOD. EVEN MORE REAL THAN THE FLOWERS OR THE FEAR MONSTERS.

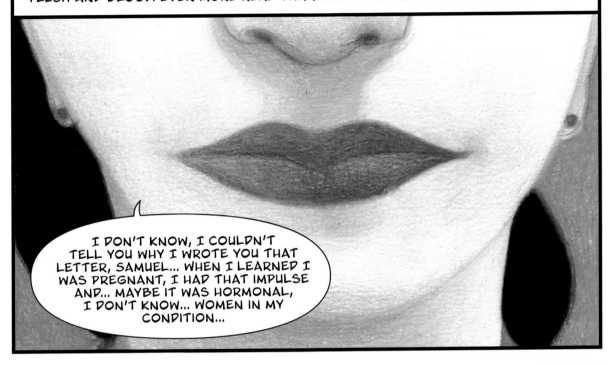

I DON'T KNOW, I COULDN'T TELL YOU WHY I WROTE YOU THAT LETTER, SAMUEL... WHEN I LEARNED I WAS PREGNANT, I HAD THAT IMPULSE AND... MAYBE IT WAS HORMONAL, I DON'T KNOW... WOMEN IN MY CONDITION...

ALICE, QUITE SIMPLY, WAS THERE. THE INTENSITY OF HER PRESENCE SEEMED OVERWHELMING TO ME. ALL OF HER REALITY AS A WOMAN COVERED ME, ENVELOPED ME... TO THE POINT OF TRANSFORMING ME TOO, INTO SOMETHING -- INTO SOMEONE -- REAL. IN MY OWN EYES, THAT IS.

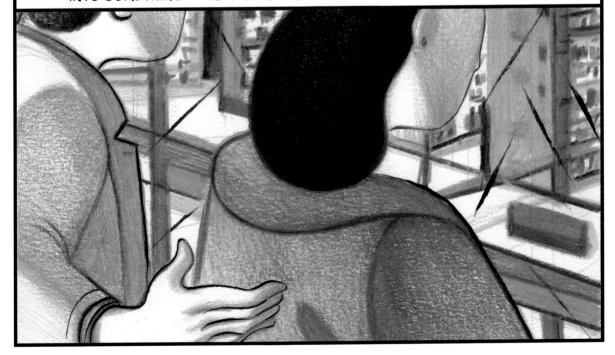

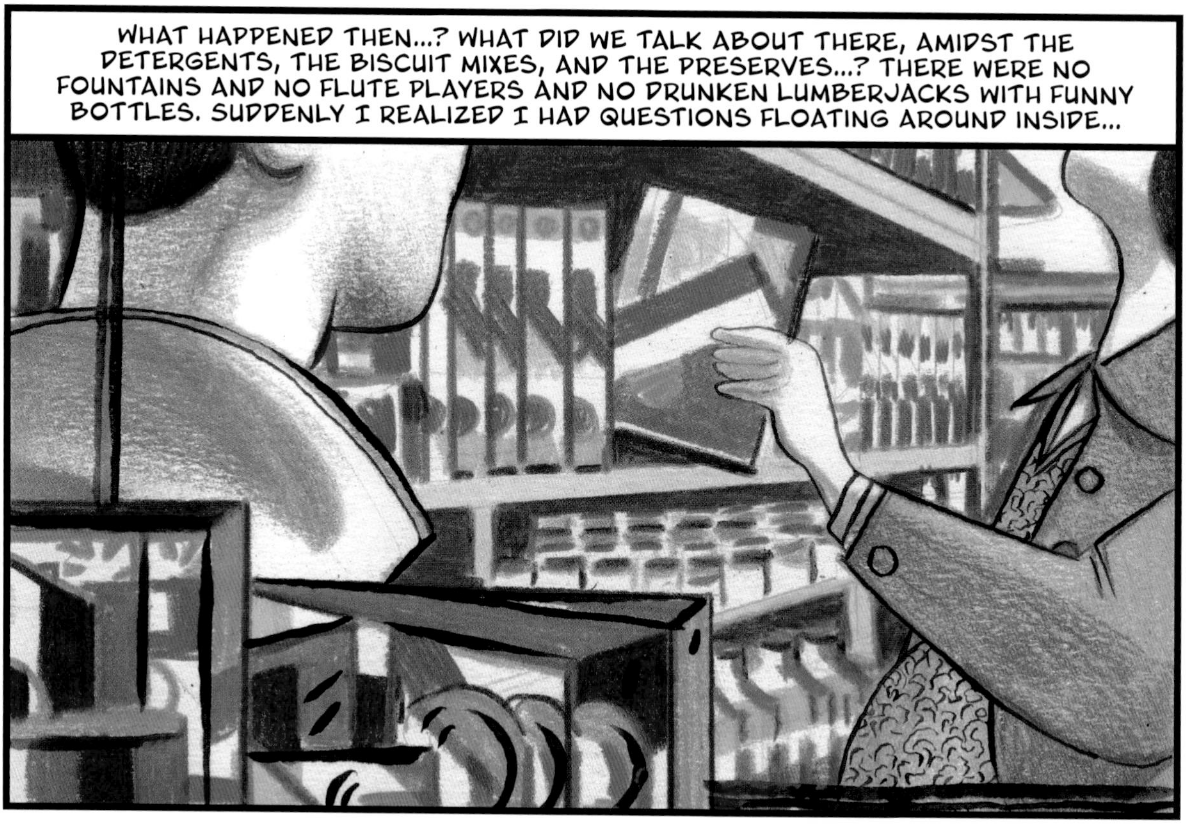
WHAT HAPPENED THEN...? WHAT DID WE TALK ABOUT THERE, AMIDST THE DETERGENTS, THE BISCUIT MIXES, AND THE PRESERVES...? THERE WERE NO FOUNTAINS AND NO FLUTE PLAYERS AND NO DRUNKEN LUMBERJACKS WITH FUNNY BOTTLES. SUDDENLY I REALIZED I HAD QUESTIONS FLOATING AROUND INSIDE...

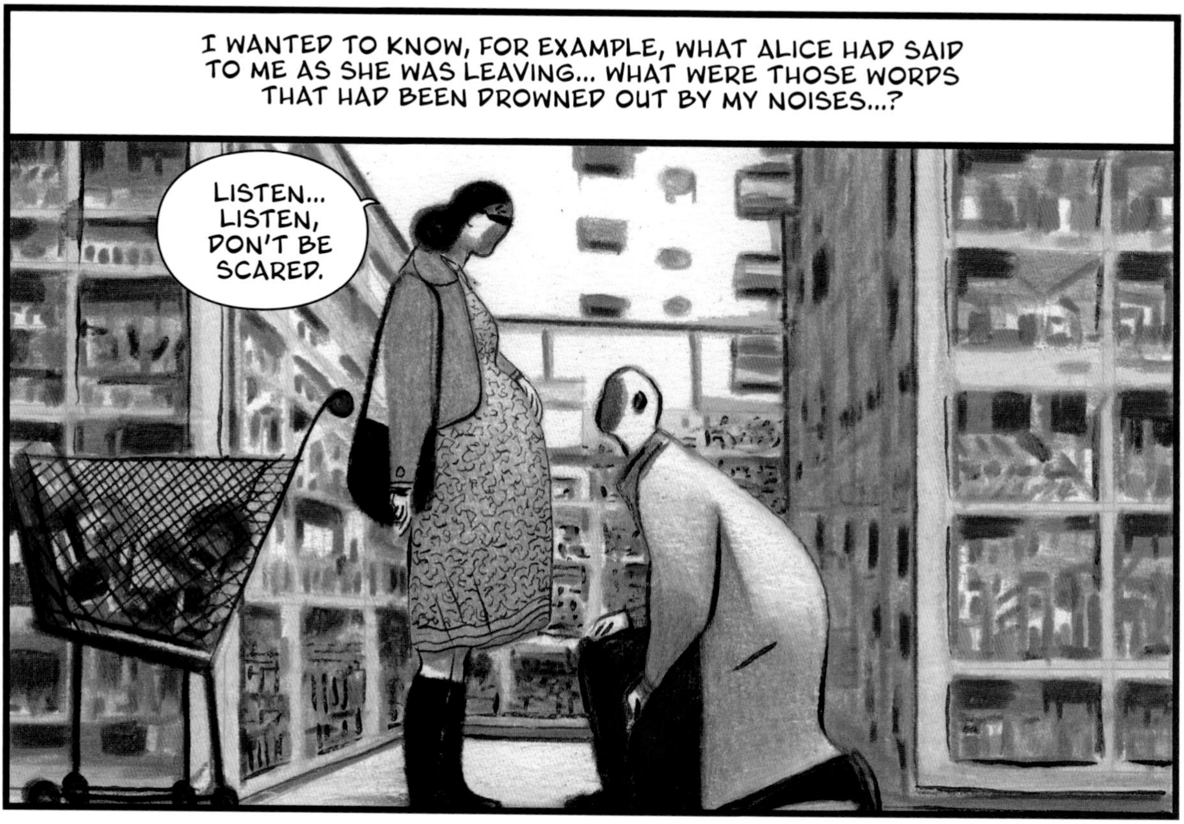
I WANTED TO KNOW, FOR EXAMPLE, WHAT ALICE HAD SAID TO ME AS SHE WAS LEAVING... WHAT WERE THOSE WORDS THAT HAD BEEN DROWNED OUT BY MY NOISES...?
LISTEN... LISTEN, DON'T BE SCARED.

I LISTENED...

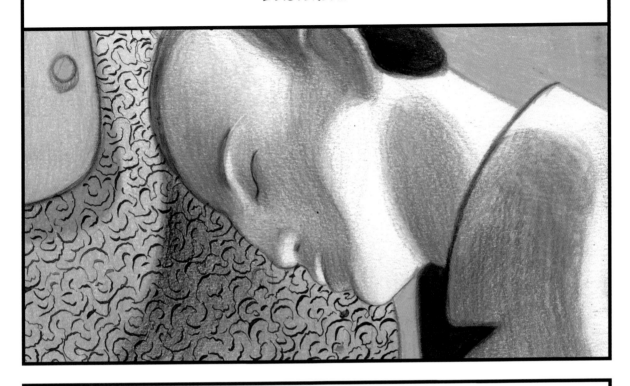

...WITHOUT FEAR...

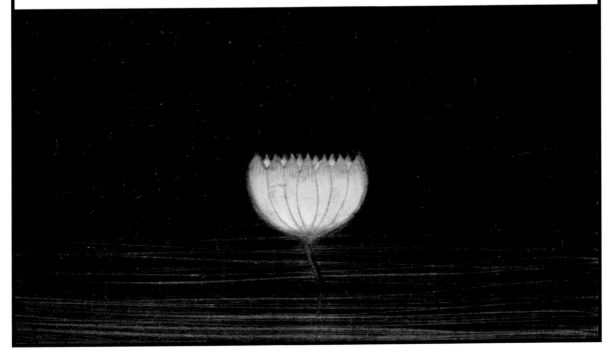

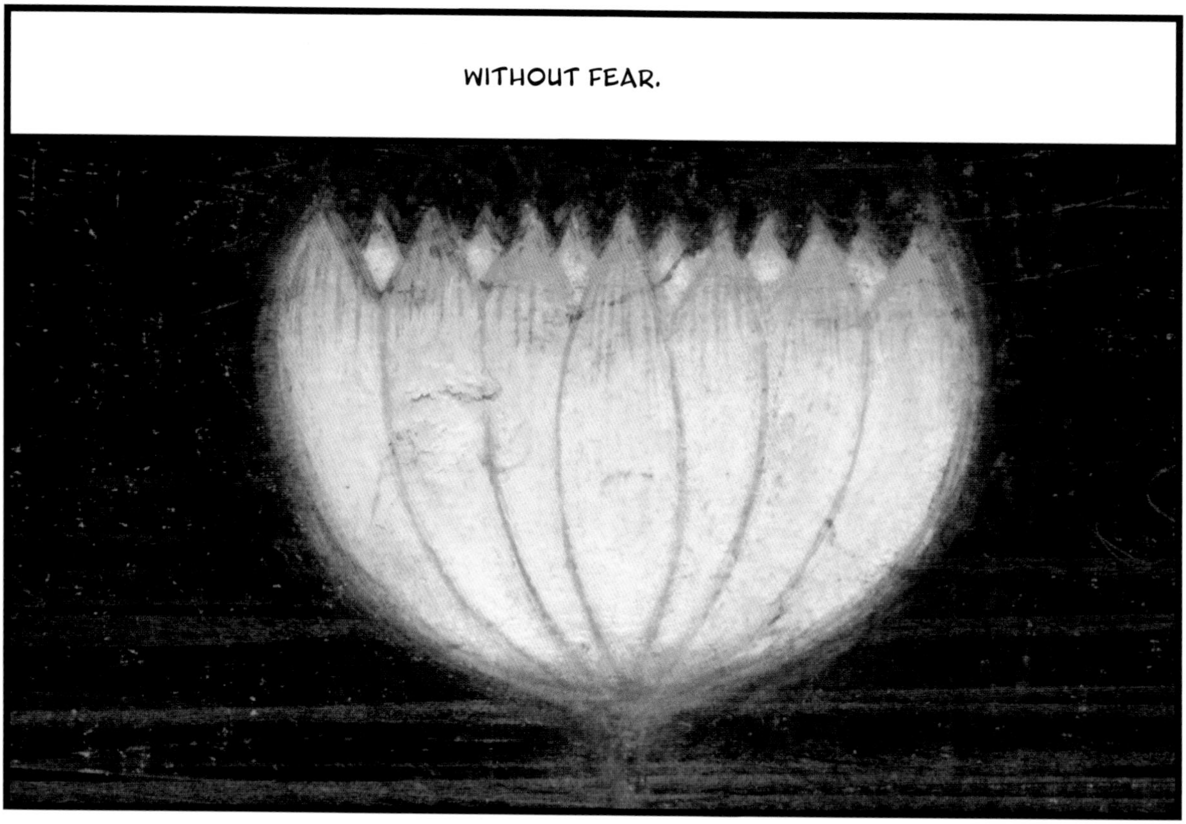
WITHOUT FEAR.

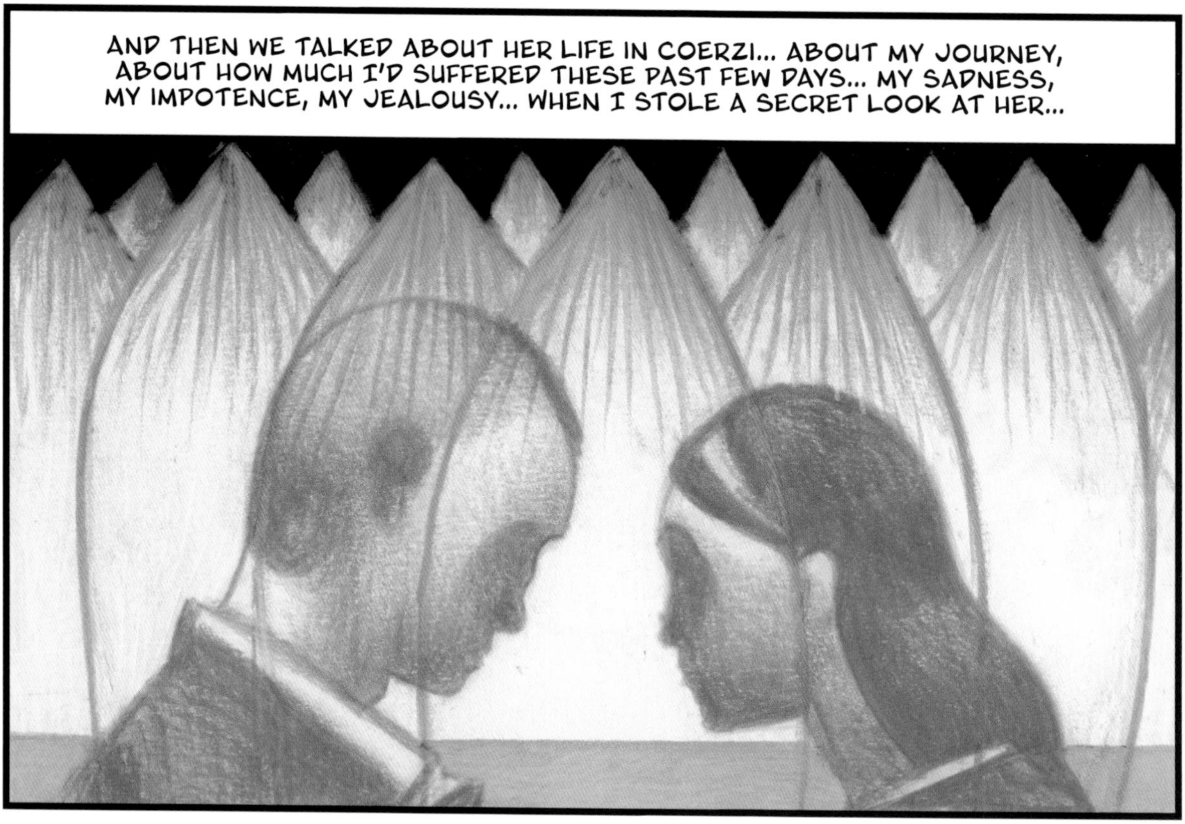
AND THEN WE TALKED ABOUT HER LIFE IN COERZI... ABOUT MY JOURNEY, ABOUT HOW MUCH I'D SUFFERED THESE PAST FEW DAYS... MY SADNESS, MY IMPOTENCE, MY JEALOUSY... WHEN I STOLE A SECRET LOOK AT HER...

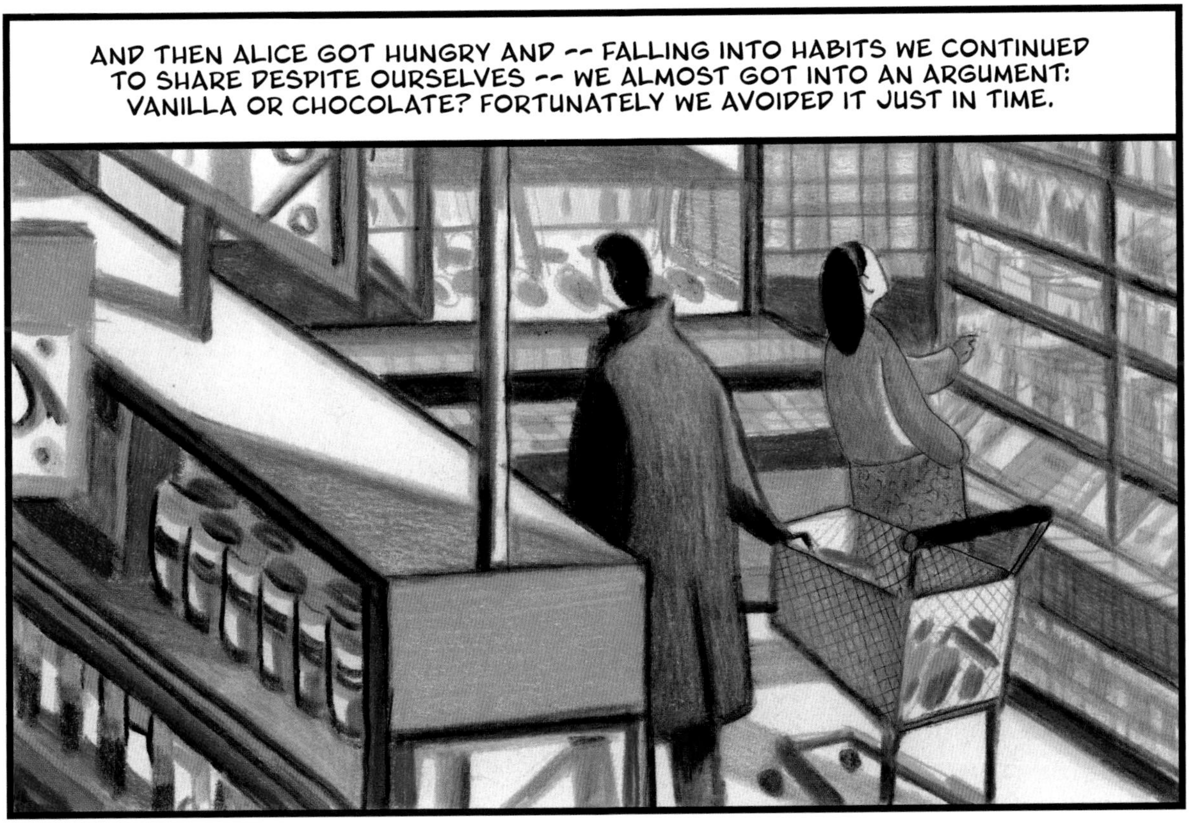
AND THEN ALICE GOT HUNGRY AND -- FALLING INTO HABITS WE CONTINUED TO SHARE DESPITE OURSELVES -- WE ALMOST GOT INTO AN ARGUMENT: VANILLA OR CHOCOLATE? FORTUNATELY WE AVOIDED IT JUST IN TIME.

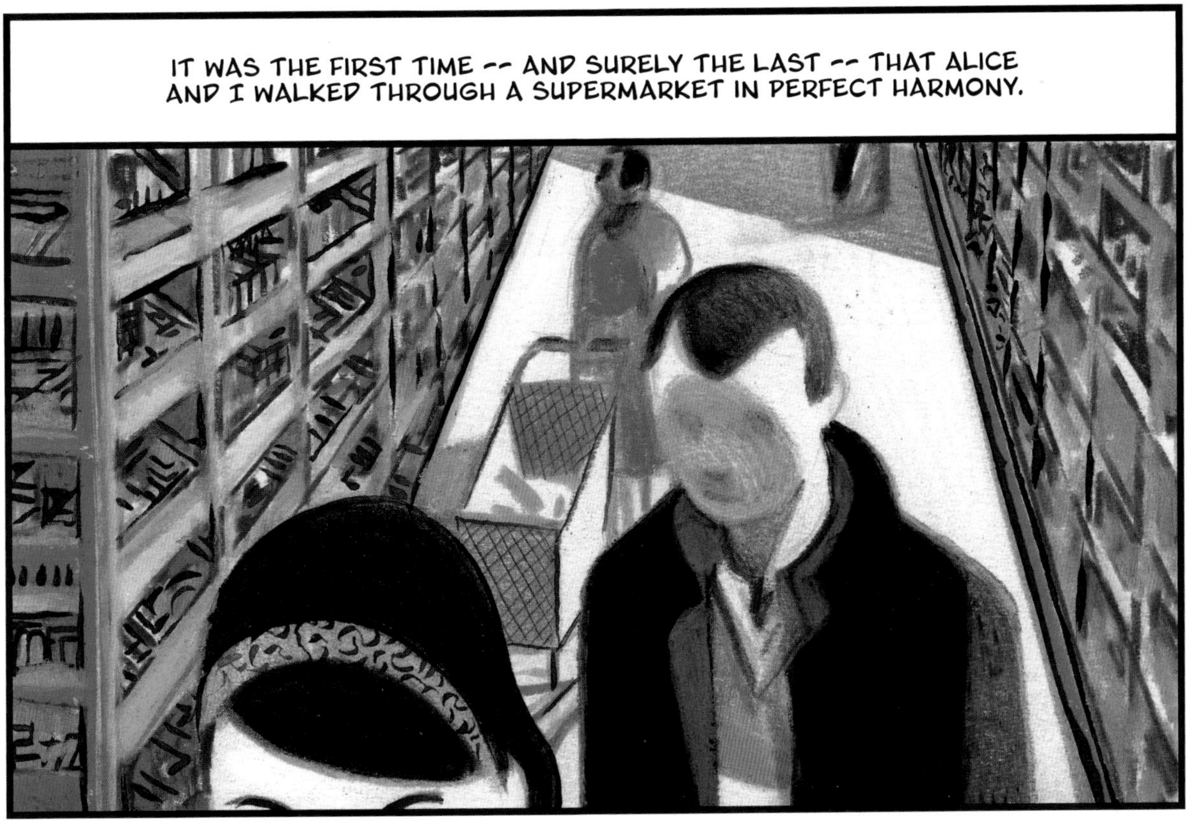
IT WAS THE FIRST TIME -- AND SURELY THE LAST -- THAT ALICE AND I WALKED THROUGH A SUPERMARKET IN PERFECT HARMONY.

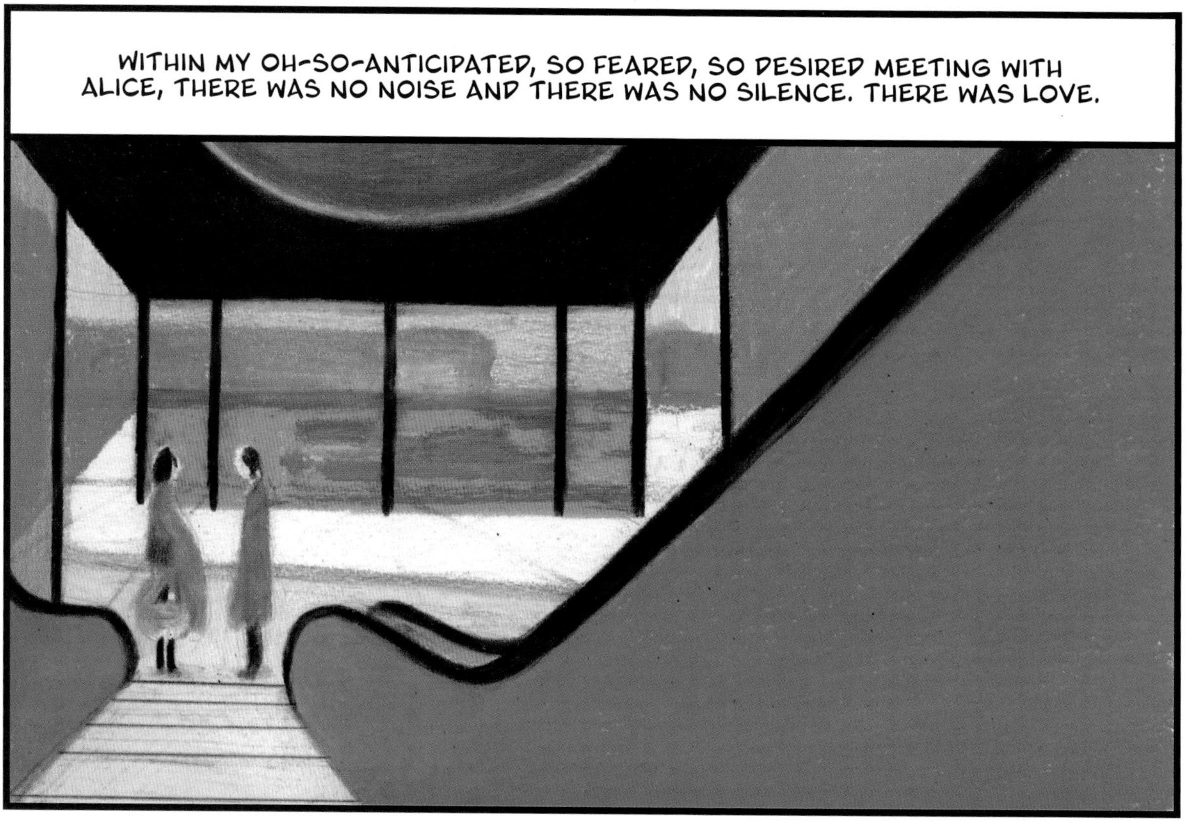
WITHIN MY OH-SO-ANTICIPATED, SO FEARED, SO DESIRED MEETING WITH ALICE, THERE WAS NO NOISE AND THERE WAS NO SILENCE. THERE WAS LOVE.

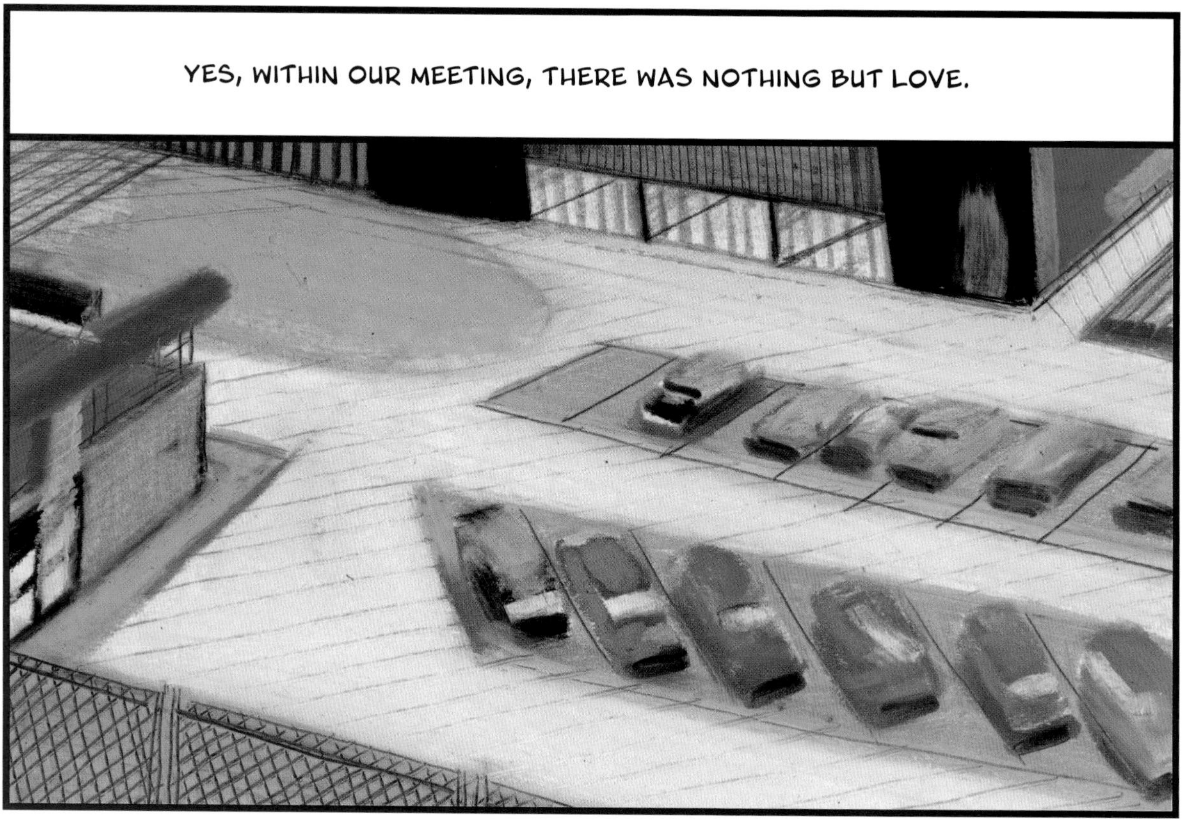
YES, WITHIN OUR MEETING, THERE WAS NOTHING BUT LOVE.

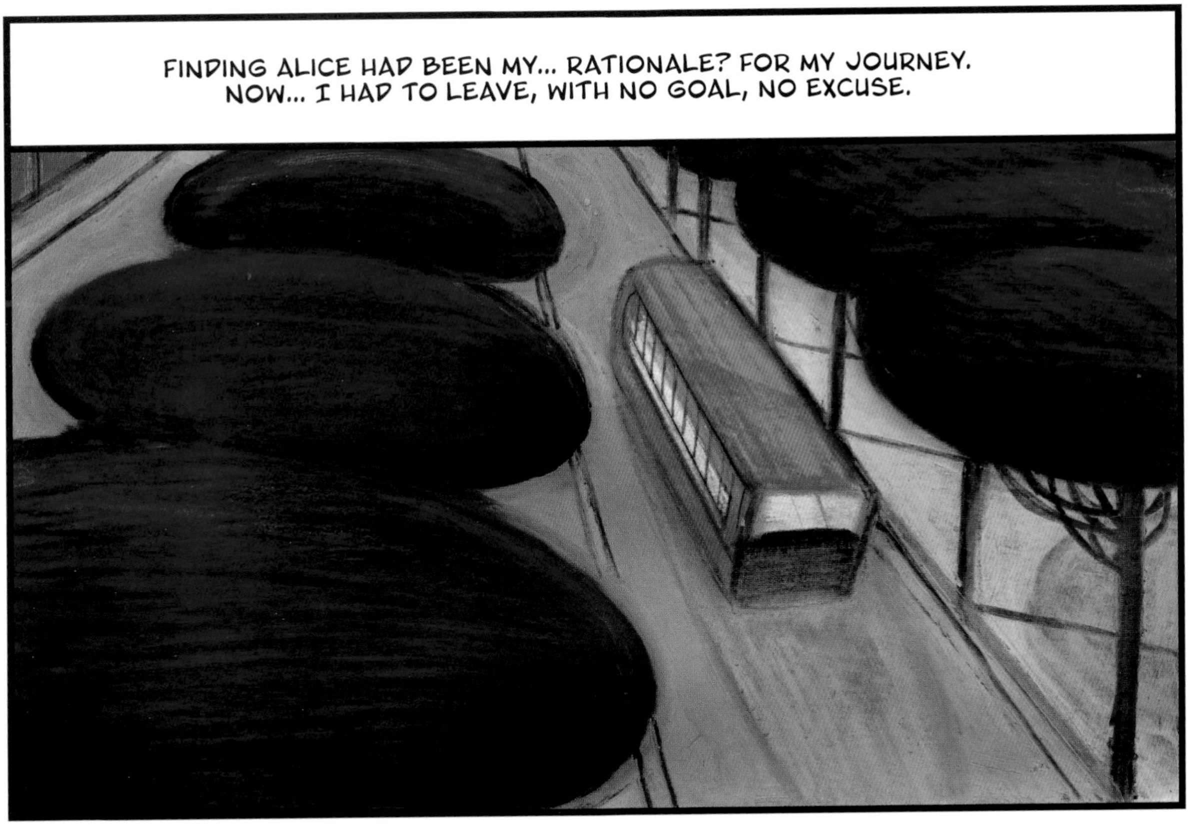
FINDING ALICE HAD BEEN MY... RATIONALE? FOR MY JOURNEY.
NOW... I HAD TO LEAVE, WITH NO GOAL, NO EXCUSE.

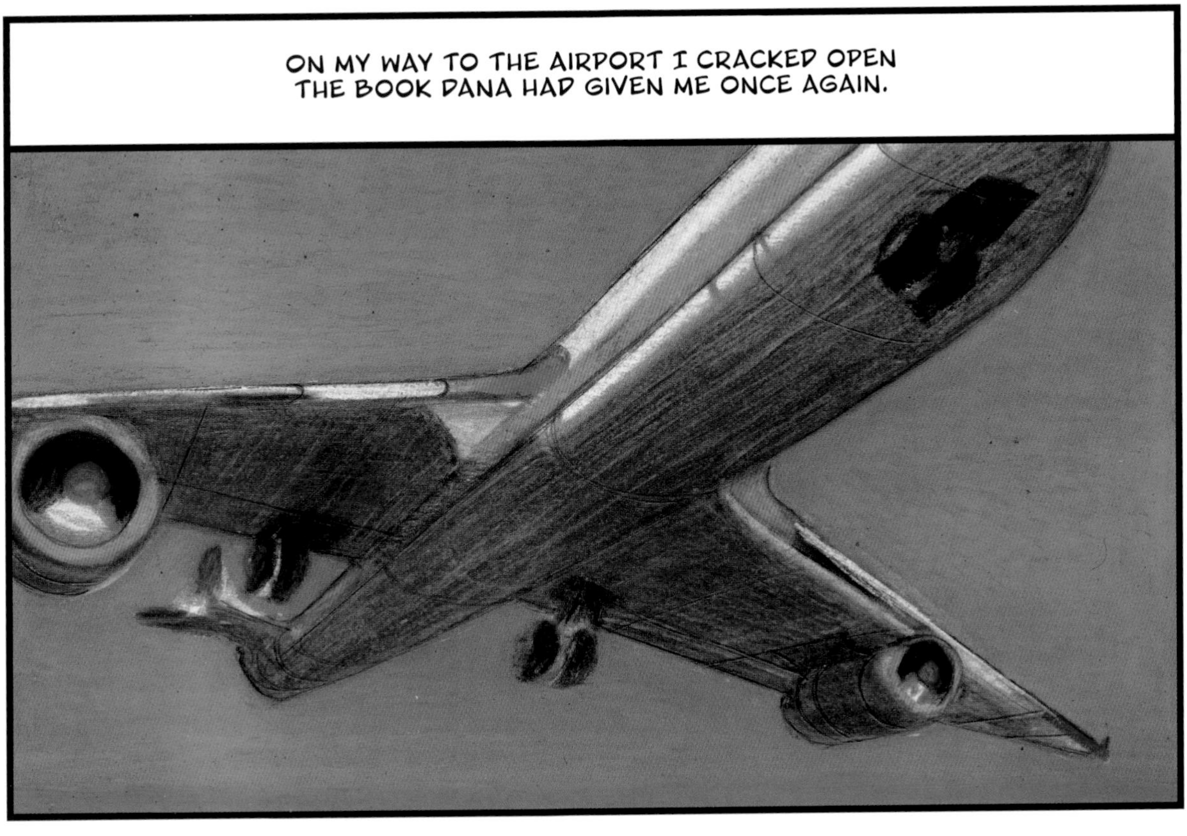
ON MY WAY TO THE AIRPORT I CRACKED OPEN
THE BOOK DANA HAD GIVEN ME ONCE AGAIN.

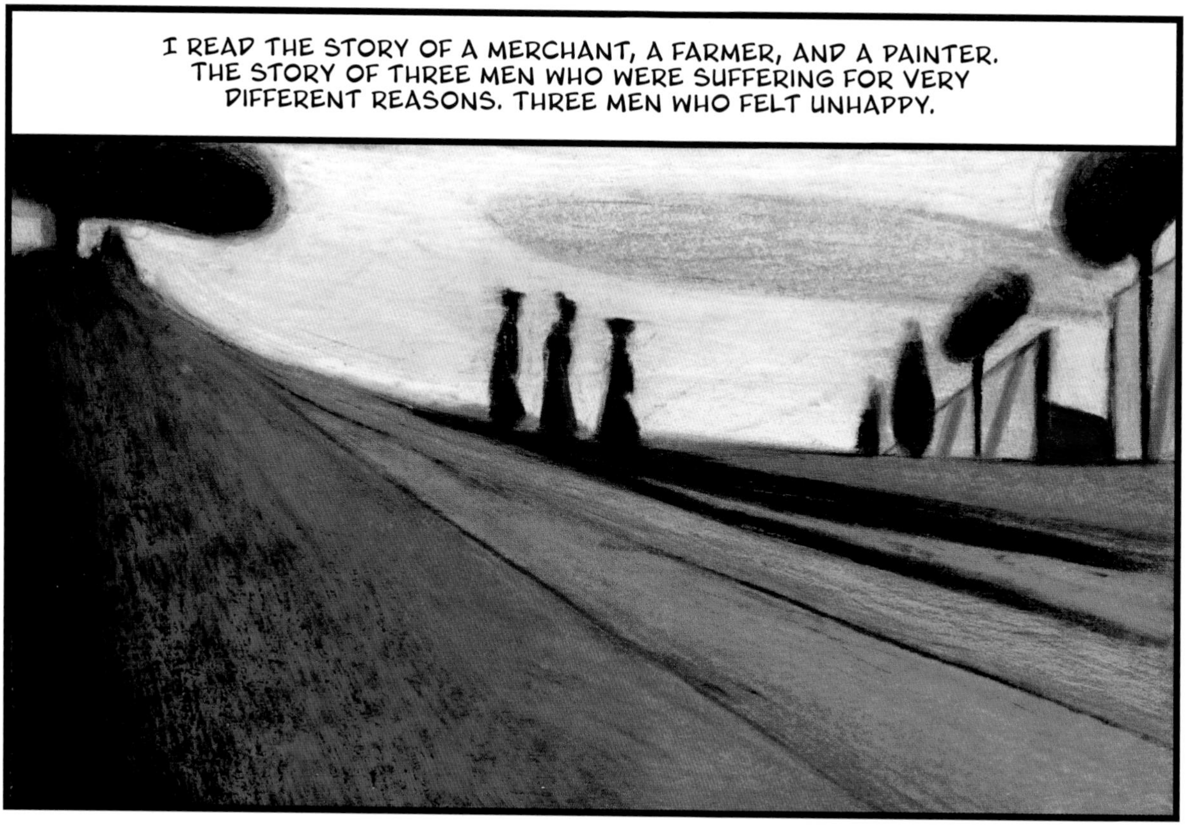
I READ THE STORY OF A MERCHANT, A FARMER, AND A PAINTER. THE STORY OF THREE MEN WHO WERE SUFFERING FOR VERY DIFFERENT REASONS. THREE MEN WHO FELT UNHAPPY.

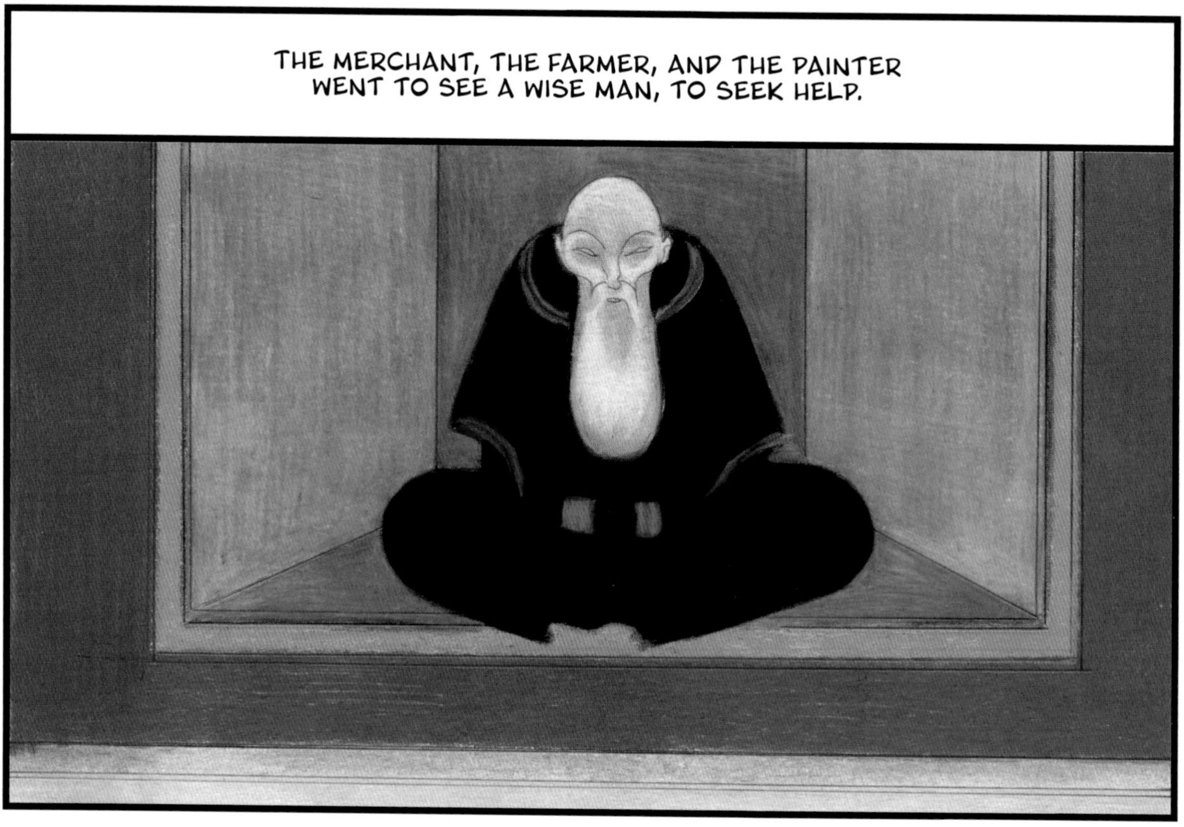
THE MERCHANT, THE FARMER, AND THE PAINTER WENT TO SEE A WISE MAN, TO SEEK HELP.

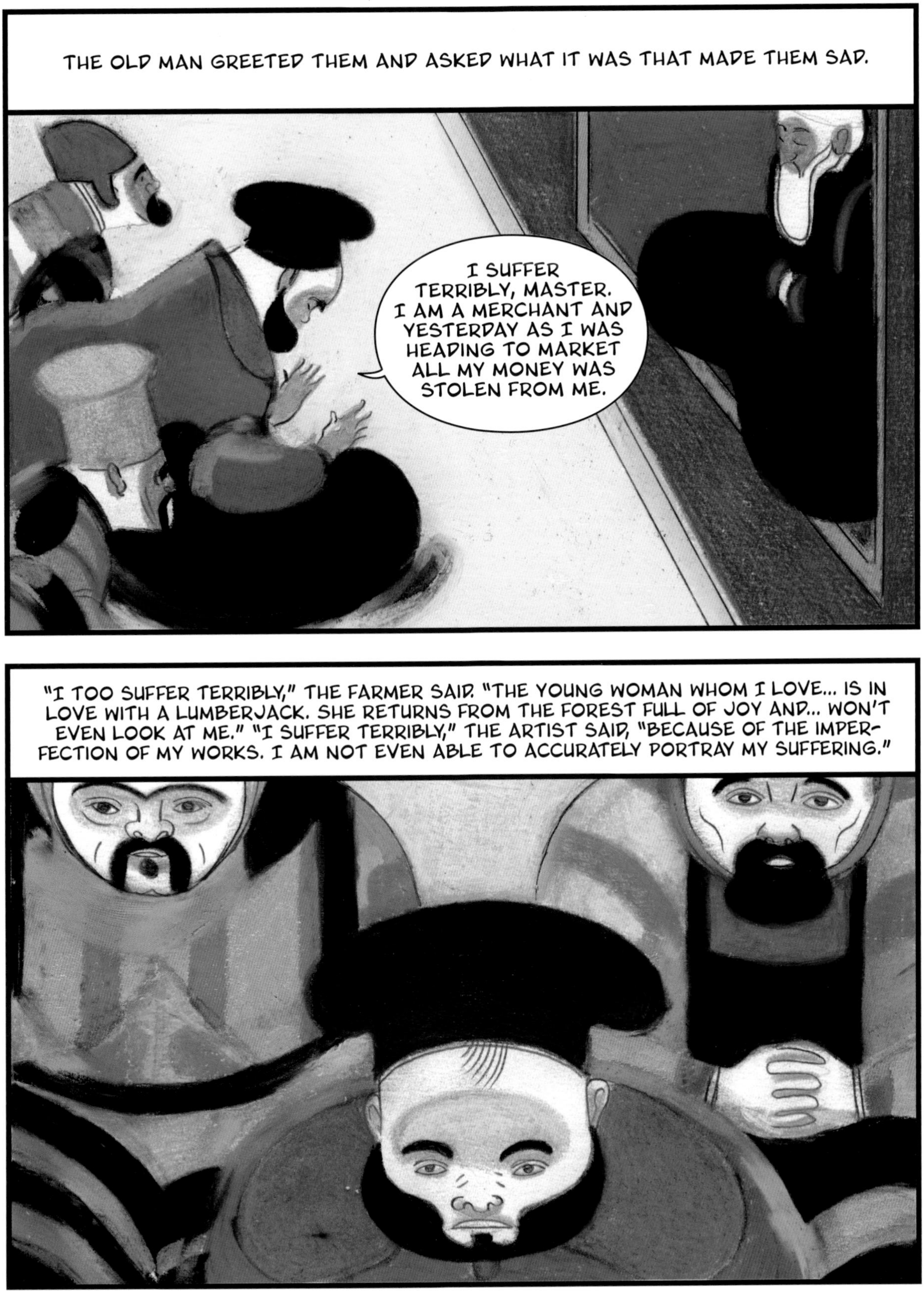
THE OLD MAN GREETED THEM AND ASKED WHAT IT WAS THAT MADE THEM SAD.
I SUFFER TERRIBLY, MASTER. I AM A MERCHANT AND YESTERDAY AS I WAS HEADING TO MARKET ALL MY MONEY WAS STOLEN FROM ME.
"I TOO SUFFER TERRIBLY," THE FARMER SAID. "THE YOUNG WOMAN WHOM I LOVE... IS IN LOVE WITH A LUMBERJACK. SHE RETURNS FROM THE FOREST FULL OF JOY AND... WON'T EVEN LOOK AT ME." "I SUFFER TERRIBLY," THE ARTIST SAID, "BECAUSE OF THE IMPERFECTION OF MY WORKS. I AM NOT EVEN ABLE TO ACCURATELY PORTRAY MY SUFFERING."

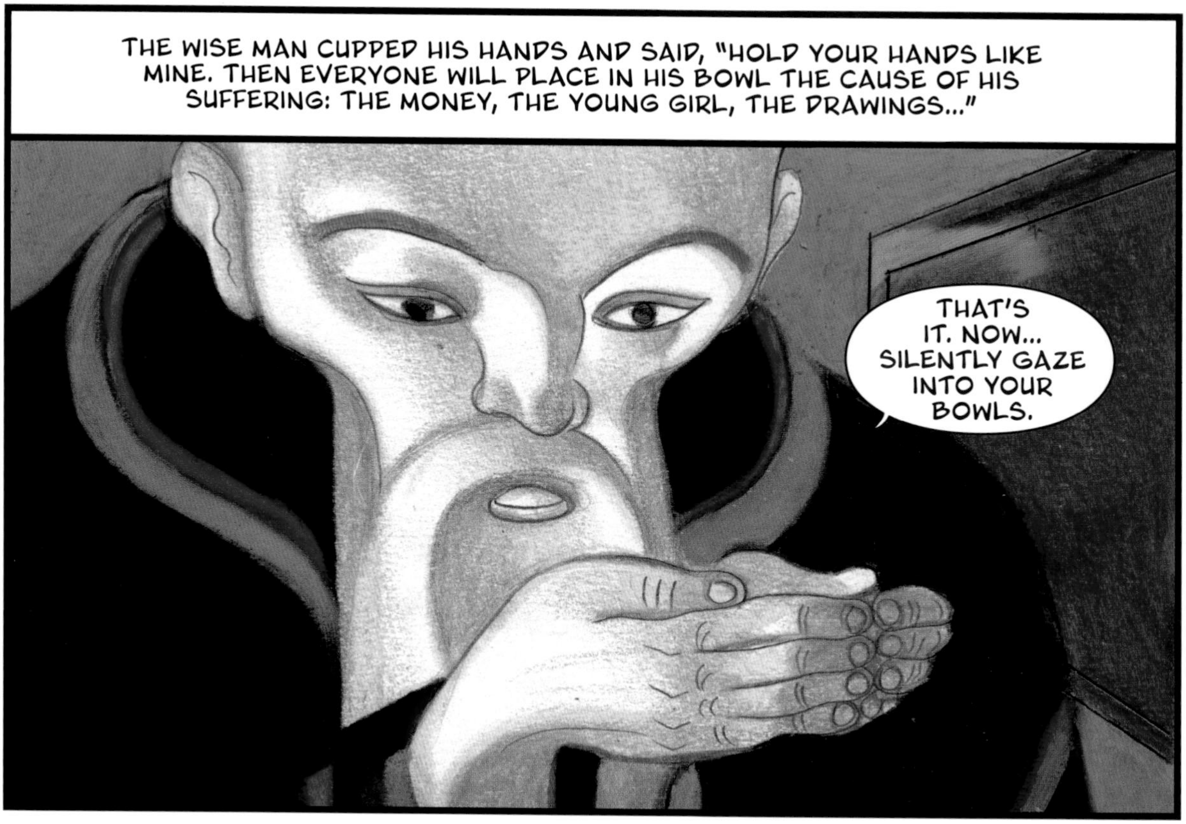
THE WISE MAN CUPPED HIS HANDS AND SAID, "HOLD YOUR HANDS LIKE MINE. THEN EVERYONE WILL PLACE IN HIS BOWL THE CAUSE OF HIS SUFFERING: THE MONEY, THE YOUNG GIRL, THE DRAWINGS..."
THAT'S IT. NOW... SILENTLY GAZE INTO YOUR BOWLS.

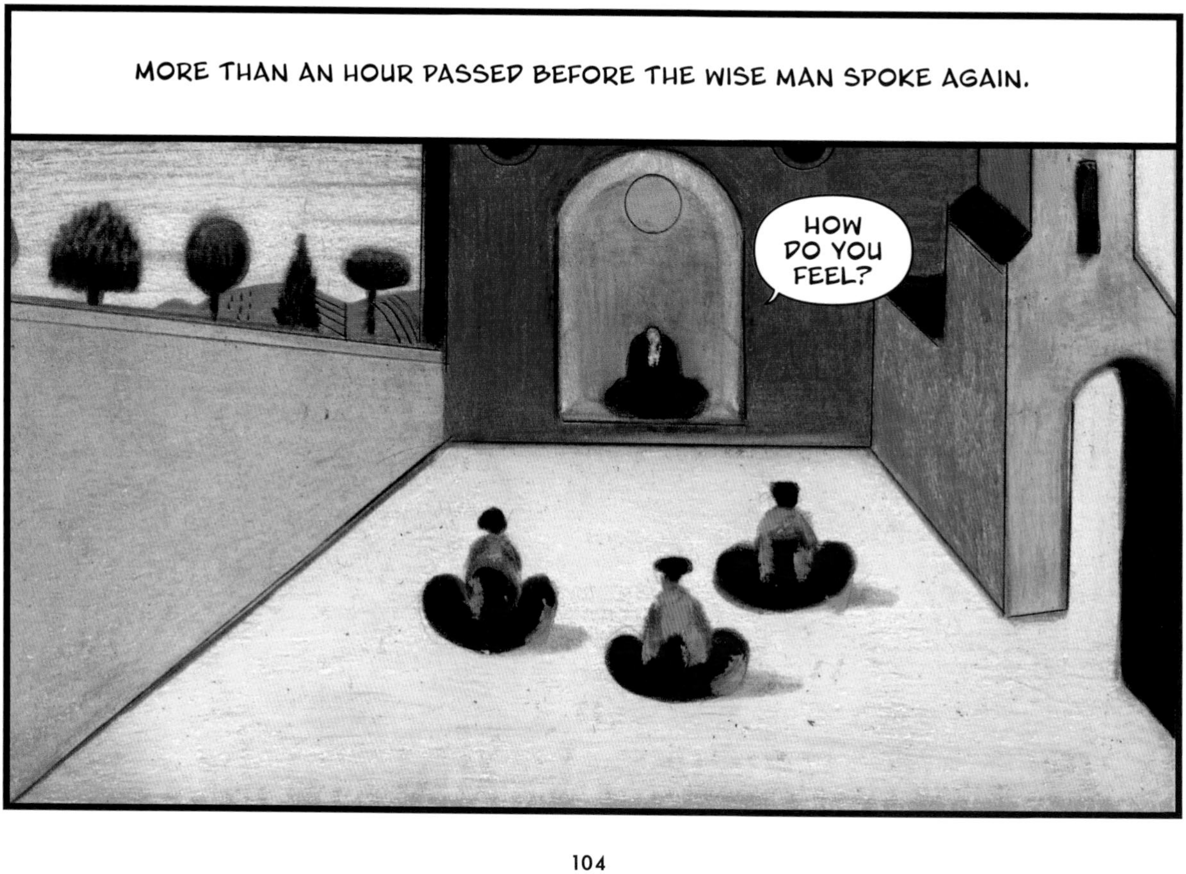
MORE THAN AN HOUR PASSED BEFORE THE WISE MAN SPOKE AGAIN.
HOW DO YOU FEEL?

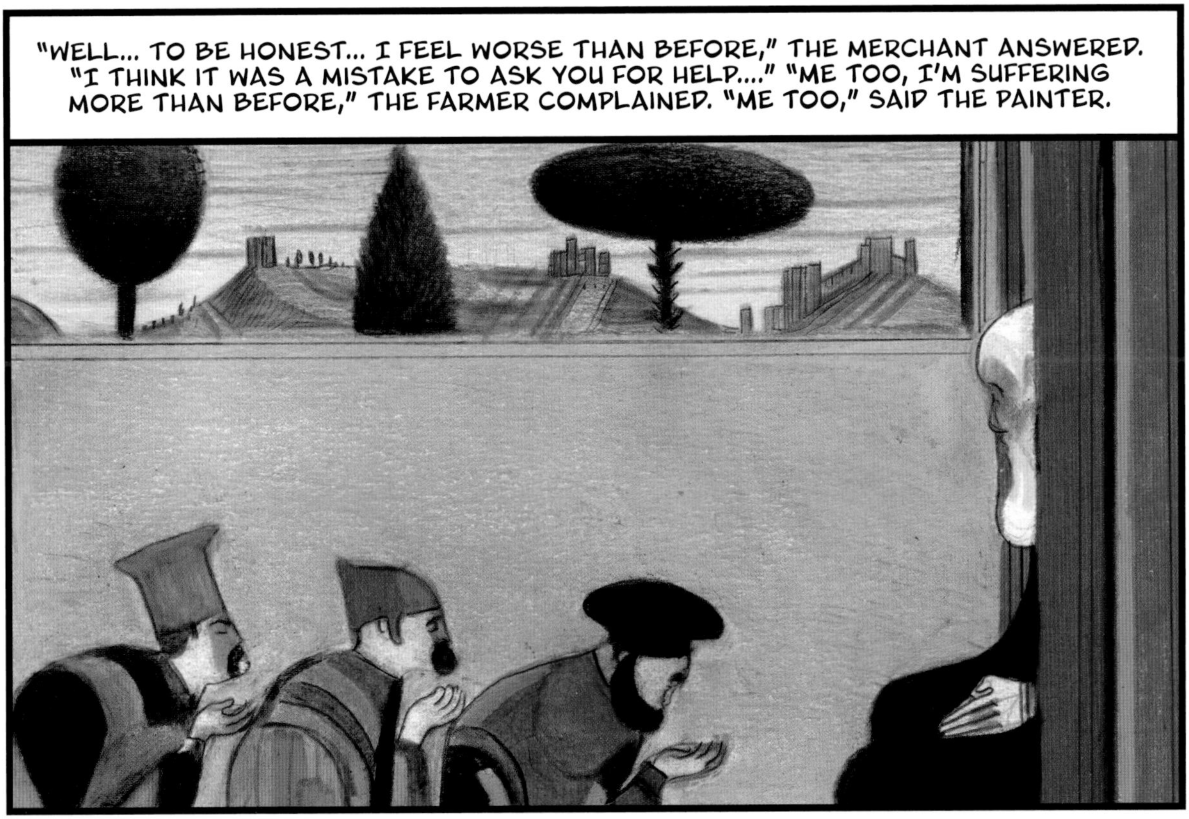
"WELL... TO BE HONEST... I FEEL WORSE THAN BEFORE," THE MERCHANT ANSWERED. "I THINK IT WAS A MISTAKE TO ASK YOU FOR HELP...." "ME TOO, I'M SUFFERING MORE THAN BEFORE," THE FARMER COMPLAINED. "ME TOO," SAID THE PAINTER.

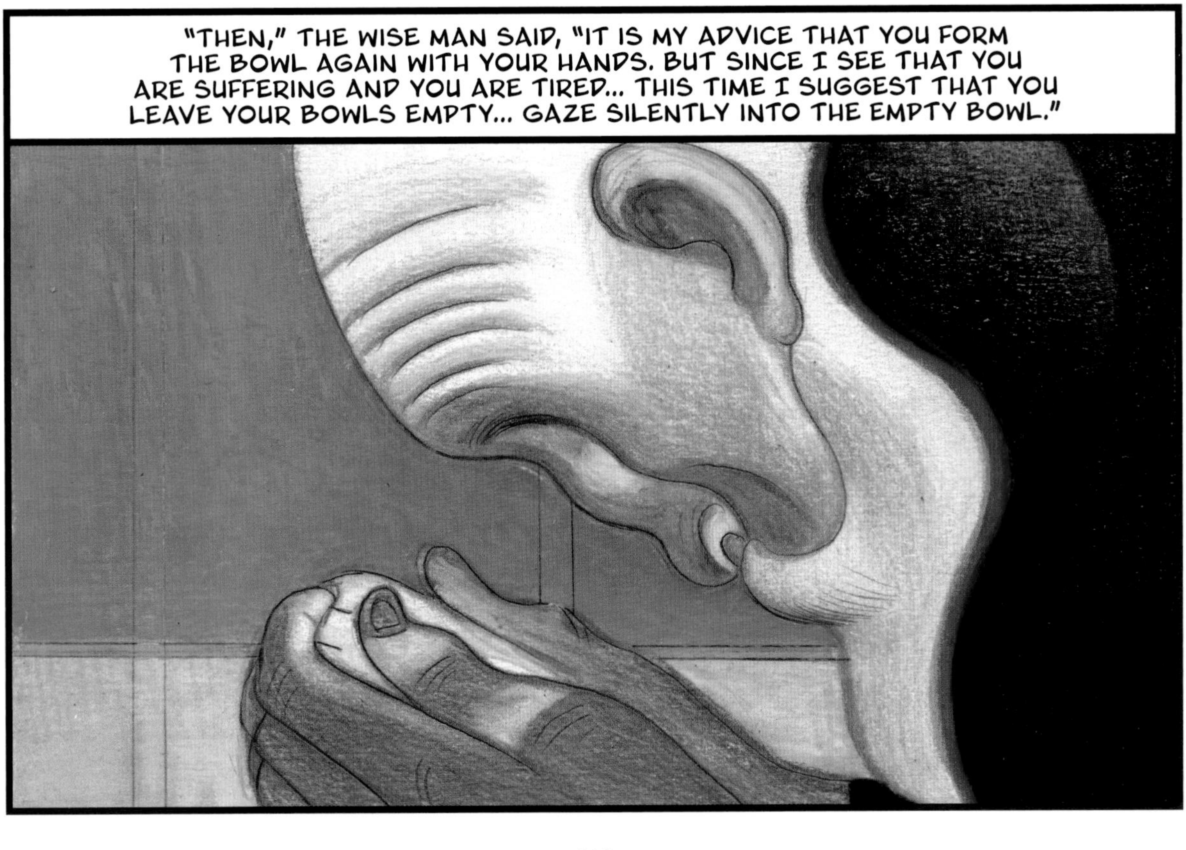
"THEN," THE WISE MAN SAID, "IT IS MY ADVICE THAT YOU FORM THE BOWL AGAIN WITH YOUR HANDS. BUT SINCE I SEE THAT YOU ARE SUFFERING AND YOU ARE TIRED... THIS TIME I SUGGEST THAT YOU LEAVE YOUR BOWLS EMPTY... GAZE SILENTLY INTO THE EMPTY BOWL."

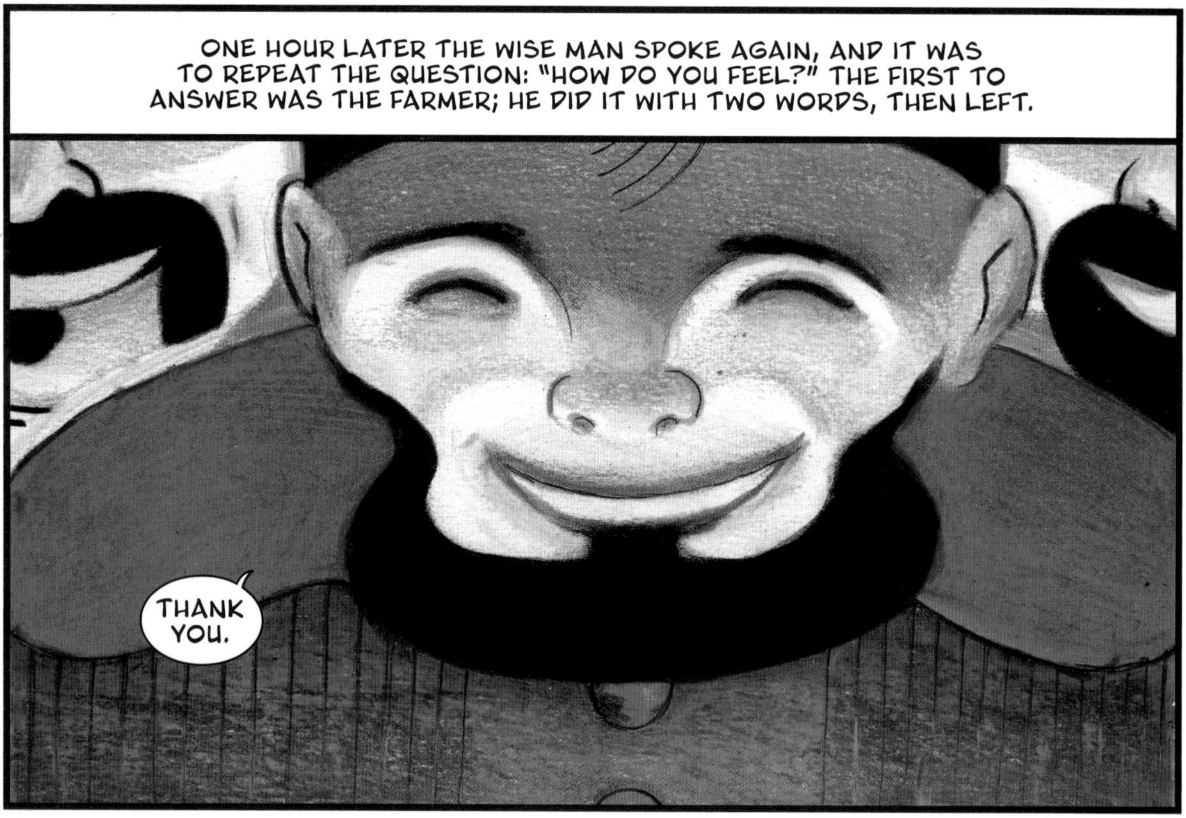
ONE HOUR LATER THE WISE MAN SPOKE AGAIN, AND IT WAS TO REPEAT THE QUESTION: "HOW DO YOU FEEL?" THE FIRST TO ANSWER WAS THE FARMER; HE DID IT WITH TWO WORDS, THEN LEFT.
THANK YOU.

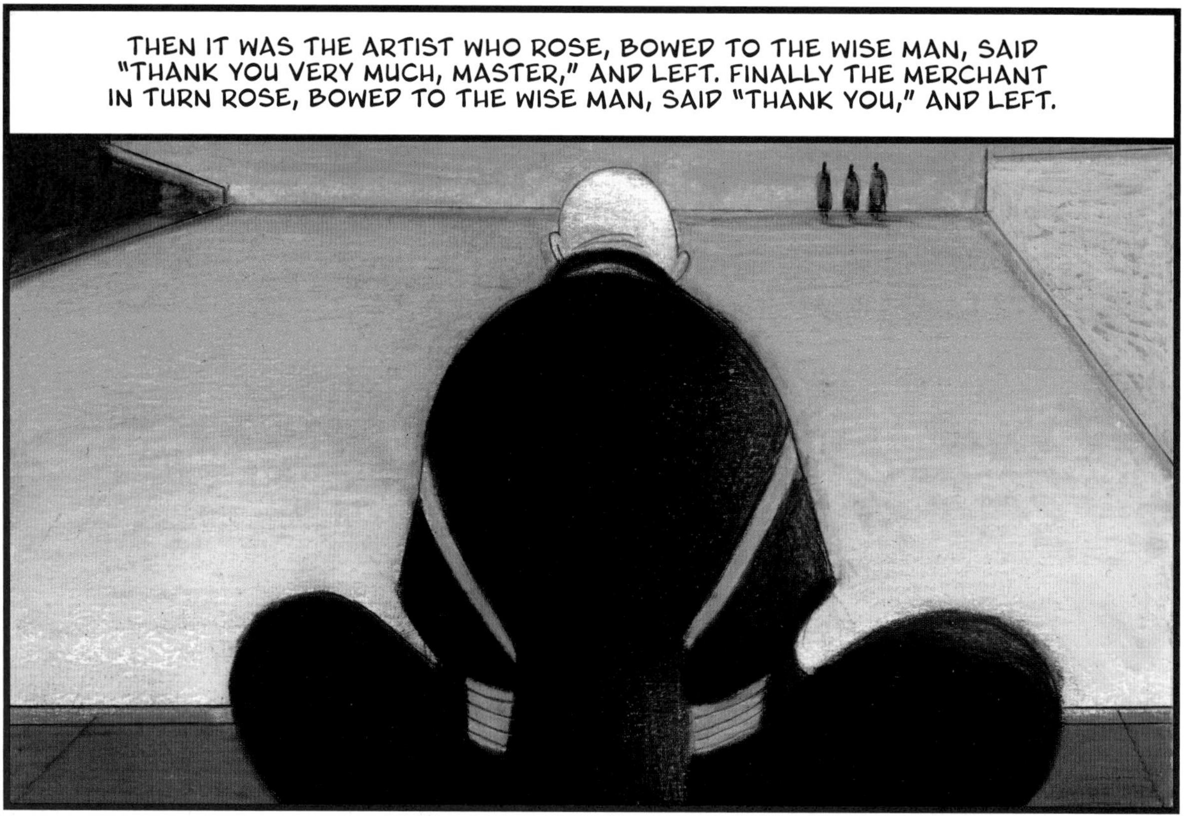
THEN IT WAS THE ARTIST WHO ROSE, BOWED TO THE WISE MAN, SAID "THANK YOU VERY MUCH, MASTER," AND LEFT. FINALLY THE MERCHANT IN TURN ROSE, BOWED TO THE WISE MAN, SAID "THANK YOU," AND LEFT.

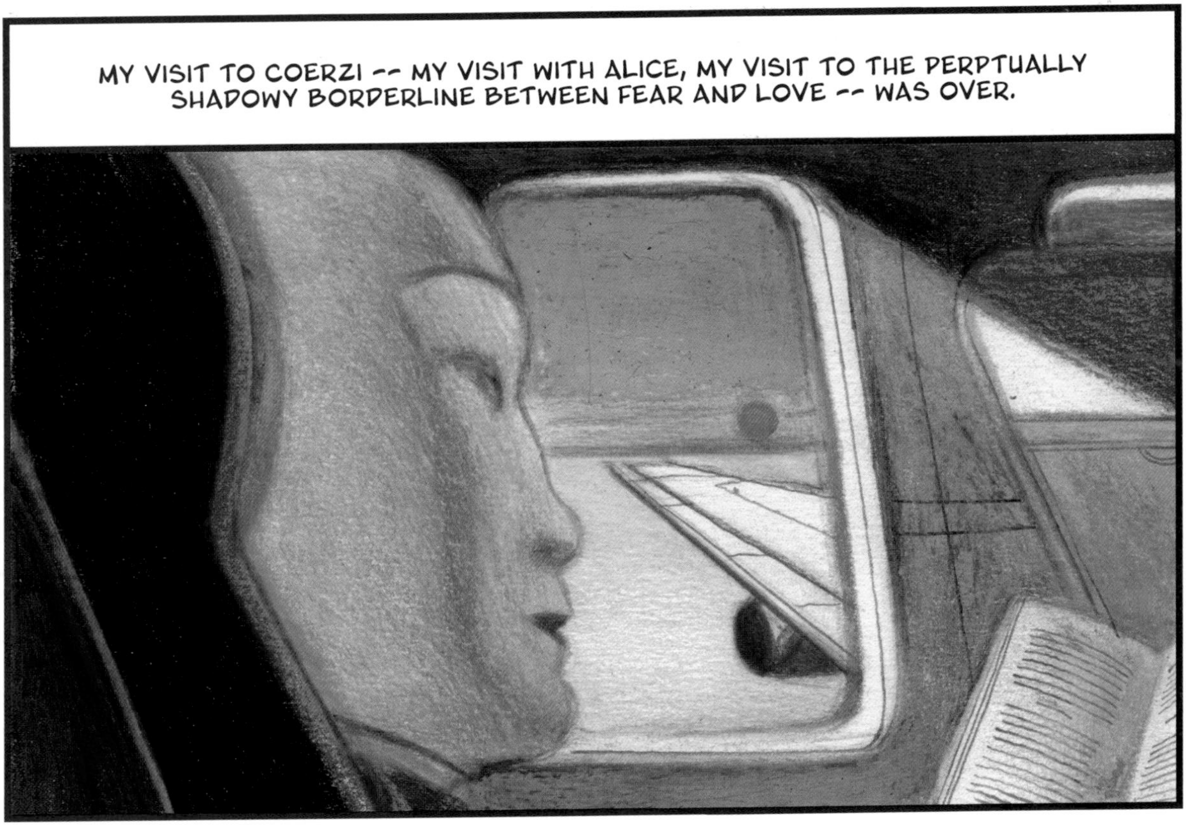
MY VISIT TO COERZI -- MY VISIT WITH ALICE, MY VISIT TO THE PERPTUALLY SHADOWY BORDERLINE BETWEEN FEAR AND LOVE -- WAS OVER.

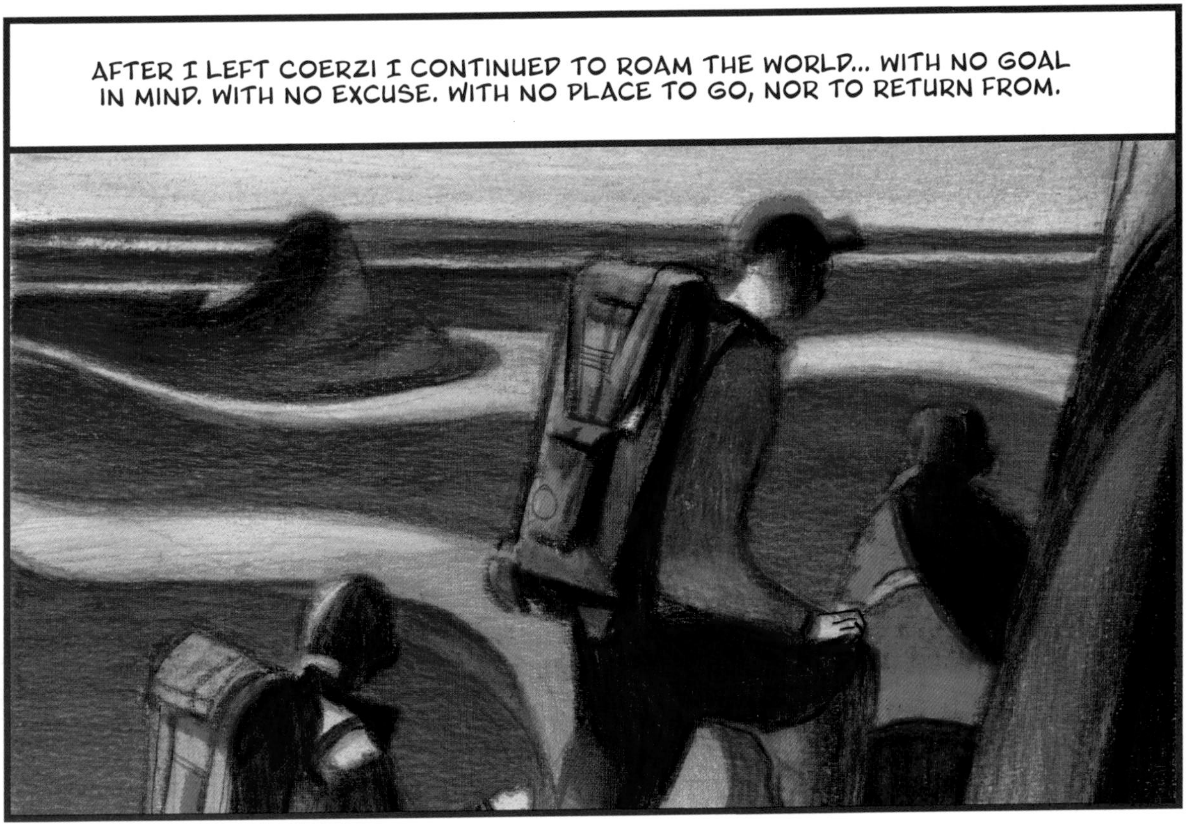
AFTER I LEFT COERZI I CONTINUED TO ROAM THE WORLD... WITH NO GOAL IN MIND. WITH NO EXCUSE. WITH NO PLACE TO GO, NOR TO RETURN FROM.

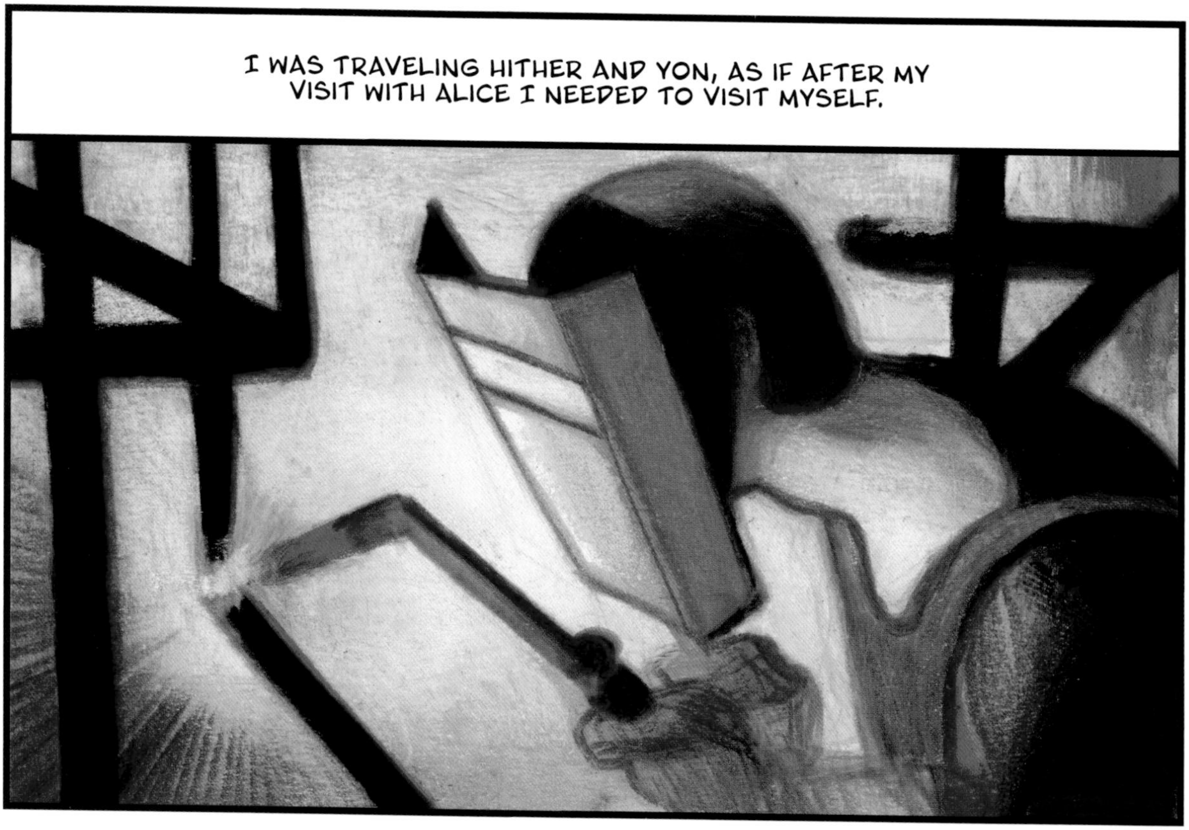
I WAS TRAVELING HITHER AND YON, AS IF AFTER MY VISIT WITH ALICE I NEEDED TO VISIT MYSELF.

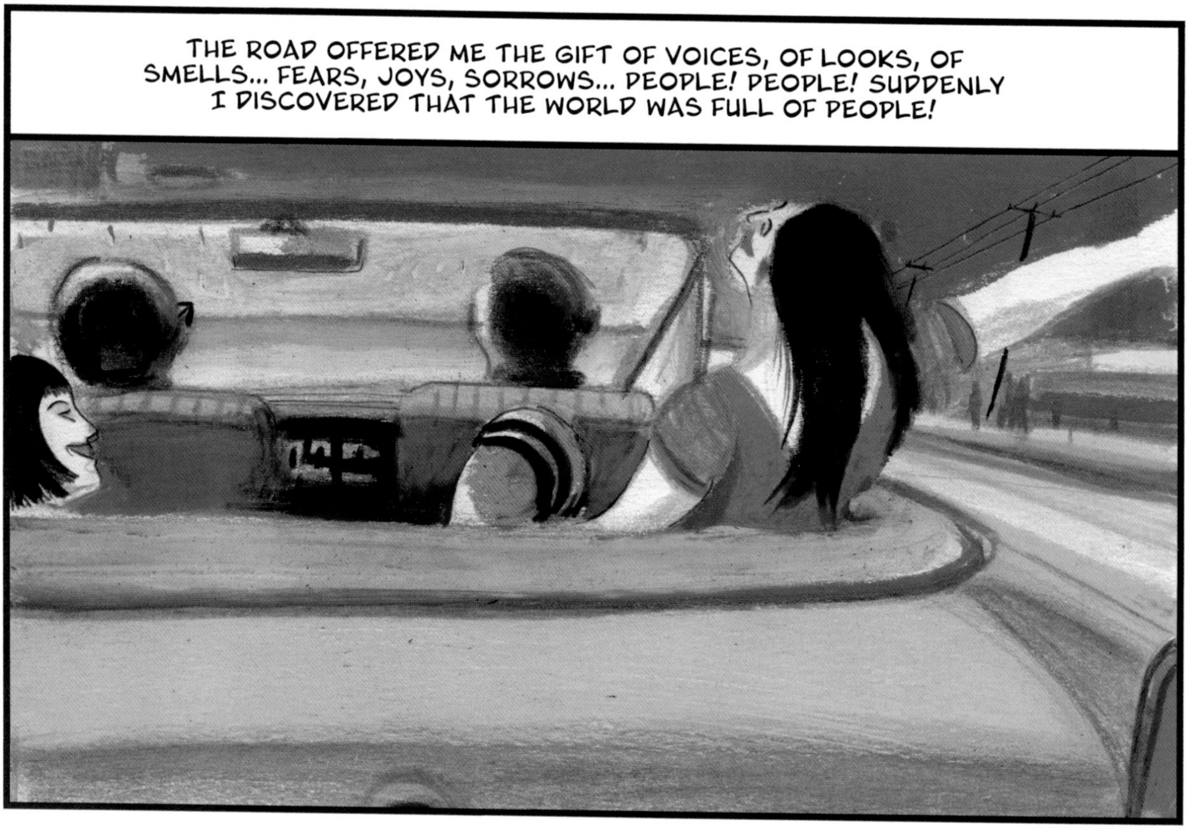
THE ROAD OFFERED ME THE GIFT OF VOICES, OF LOOKS, OF SMELLS... FEARS, JOYS, SORROWS... PEOPLE! PEOPLE! SUDDENLY I DISCOVERED THAT THE WORLD WAS FULL OF PEOPLE!

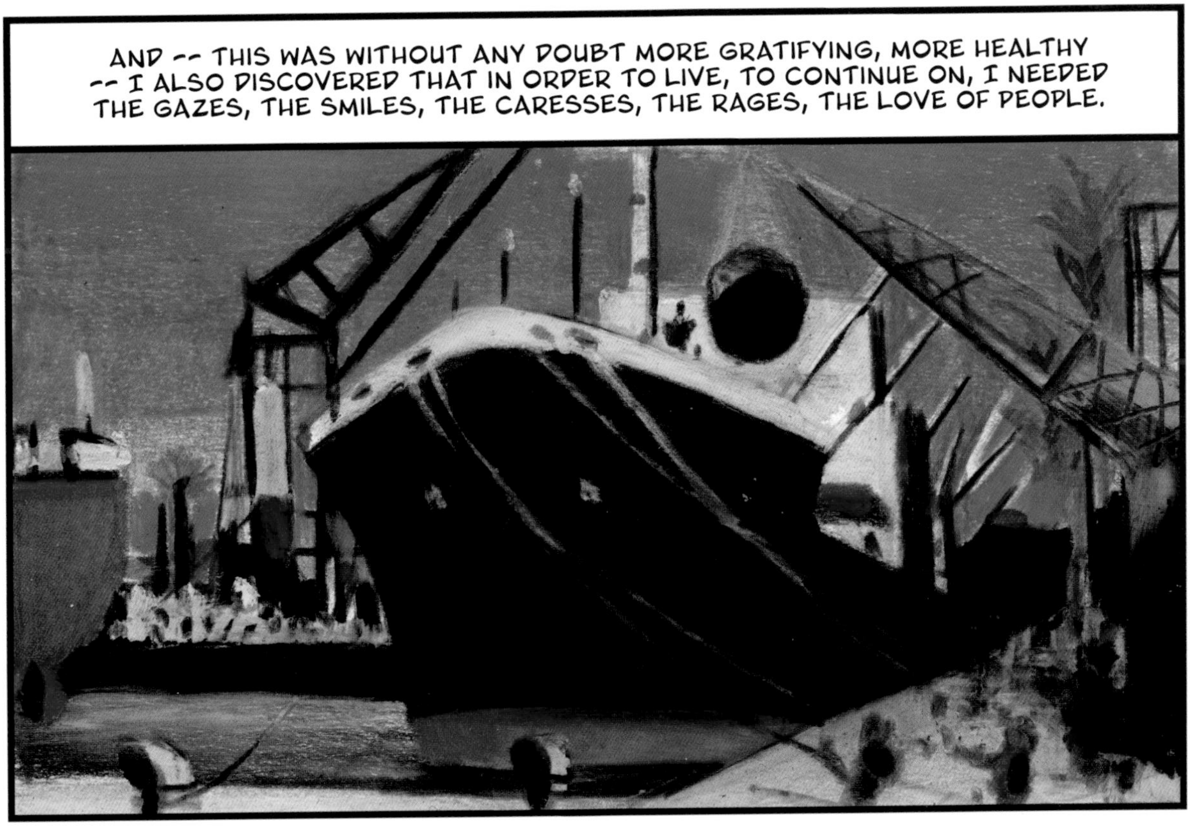
AND -- THIS WAS WITHOUT ANY DOUBT MORE GRATIFYING, MORE HEALTHY -- I ALSO DISCOVERED THAT IN ORDER TO LIVE, TO CONTINUE ON, I NEEDED THE GAZES, THE SMILES, THE CARESSES, THE RAGES, THE LOVE OF PEOPLE.

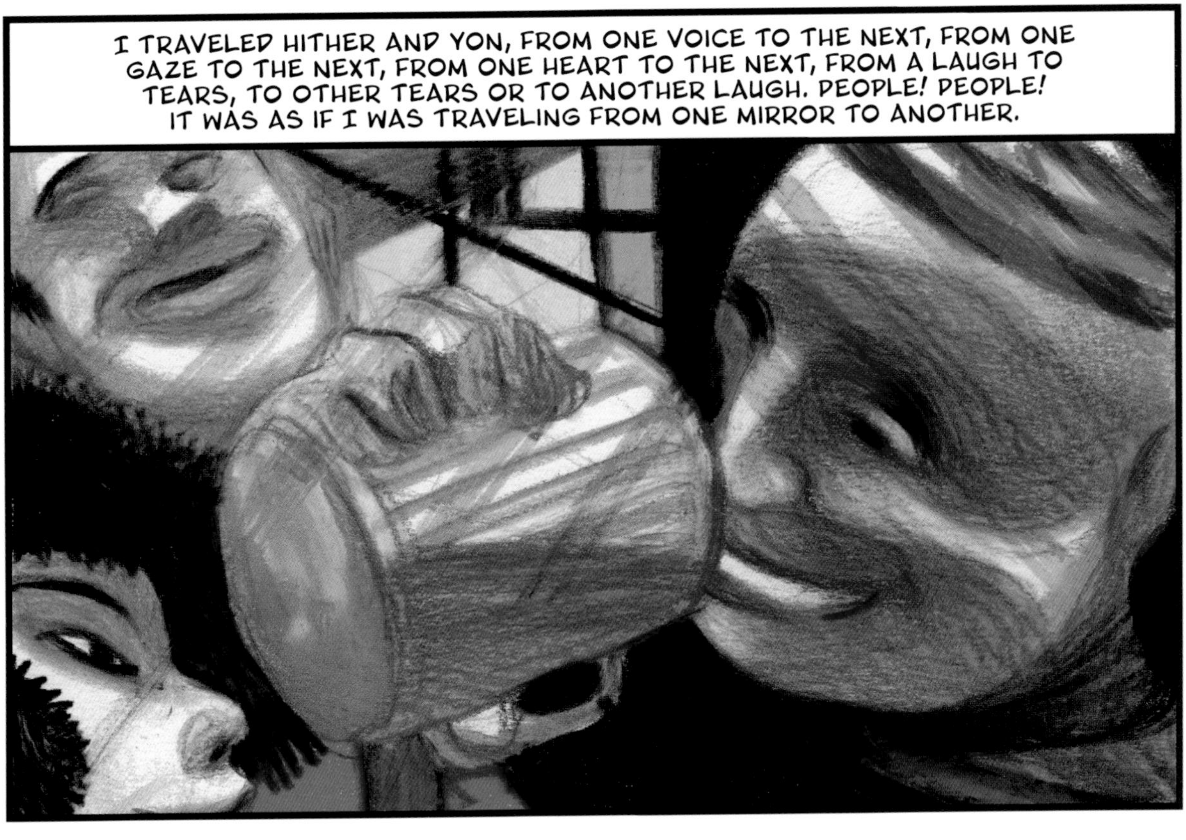
I TRAVELED HITHER AND YON, FROM ONE VOICE TO THE NEXT, FROM ONE GAZE TO THE NEXT, FROM ONE HEART TO THE NEXT, FROM A LAUGH TO TEARS, TO OTHER TEARS OR TO ANOTHER LAUGH. PEOPLE! PEOPLE! IT WAS AS IF I WAS TRAVELING FROM ONE MIRROR TO ANOTHER.

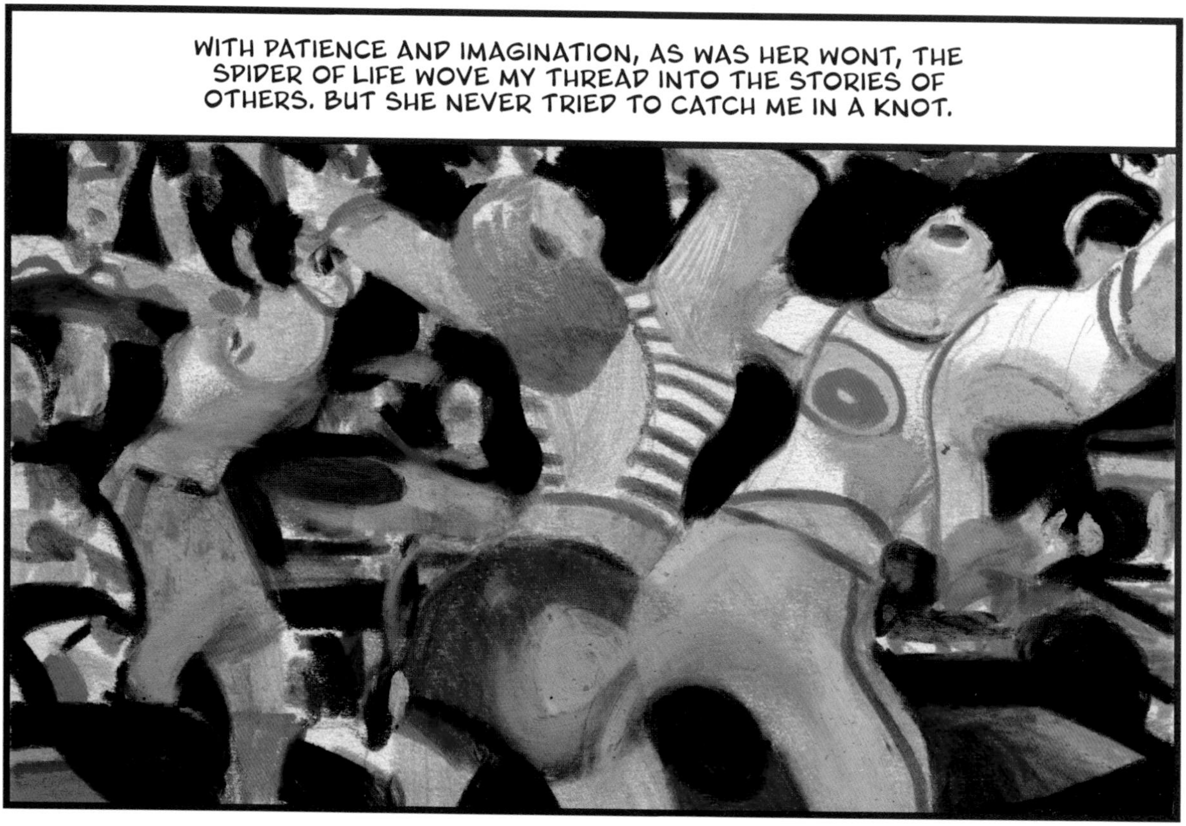
WITH PATIENCE AND IMAGINATION, AS WAS HER WONT, THE SPIDER OF LIFE WOVE MY THREAD INTO THE STORIES OF OTHERS. BUT SHE NEVER TRIED TO CATCH ME IN A KNOT.

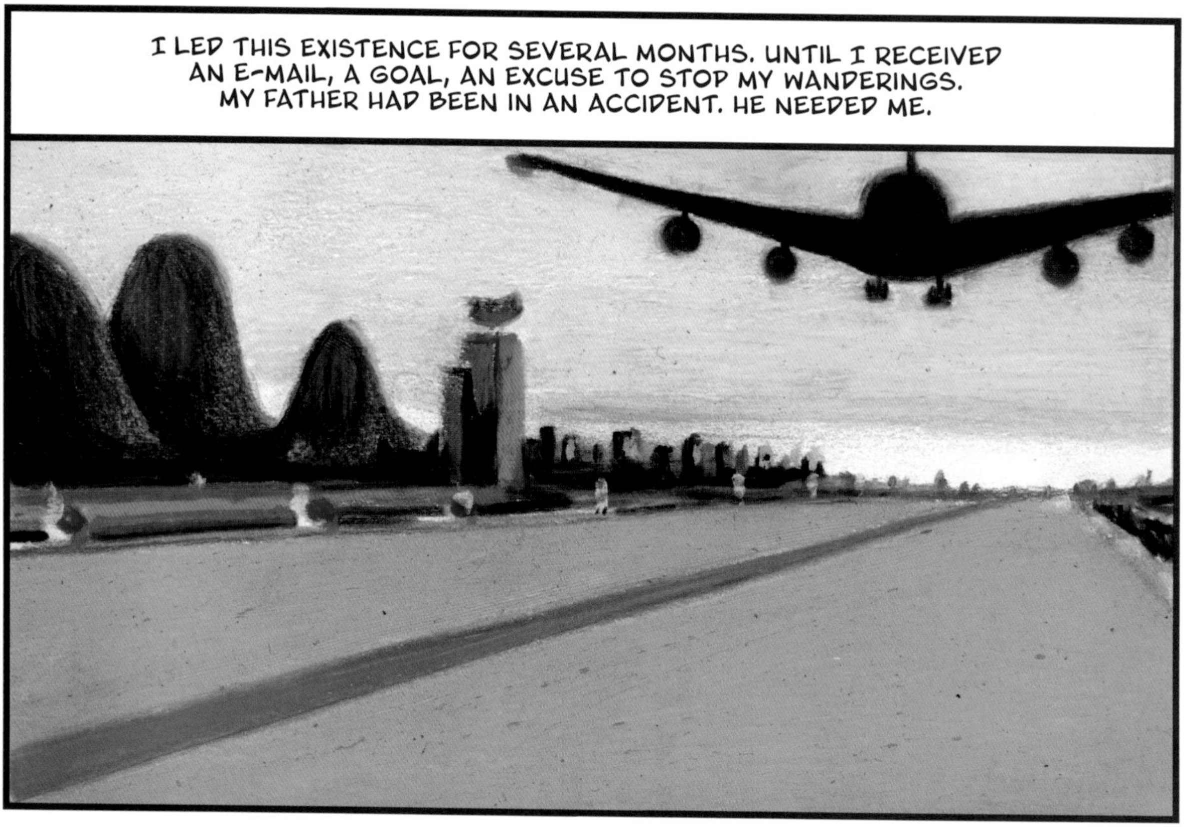
I LED THIS EXISTENCE FOR SEVERAL MONTHS. UNTIL I RECEIVED AN E-MAIL, A GOAL, AN EXCUSE TO STOP MY WANDERINGS. MY FATHER HAD BEEN IN AN ACCIDENT. HE NEEDED ME.

MY FATHER HAD PURCHASED, AT THE AGE OF EIGHTY-FOUR, HIS FIRST BICYCLE.
HIS DOCTOR HAD ADVISED HIM, FOR THE NTH TIME THESE PAST TEN YEARS,
TO GET A LITTLE EXERCISE... A LITTLE MORNING WALK IN THE COUNTRYSIDE.

MY FATHER, BY NATURE A NERVOUS MAN, A LOVER OF SPEED AND AUTOMOBILES,
HAD NEVER WALKED. HIS DOCTOR HAD SUGGESTED A STATIONARY BIKE. "I'VE
LOST MY HEARING, MY SIGHT, MY MEMORY AND MY SEXUAL POTENCY, BUT NOT
MY SENSE OF THE RIDICULOUS." AN ANSWER WORTHY OF MY FATHER.

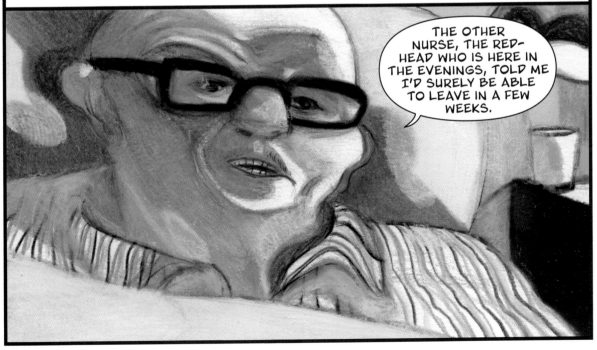

THE OTHER NURSE, THE RED-HEAD WHO IS HERE IN THE EVENINGS, TOLD ME I'D SURELY BE ABLE TO LEAVE IN A FEW WEEKS.

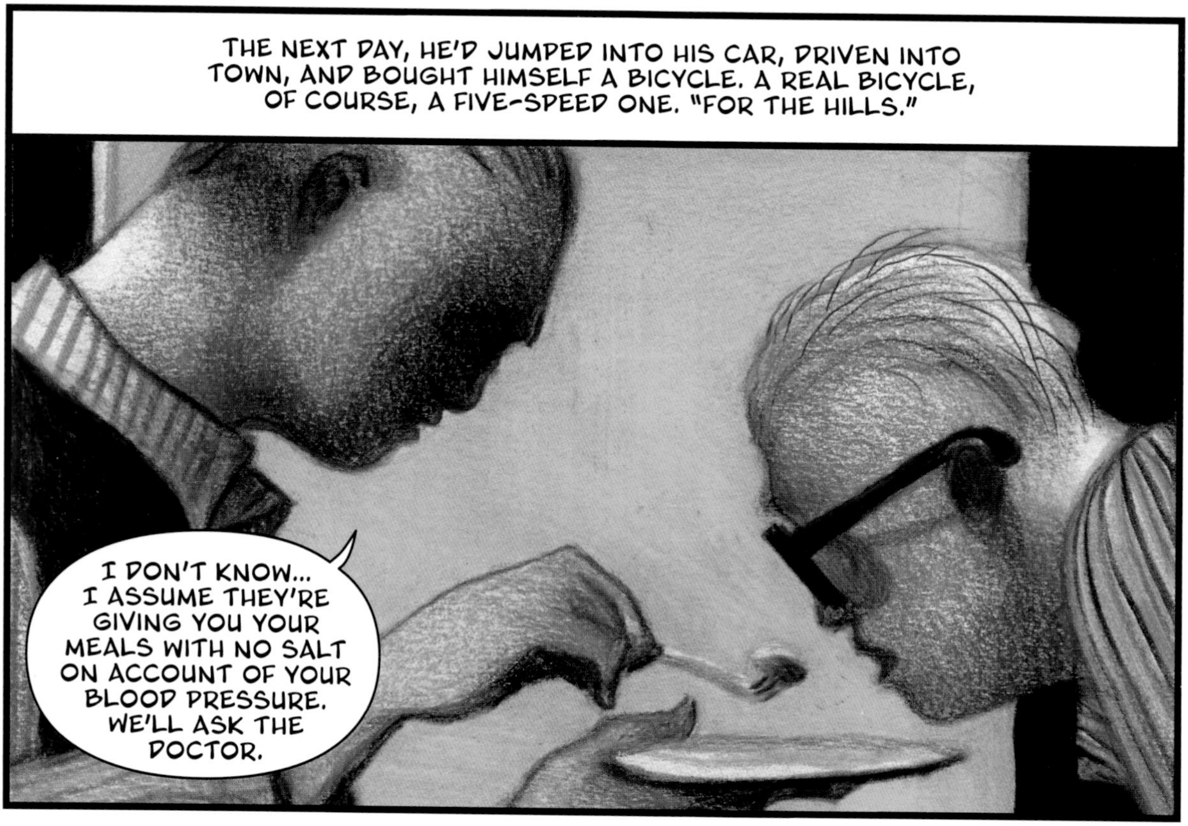
THE NEXT DAY, HE'D JUMPED INTO HIS CAR, DRIVEN INTO TOWN, AND BOUGHT HIMSELF A BICYCLE. A REAL BICYCLE, OF COURSE, A FIVE-SPEED ONE. "FOR THE HILLS."
I DON'T KNOW... I ASSUME THEY'RE GIVING YOU YOUR MEALS WITH NO SALT ON ACCOUNT OF YOUR BLOOD PRESSURE. WE'LL ASK THE DOCTOR.

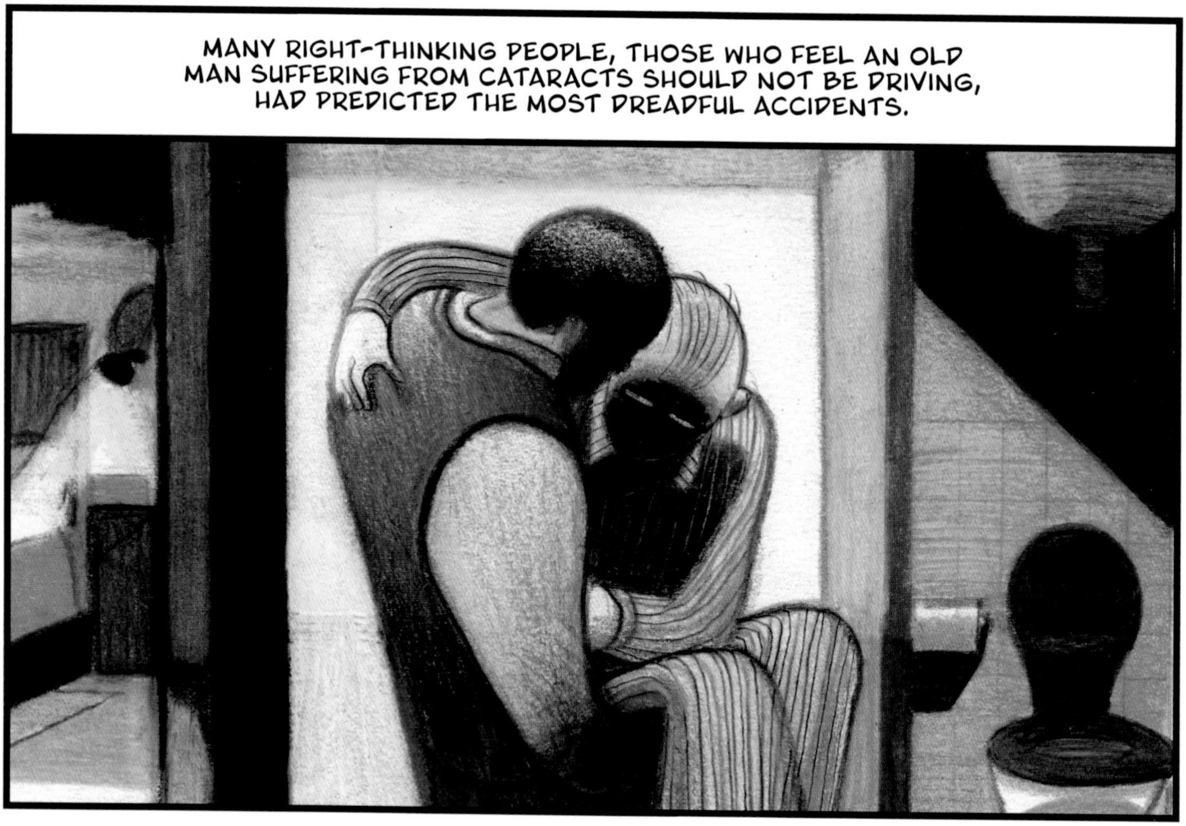
MANY RIGHT-THINKING PEOPLE, THOSE WHO FEEL AN OLD MAN SUFFERING FROM CATARACTS SHOULD NOT BE DRIVING, HAD PREDICTED THE MOST DREADFUL ACCIDENTS.

TWO MONTHS LATER, AS MY FATHER WAS TRYING TO CLIMB ONTO THE ROOF OF HIS HOUSE, IN ORDER TO INSTALL SOMETHING THAT WOULD INDUCE HIS CANARIES TO MATE, HE LOST HIS BALANCE AND FELL OFF HIS LADDER. THE DOCTORS HAD TOLD HIM THAT HE WOULD NEVER WALK AGAIN.

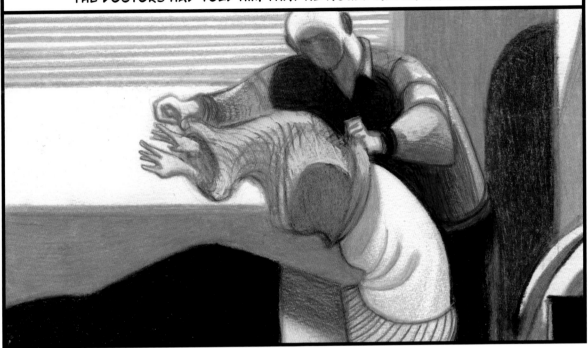

MY FATHER'S ACCIDENT HAD TRANSPORTED ME -- LIKE A SPACESHIP -- TO ANOTHER PLANET. THE HOSPITAL PLANET. THE PLANET OF INJURED FLESH, OF COMPASSION, OF HOPE.

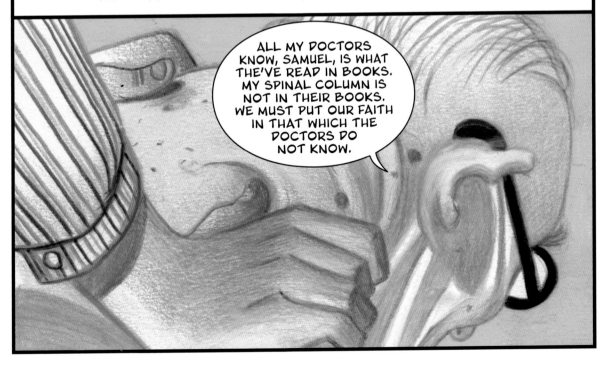

ALL MY DOCTORS KNOW, SAMUEL, IS WHAT THE'VE READ IN BOOKS. MY SPINAL COLUMN IS NOT IN THEIR BOOKS. WE MUST PUT OUR FAITH IN THAT WHICH THE DOCTORS DO NOT KNOW.

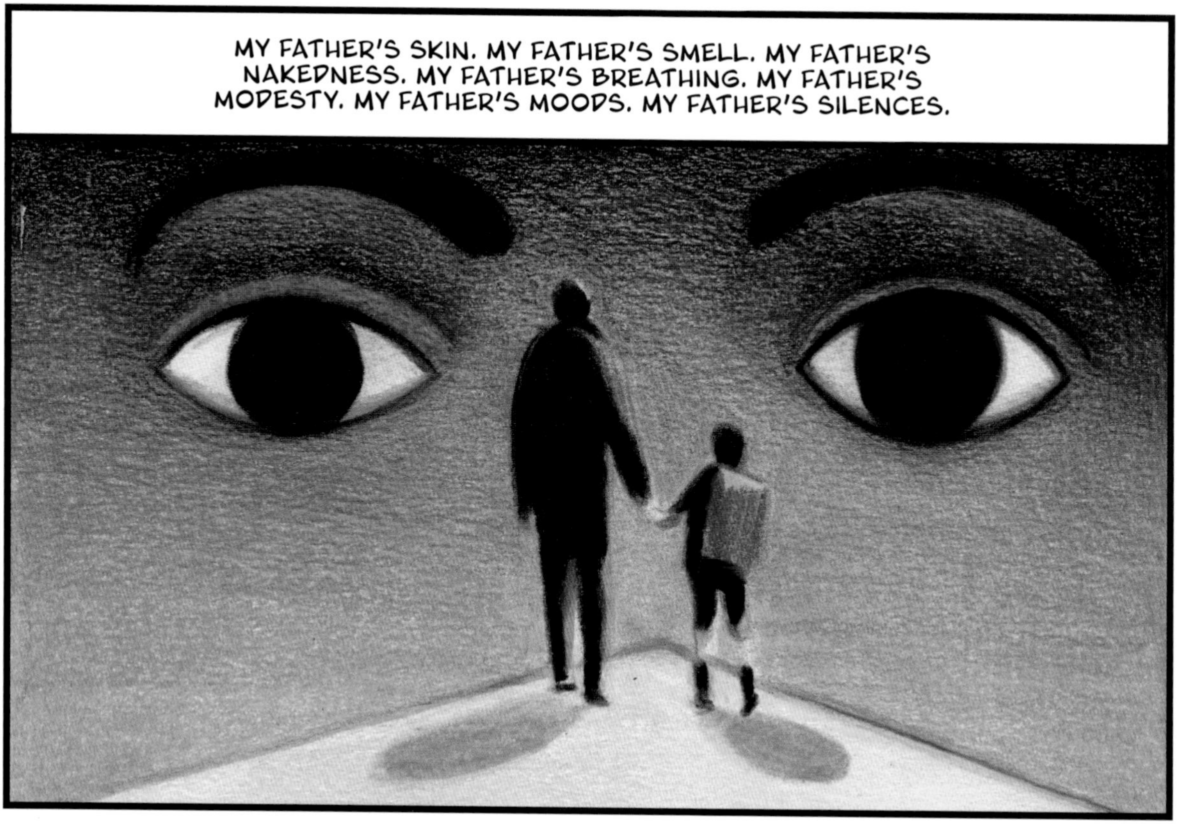
MY FATHER'S SKIN. MY FATHER'S SMELL. MY FATHER'S NAKEDNESS. MY FATHER'S BREATHING. MY FATHER'S MODESTY. MY FATHER'S MOODS. MY FATHER'S SILENCES.

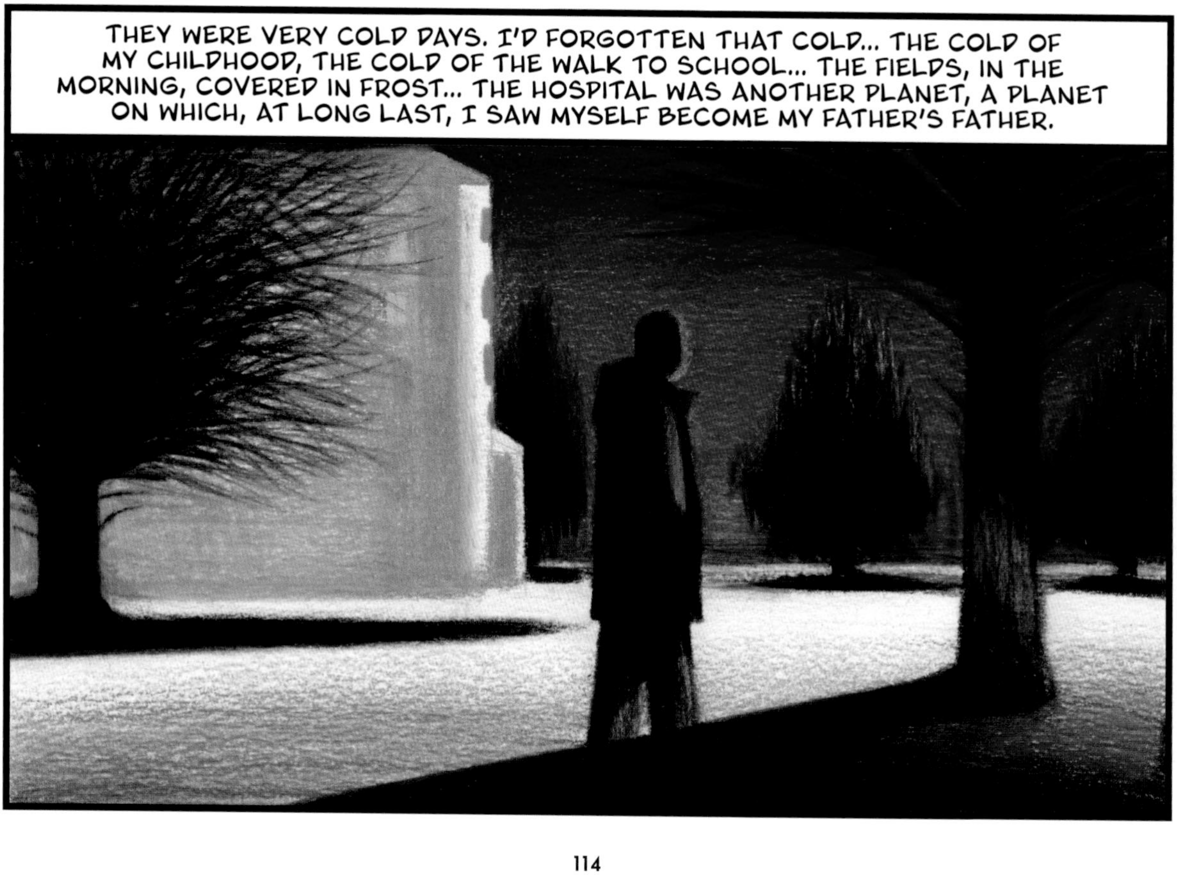
THEY WERE VERY COLD DAYS. I'D FORGOTTEN THAT COLD... THE COLD OF MY CHILDHOOD, THE COLD OF THE WALK TO SCHOOL... THE FIELDS, IN THE MORNING, COVERED IN FROST... THE HOSPITAL WAS ANOTHER PLANET, A PLANET ON WHICH, AT LONG LAST, I SAW MYSELF BECOME MY FATHER'S FATHER.

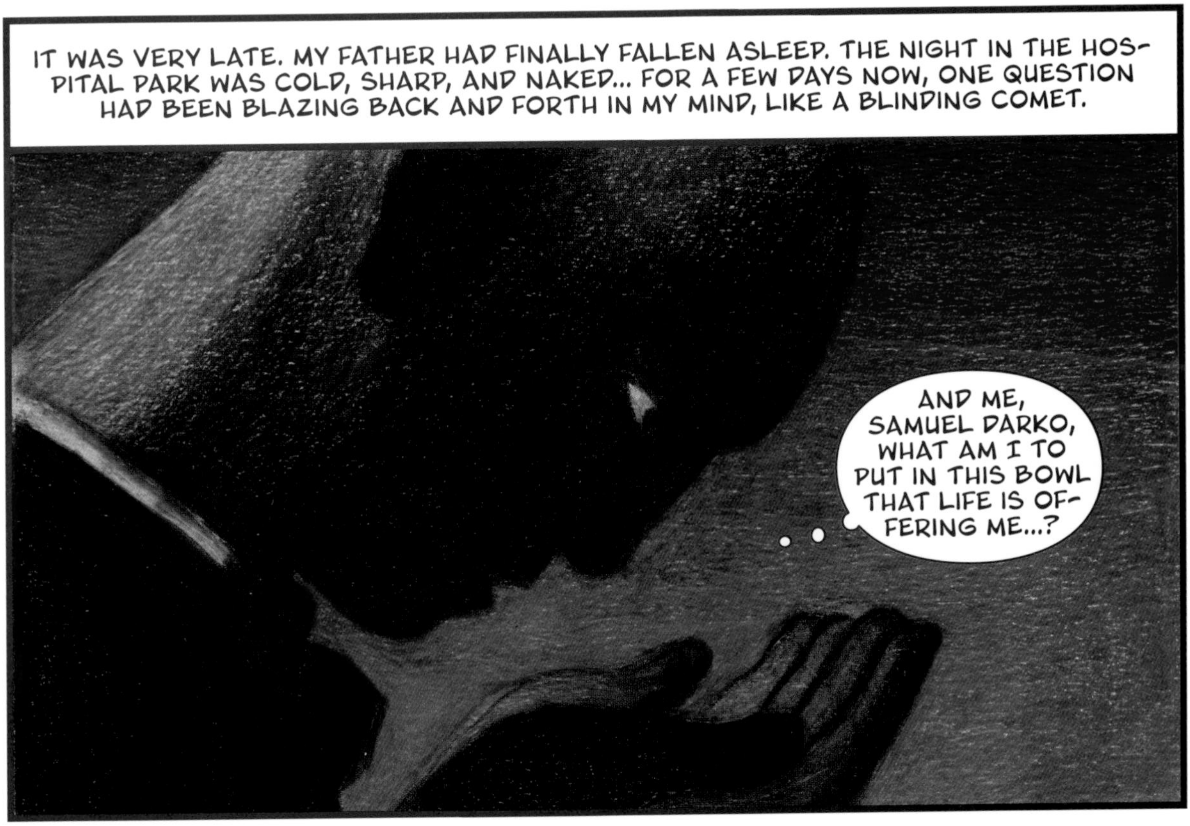
IT WAS VERY LATE. MY FATHER HAD FINALLY FALLEN ASLEEP. THE NIGHT IN THE HOSPITAL PARK WAS COLD, SHARP, AND NAKED... FOR A FEW DAYS NOW, ONE QUESTION HAD BEEN BLAZING BACK AND FORTH IN MY MIND, LIKE A BLINDING COMET.
AND ME, SAMUEL DARKO, WHAT AM I TO PUT IN THIS BOWL THAT LIFE IS OFFERING ME...?

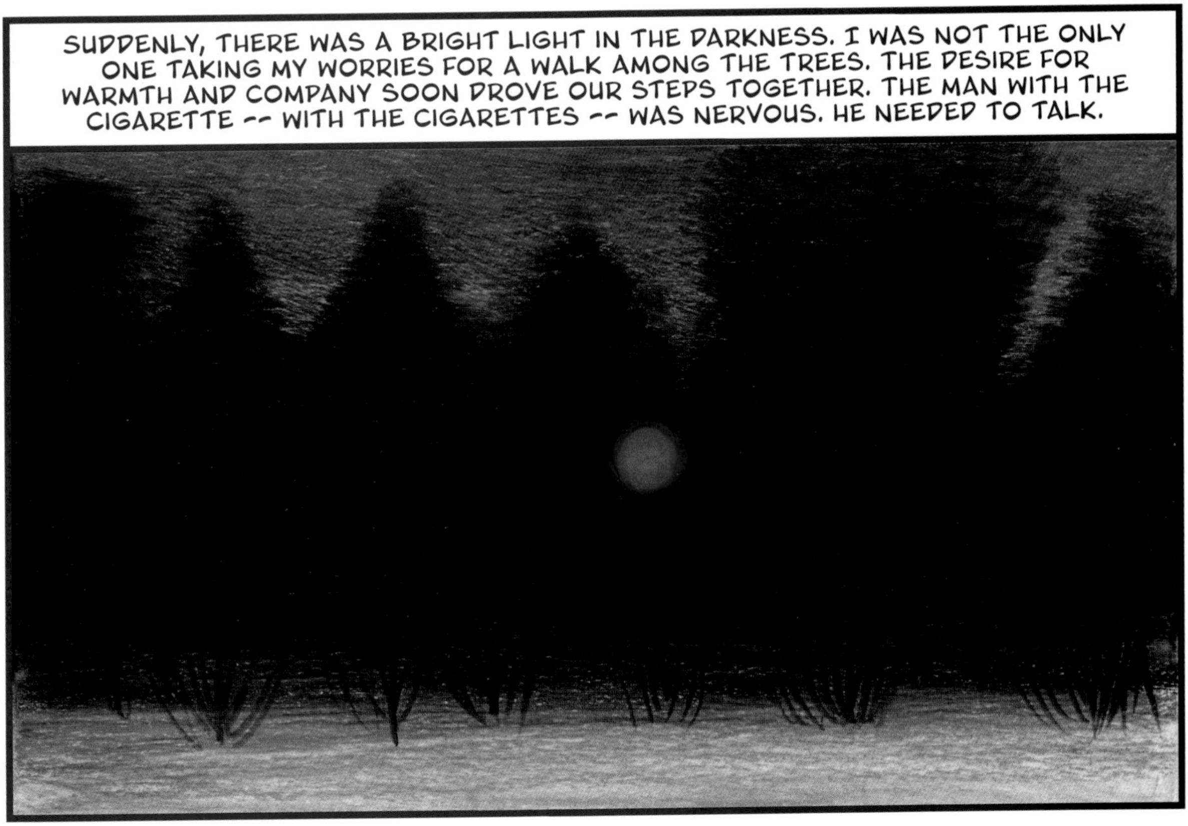
SUDDENLY, THERE WAS A BRIGHT LIGHT IN THE DARKNESS. I WAS NOT THE ONLY ONE TAKING MY WORRIES FOR A WALK AMONG THE TREES. THE DESIRE FOR WARMTH AND COMPANY SOON DROVE OUR STEPS TOGETHER. THE MAN WITH THE CIGARETTE -- WITH THE CIGARETTES -- WAS NERVOUS. HE NEEDED TO TALK.

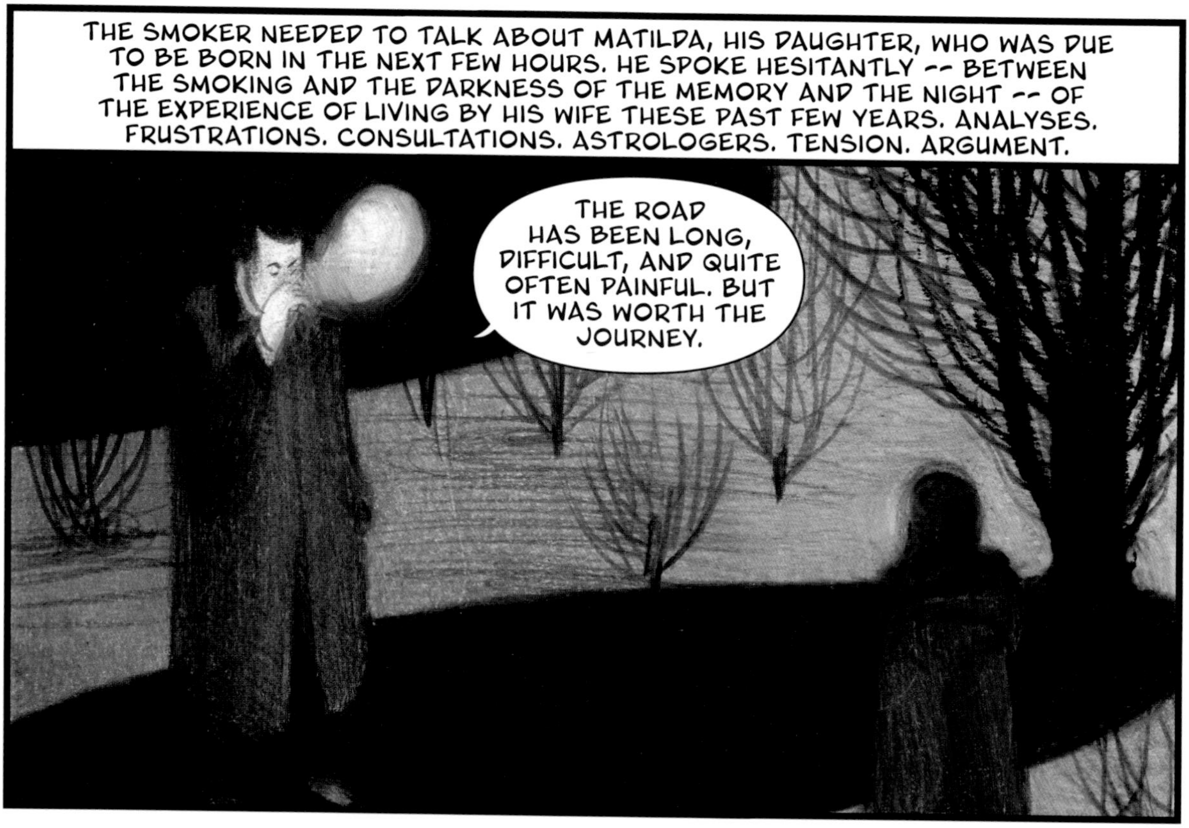
THE SMOKER NEEDED TO TALK ABOUT MATILDA, HIS DAUGHTER, WHO WAS DUE TO BE BORN IN THE NEXT FEW HOURS. HE SPOKE HESITANTLY -- BETWEEN THE SMOKING AND THE DARKNESS OF THE MEMORY AND THE NIGHT -- OF THE EXPERIENCE OF LIVING BY HIS WIFE THESE PAST FEW YEARS. ANALYSES. FRUSTRATIONS. CONSULTATIONS. ASTROLOGERS. TENSION. ARGUMENT.
THE ROAD HAS BEEN LONG, DIFFICULT, AND QUITE OFTEN PAINFUL. BUT IT WAS WORTH THE JOURNEY.

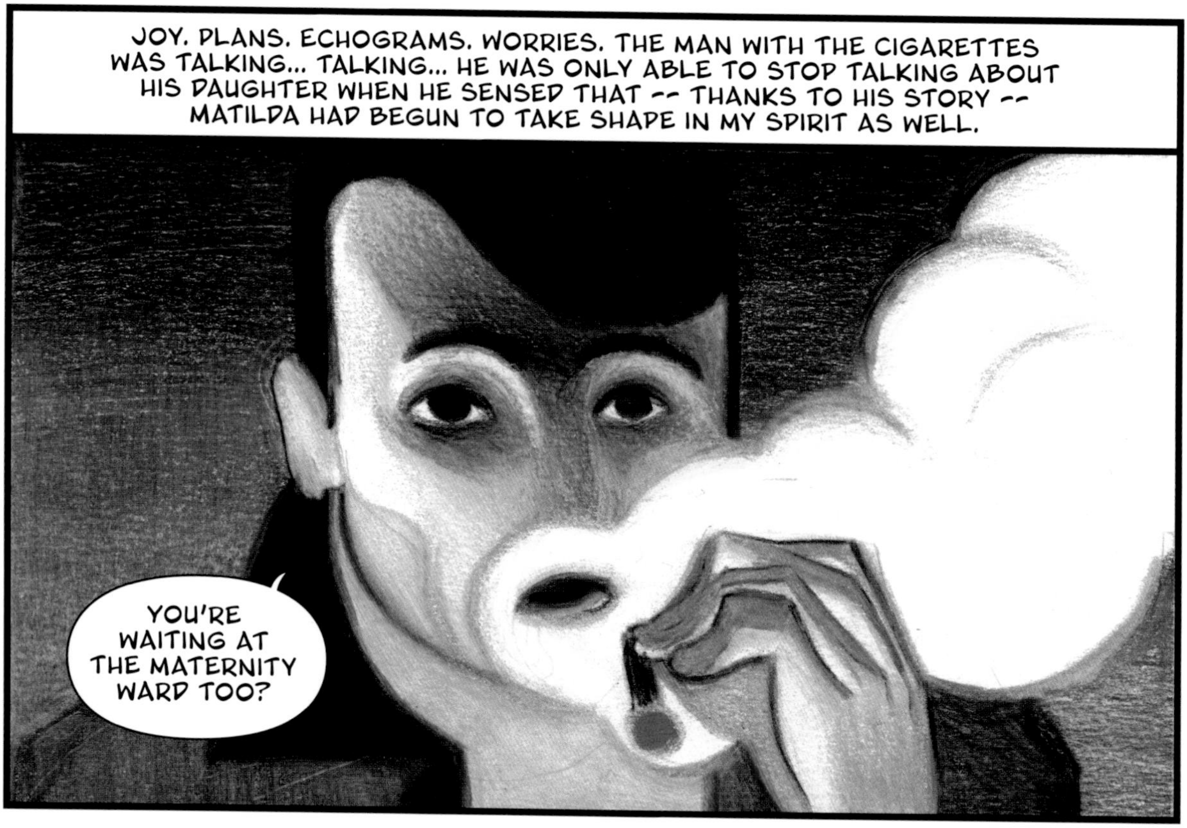
JOY. PLANS. ECHOGRAMS. WORRIES. THE MAN WITH THE CIGARETTES WAS TALKING... TALKING... HE WAS ONLY ABLE TO STOP TALKING ABOUT HIS DAUGHTER WHEN HE SENSED THAT -- THANKS TO HIS STORY -- MATILDA HAD BEGUN TO TAKE SHAPE IN MY SPIRIT AS WELL.
YOU'RE WAITING AT THE MATERNITY WARD TOO?

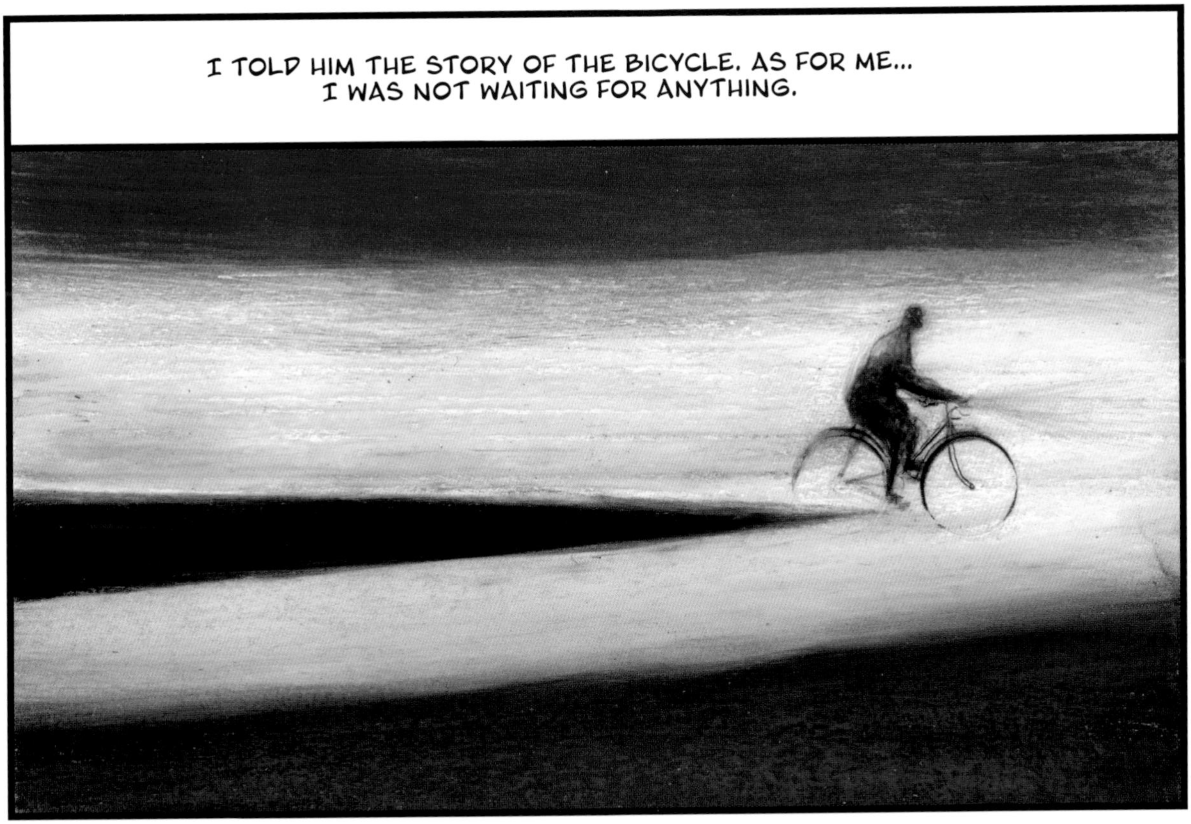
I TOLD HIM THE STORY OF THE BICYCLE. AS FOR ME...
I WAS NOT WAITING FOR ANYTHING.

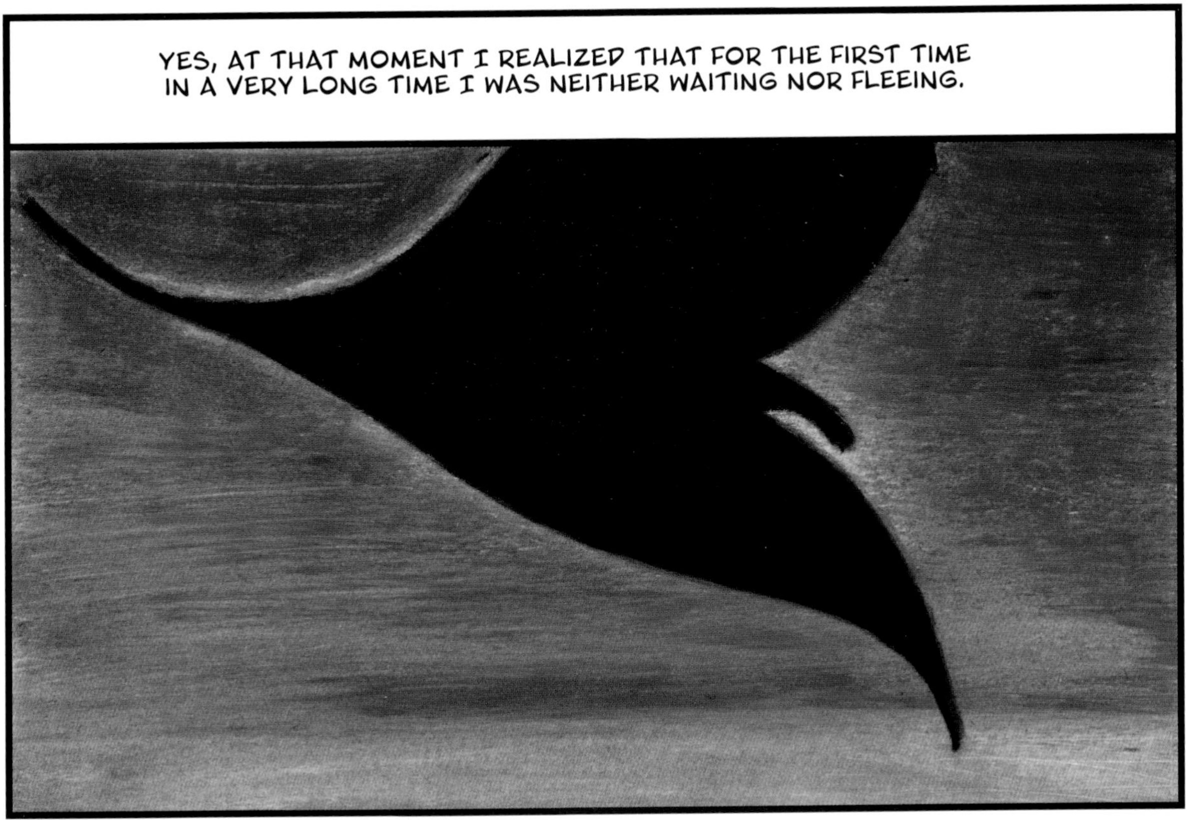
YES, AT THAT MOMENT I REALIZED THAT FOR THE FIRST TIME
IN A VERY LONG TIME I WAS NEITHER WAITING NOR FLEEING.

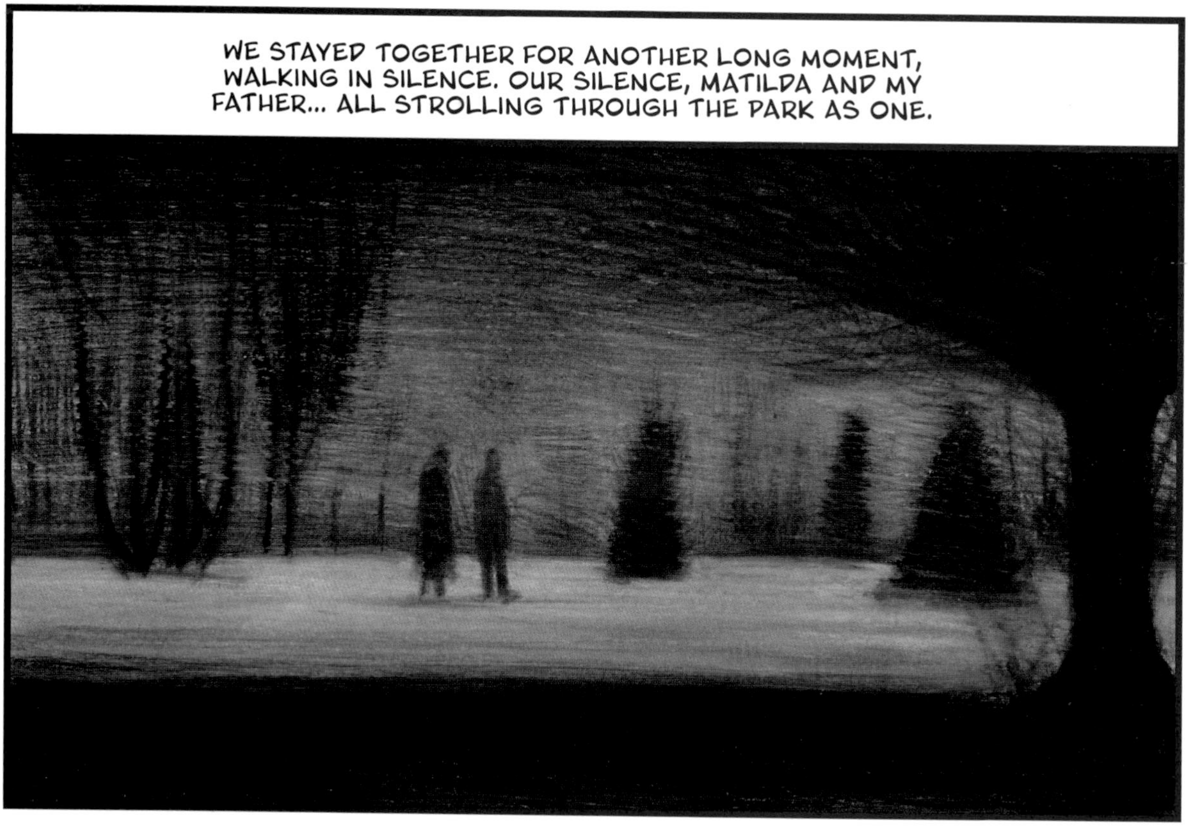
WE STAYED TOGETHER FOR ANOTHER LONG MOMENT, WALKING IN SILENCE. OUR SILENCE, MATILDA AND MY FATHER... ALL STROLLING THROUGH THE PARK AS ONE.

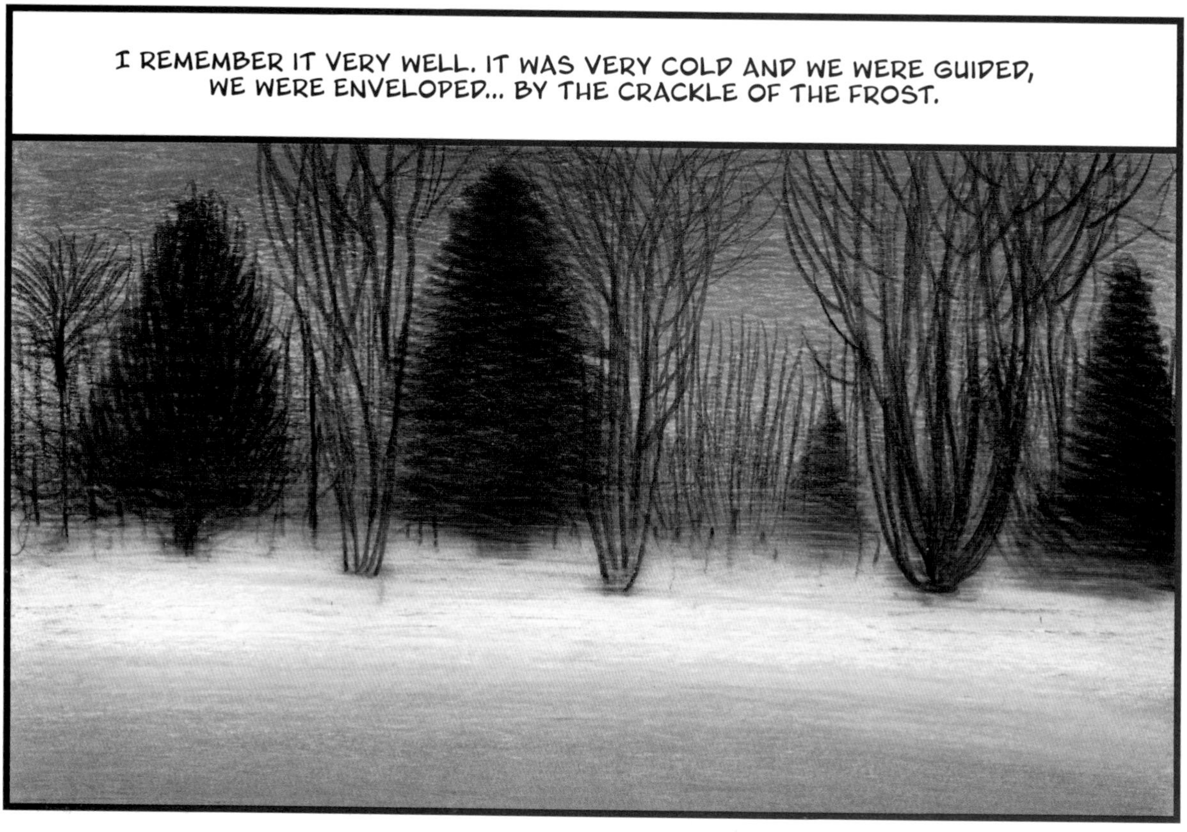
I REMEMBER IT VERY WELL. IT WAS VERY COLD AND WE WERE GUIDED, WE WERE ENVELOPED... BY THE CRACKLE OF THE FROST.